Ionian
Corfu to Zakinthos and
the adjacent mainland

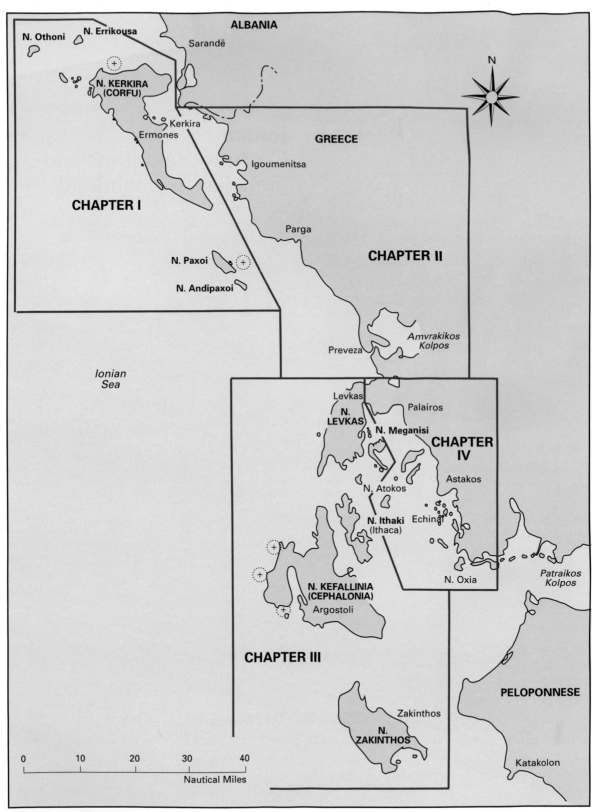

IONIAN ISLANDS AND ADJACENT COAST

Ionian

Corfu to Zakinthos and
the adjacent mainland

ROD HEIKELL

Imray Laurie Norie and Wilson Ltd
St Ives Cambridgeshire England

Published by
Imray Laurie Norie and Wilson Ltd
Wych House The Broadway St Ives Huntingdon
Cambridgeshire PE17 4BT England
☎ +(0)1480 462114 *Fax* +(0)1480 496109
E-mail ilnw@imray.com
Web www.imray.com
1999

© Rod Heikell 1999
1st edition 1992
2nd edition 1994
3rd edition 1996
4th edition 1999

British Library Cataloguing in Publication Data.
A catalogue record for this book is available from
the British Library.

ISBN 0 85288 423 0

CAUTION
While every care has been taken to ensure
accuracy, neither the Publishers nor the Author
will hold themselves responsible for errors,
omissions or alterations in this publication. They
will at all times be grateful to receive information
which tends to the improvement of the work.

PLANS
The plans in this guide are not to be used for
navigation. They are designed to support the text
and should at all times be used with navigational
charts.

Printed in Great Britain at
Bath Press Colour Books, Blantyre, Scotland

Contents

Chair repairs. Mainland

Eftilia. Levkas

Fisherman. Ithaca

Papas. Levkas

Preface

I've been meaning to write this guide for a long time. I first arrived in the Ionian in 1977, passing through as I thought, but like many others ended up staying for the rest of the summer there. Some of it has changed radically in that time and there are certainly more yachts around, but it retains a charm which brings me back and holds others locked in its geographical fist.

There are good reasons why travellers feel loath to move from the place. It is hard to imagine a more perfect sailing area. In the summer the wind gets up at midday, blows through the afternoon, and dies at night. A perfect gentleman's wind which lets you sail through the afternoon and get a good night's sleep without worrying about the anchor holding. It lets you motor against the prevailing wind direction in the morning calm. I have had the best sailing anywhere in the Ionian and still have my favourite legs where you can rip along on a close reach in near flat water. Ashore this western strip has an Italianate feel to it reflected in Venetian castles, odd belfries, red-roofed houses, a bit of neo-Baroque here and there, and inhabitants who enjoy their pasta as much as their *moussaka*. You have to dig a bit for the Italian connection and travel in other parts of Greece to make comparisons, but it is there though the area is still indubitably Greek.

The name of the area and the sea comes from Io, a priestess to Hera who briefly had a fling with her employer's husband Zeus. Hera found out about the affair and Zeus, worried about what his wife might do, changed Io into a white cow. Cunning Hera sent a gadfly to torment the cow and Io galloped around Europe attempting to escape her persecutor, eventually plunging into the sea now called the Ionian after her. One confusion which sometimes crops up is between the Ionian Sea and the colony of ancient Ionia on the coast of Asia Minor in present day Turkey. The Ionians (properly the Ionics) here were named after Ion, son of Creusa and the Sun God Apollo, and have no mythopaeic connections to the area described in this book.

It has taken me a long time to get around to writing this guide. I hope it provides sound sailing directions and gives a taste of the varied history and geography of the area - if you need more there is a list of a few books which may be useful in the appendix. If things have changed in the time between writing and going to print then please let me know care of the publishers. To those who helped me put this book together my thanks. I would especially like to thank Willie Wilson of Imrays; Julia who re-arranged the text for printing on screen; Debbie who painstakingly perfected the plans; Graham and Katrina Sewell of *Songline* who looked at some of the harbours and read the first proofs; Joe and Robin Charlton of Contract Yacht Services in Levkas who provided a base and good barbecues; Adonis Fotinos of Christo's Boatyard in Levkas; Sotos Kouvaras of Greek Sails; and Odile who did the draft lay-out, compiled the index, read proofs, and crewed *Tetranora* as we pottered around the Ionian.

PREFACE TO THE FOURTH EDITION

Returning to the Ionian after some time away is like coming home. The landscape is at once familiar but half-remembered: old friends in familiar places with extensions to family and homes;. the sun still hot overhead and the evening skies in pastel hues as the sun goes down. Strange too, to arrive in a new boat, *seven tenths*, both of us still bearing the scars of 8000 odd miles of cruising around Cuba and Haiti and the Leewards before crossing the pond to the Mediterranean.

The area has changed little since the first edition of this book was published and that in itself is a joy. There are new buildings, improvements to harbours and marinas, a new pontoon here and some water points there, but overall the look and feel of the area, the soul of the place, has not changed radically. It is too easy to criticise some development of the ubiquitous pour-and-fill variety, but in the end the area has escaped lightly from the sort of the development that blights other parts of the world. Let us hope it remains so.

For this edition I would like to thank Barry Nielson of Sailing Holidays, Joe Charlton and Laurie Campbell of Contract Yacht Services, Captain Y Elren of M.Y *Deianeira* for local information, Nigel Patten and Willie Wilson, Julia Knight, Elaine Sharples and all at Imrays who beavered away to get this edition out. My thanks and as ever the mistakes are mine.

Rod Heikell
London 1999

Also by Rod Heikell
Mediterranean France & Corsica Pilot
Italian Waters Pilot
Greek Waters Pilot
Saronic
Turkish Waters & Cyprus Pilot
Imray Mediterranean Almanac Editor
Mediterranean Cruising Handbook
Danube - A River Guide
Yacht Charter Handbook
Indian Ocean Cruising Guide Turkey's Turquoise Coast NET
Mediterranean Sailing A & C Black

Imray Books for the Mediterranean Sea

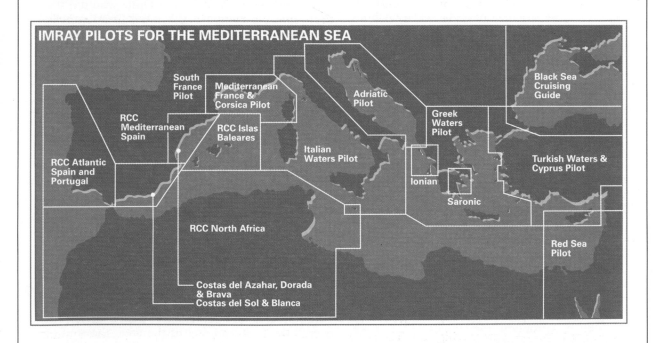

The Ionian

About Greece

History

One of the problems I constantly encounter in Greece is putting historical events into perspective. When did the Venetians colonise the Greek islands? And which islands? When was the classical period in Greek antiquity? Who were the Myceneans? I am not going to elaborate on any of these, but I have assembled the following historical order of things in Greece (with a slight bias to the Ionian) in order to give some perspective to historical events. For detail, wrangling over dates and places, and for explanations of what went on, the reader will have to consult other sources.

Neolithic period Little is known of early Neolithic life in Greece. Around 6500 BC early stone-age settlers crossed the Bosphorus to mainland Europe and probably used primitive boats and rafts to get to islands close to the Asian shore. Flint tools used by these settlers dating from around 6000 BC have been found on Cephalonia and Zakinthos. Around 4000 BC the Cycladic civilisation was well established and from the wide distribution of their distinctive geometric designs we know that there was communication between the islands on a regular basis.

Minoan period (2000 to 1450? BC) Around 2500 BC new colonists moved down into Greece from the Balkans and Turkey bringing bronze weapons and tools with them. The Minoan civilisation was concentrated on Crete and Thira where the art of pottery and metalwork was brought to a high art. They also seem to have brought the art of comfortable and civilised living to a high art as well. The Minoans colonised few places and appeared happy to police the seas with their vessels and so procure order and peace while permitting other peoples to go about their business. The Minoans are not thought to have colonised any of the Ionian islands. The civilisation ended abruptly around 1450 BC, it is thought from one of the biggest eruptions known, when Thira exploded and tidal waves estimated to be 70ft, earthquakes and ash, destroyed the civilisation overnight.

Mycenean period (1500 to 1100 BC) With the demise of the Minoans, the Myceneans, a Greek-speaking race based at Mycenae in the Peloponnese, stepped into the power vacuum. These are the Aecheans of Homer and the Trojan War, fought around 1200 BC, is thought to be a battle brought about by the Myceneans seeking trade outlets in the Black Sea. Mycenean artefacts have been found on some of the Ionian islands (Levkas, Cephalonia, Ithaca, Zakinthos) and it is likely that the expedition from the Ionian islands described by Homer is derived from real Mycenean settlements, though it is the location of these settlements that causes problems (see the section on Homer and the *Odyssey*). The Myceneans were displaced by the Dorians who invaded from the north bringing with them Iron-Age technology.

Greek civilisation (1100 to 200 BC) This title covers a multitude of sins. From around 1100 to 900 BC the Greek 'Dark Age' wiped out not only culture, but also written language. While the Greek-speaking Dorians existed in this dark twilight, the Phoenicians from the Levant (Syria? Lebanon?) took control of the sea routes. By 800 BC a written language was emerging and Homer, possibly a native of Khios, penned the *Iliad* and the *Odyssey*.

From 750 to 500 BC (the Archaic or Classical period) city-states (*Polis*) sprang up all over Greece, some more powerful than others, some in alliance with others, but all trading with one another and bound together in a loose defence pact. Colonies were established all around the Mediterranean. Corinth, the nearest powerful city-state to the Ionian, colonised most of the major Ionian islands.

The Persian Wars (500 to 478 BC) pulled the city-states together around Athens and cemented the Delian league – though the Ionian was little affected by it all. The Hellenic period arrived with the final defeat of the Persians and the establishment of Athens as the power base. The Ionian islands were effectively under control of Athens and naval bases were established to counter any threat from nearby Sparta. The Peloponnesian War (431 to 404 BC) between Athens and Sparta divided the Ionian islands and caused much hardship for the inhabitants. The war weakened both Athens and Sparta leaving the way open for Phillip II of Macedonia and later his son Alexander the Great to take control, though these tumultuous times hardly touched the Ionian islands.

The Romans (200 BC to AD 295) A weak Greece was easy prey for the Romans and they declared war on Phillip V of Macedonia in 202 BC. The Ionian islands, being closest to Italy, were among the first to fall: Corfu in 200 BC, Levkas in 197, Zakinthos in 191, and Cephalonia in 188. In 31 BC Octavius defeated Anthony and Cleopatra at Actium near Preveza and cemented the Roman Empire into a whole after a decade of infighting. Roman rule had little cultural influence on Greece while things Greek, everything from architectural style to cuisine, had a profound effect on the Roman way of life. Greek cities were largely autonomous owing allegiance to Rome and Greek remained the official language. In AD 295, weakened by attacks from tribes on the edges of the empire and beset by difficulties within, Diocletian split the empire into two.

Byzantium (AD 330 to 1204) The foundation of Constantinople and the rise of Byzantium marks the rise of the first Christian Empire. Byzantine rule of most of its empire, including the Ionian islands, was constantly beset by invasions from the north and south. The Slavs, Avars, Goths, Huns, Vandals and Bulgars came down from the north while the Saracens sailed across from the south. The islands were depopulated and towns and villages contracted in size and moved away from a precarious shoreline. At times the Byzantines drove the invaders out, in the 9th century Emperor Leo VI (the Wise) compacted all the Ionian islands into one province under Cephalonia, but Byzantine power was on the wane and new invaders were afoot.

The Normans (1081 to 1194) In the Ionian the Normans under Robert Guiscard, an obscure Knight with a license to pillage, quickly demolished any Byzantine resistance, but he died of fever before he could enjoy his success. The Normans occupied the Ionian islands until their power base in Italy waned towards the end of the 12th century.

The Venetians (1204 to 1550) In 1204 the Fourth Crusade sacked Constantinople (ostensibly their allies!) and parts of the Byzantine Empire were parcelled out to adventurers from the European nobility. The Venetians, who had transported the crusaders, emerged with a large chunk of Byzantine territory as their prize, including the Ionian islands. Most of the Ionian islands were leased out to Venetian families with the Orsini family getting Cephalonia, Ithaca, and Zakinthos.

Wherever the Venetians went they stamped their standard, the Lion of Saint Mark, on their castles and forts

During this period the Venetians established castles and forts at the principal ports along their trade routes. Most of these massive structures remain intact to this day and nearly every fort or castle you come across will be Venetian, at least in origin.

The Turks (1460 to 1830) In 1453 the Ottoman Turks took Constantinople and ended the rule of Byzantium. By the end of the 16th century most of Greece was under Turkish control. In the Ionian and elsewhere the Venetians continued to battle the Turks for territory and managed to hold onto most of the Ionian islands until Napoleon attacked the heart of the empire and by proxy obtained her possessions.

With the British defeat of the French in the Battle of the Nile, the Ionian islands, but not the mainland, came under British and Russian administration. In 1815 the islands came under sole British administration. The mainland opposite and most of the rest of Greece remained under Turkish control.

The War of Independence (1822 to 1830) In 1821 the Greek flag was raised at Kalavrita in the Peloponnese. In 1822 the Turks massacred 25,000 people on the island of Khios and so aroused Greek passions that many took up arms against the Turks throughout Greece. Under British rule the Ionian islands had a neutral status and many Greeks fled here from the fighting on the mainland. The islands also served as a convenient base for Greek resistance groups to operate from and for British and other European eccentrics to hop across to the mainland to aid the cause. Byron was only one of many who used this route, leaving Cephalonia for Mesolongion on New Year's Eve, 1823. The war was effectively won when a combined English, French and Russian fleet destroyed the larger Turkish and Egyptian fleet at Navarino. The Ionian islands remained under British rule.

Modern Greece The newly born republic got off to a shaky start and after a series of assassinations the western powers put a Bavarian prince on the throne. He proved an insensitive and unpopular ruler and was deposed by a popular revolt in 1862. In 1863 a new ruler, George I from Denmark, was chosen and the British relinquished control of the Ionian islands to encourage support. The boundaries of Greece expanded with the acquisition of Thessaly and the Epirus in 1881 and Macedonia and the northern Aegean islands in the Balkan wars (1912–13).

The Greeks fought on the Allied side in the First World War and with the defeat of the Turks on the Axis side, embarked on a disastrous campaign to acquire territory in Asia Minor. When the Greeks were finally driven out the Turkish population remaining in Greece was exchanged for Greeks in Turkey. Greece fought in the Second World War on the side of the Allies and obtained the last of her territory, the Dodecanese, from the Italians at the end of the war. Civil war split the country until 1947 when a Conservative government was elected. In 1967 the army took power with the notorious junta of the Colonels which ushered in seven years of autocratic and harsh rule. Democracy returned in 1974 with Karamanlis. The first Socialist government, PASOK, under Papandreou, was elected in 1981. In 1986 Greece joined the European Community and in common with the other EU members customs and immigration controls no longer apply at the borders for EU nationals.

Homer and the *Odyssey*

With the resurrection of writing after the Greek 'Dark Ages' there appeared, sometime in 800 BC, the two epic poems, the *Iliad* and the *Odyssey*. They are said to have been written by Homer who is thought to have been born on Khios in 800 BC. There is nothing certain about any of this. The two epics survived into later ages in different versions with the words altered and whole passages inserted or missing. Homer may have been one man or the epics may have been the work of a group of poets. The two epics differ intrinsically in style and composition. And the translations available to those of us who don't speak sufficient ancient Greek to read Homer in the raw further complicate the picture. There is plenty of room for speculation and contemplation on the epics and writers of academic tomes and popular reconstructions have plundered the opportunities available to produce literally scores of books on the interpretation of Homer and his epics.

It is the *Odyssey* we are interested in here. Odysseus came from Ithaca and this island most likely existed somewhere in the Ionian. The basic plot of the *Odyssey* concerns the attempts of Odysseus and his men to get home from the Trojan War.

Lineages play a large part in the epic. The Trojan War was ignited when Helen, wife of Menelaus, king of Sparta, eloped with Paris, son of the king of Troy. Menelaus, brother of Agamemnon, king of Mycenae, put together a vast fleet from associated city-states to besiege Troy and punish Paris. Odysseus as Lord of the Kefallenes brings twelve ships to Troy. After ten

years a ruse masterminded by Odysseus, the wooden horse, is trundled into Troy and so the city falls. Here the *Odyssey* proper starts following the fortunes and disasters that befall Odysseus on his voyage home. It takes ten years for him to return and he has many adventures along the way before he is re-united with his Penelope on Ithaca.

Dissection and commentary of the *Odyssey* began not long after the mysterious bard died. In the 3rd century BC it reached fever pitch with the

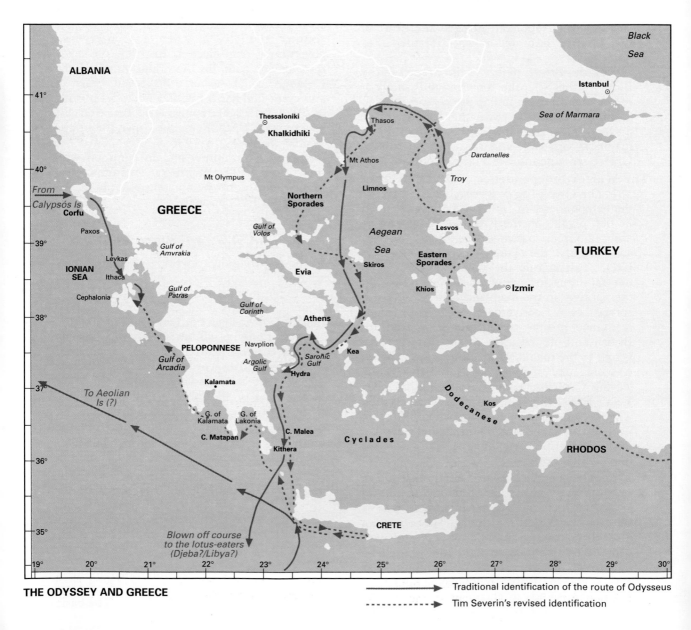

THE ODYSSEY AND GREECE

→ Traditional identification of the route of Odysseus

---→ Tim Severin's revised identification

4

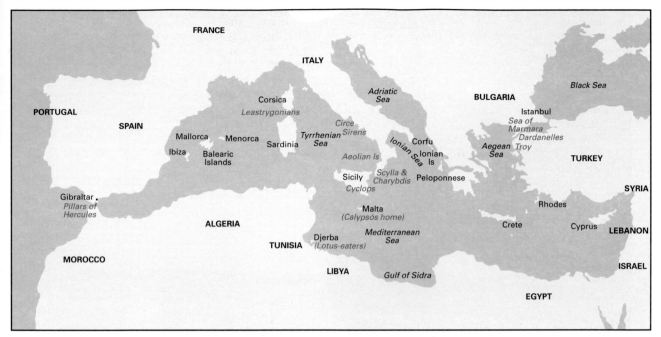

TRADITIONAL IDENTIFICATION OF PLACES VISITED IN THE ODYSSEY

great library at Alexandria filled with different versions of the epic and commentaries on it. It was the Alexandrines who divided the epics into the 24 book form that survives today. They were also of the opinion that the two epics were the product of two authors, not one. Despite the wanton destruction of the library at Alexandria, surely one of the greatest losses of the age, the tradition of analysis and commentary survived into the Roman and Byzantine periods before disappearing under the great weight of Christian censorship. Not until the 18th century was there any real revival of interest with a veritable deluge in the 19th and early 20th century as ancient sites were rediscovered and a knowledge of ancient Greece became an essential part of every young gentleman's education. Theories accumulated over just what the *Odyssey* was about – few doubted its obvious literary merits.

So does the *Odyssey* describe a real voyage by a real person? Or is it just an adventure story, a sort of *Buck Rogers* of the 8th century BC plucked from the lay poems of the times. There are many theories which can be roughly divided into the following categories.

1. The events in the epic are a fictional mishmash that do not have any particular geographical location. In effect it is ancient science fiction stroke adventure story and any attempt to identify the places in it would be like trying to locate where a fictional planet or a fictional country was. There may be threads of known geography included but the essence of the geography is fictional. This category also includes all those commentaries that tail off into long diatribes against the futility of trying to locate the geography of the *Odyssey* because it detracts from the literary and mythic qualities of the epic, a position I find difficult to understand when so often a geographical location, however vague, can enhance the poetry.

2. The geography described in the epic belongs not to the Mediterranean but variously to the Black Sea, the Atlantic, the Indian Ocean, the North Sea and the Baltic, or in variations to specific parts of the Mediterranean such as Spain or the Adriatic. Some of these locations are just cranky and are used to bolster theories of previous master-races, some of whom arrived on spaceships, and are recorded in the *Odyssey*. Some of the geographical locations, especially those placing the *Odyssey* in the Atlantic or Indian Oceans are just silly.

3. The geography described in the *Odyssey* is all real and relates to the known world of the time,

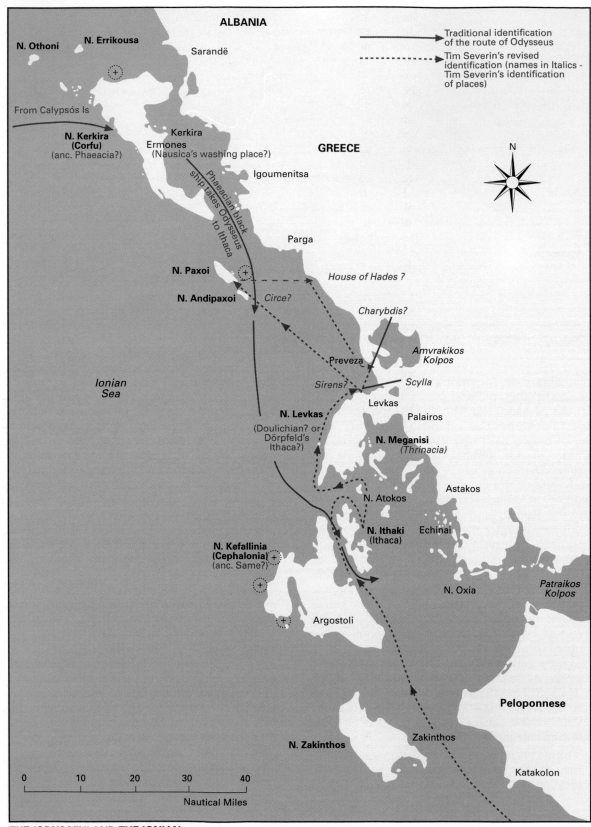

THE 'ODYSSEY' AND THE IONIAN

but the adventures of Odysseus are tailored to take us on a tour of the Mediterranean known to Homer and neither he nor his adventures existed as such, but are a fictional web holding the geography together. Thus all the places mentioned exist and can be located in the Mediterranean from the Pillars of Hercules at Gibraltar to Ithaca in the Ionian.

4. The geography and the hero and his voyage are Homers account of real events and a real person, perhaps embellished here and there, but basically a true story. Accounts like Ernle Bradford's excellent *Ulysses Found* take more or less this line. The geography of the *Odyssey* is located in the Mediterranean and can be traced to present-day places that bear the names mentioned in the epic as above.

5. A recent theory propounded by Tim Severin in *The Ulysses Voyage* (Ulysses is the Latinised version of Odysseus) states that Odysseus took the logical route home and all the places mentioned in the *Odyssey* can be located in present-day Greece.

So where does this leave us? There is no definitive proof for any of them. I have sailed around all of the geographical areas described in the various theories (except the silly ones) on numerous occasions and in all sorts of weather and as a personal preference I plump for number three, the rather woolly version that locates the geography in the Mediterranean in specific places, many of which bear the same name to this day, but which allows Homer a bit of license when dealing with his hero. Odysseus may well have existed and one interesting theory paints him as a successful pirate, a sort of Robin Hood from the Dark Ages. As Thucydides (460–399 BC) later commented on piracy in the Dark Ages, it was a respectable profession.

'The leading pirates were powerful men, acting both out of self-interest and in order to support the weak among their own people. They would descend upon cities which were unprotected by walls and indeed consisted only of scattered settlements: and by plundering such places they would gain most of their livelihood. At this time such a profession, so far from being regarded as disgraceful, was considered quite honorable. And in the old poets we find the regular question always asked of those who arrived by sea is 'Are you pirates?' It is never assumed either that those who were so questioned would shrink from admitting the fact, or that those who were interested in finding out the fact would reproach them with it.'

So Homer put together his epic using material from the lay poems and quite possibly from his own experience. There are many references in the *Odyssey* which point to an author acquainted with the sea and travelling upon it. Herodotus (484–420 BC) describes Homer as a travelling man not dissimilar to his hero in the *Odyssey*. He says Homer was born in Smyrna (now Izmir in Turkey) and travelled to many parts of Greece including Ithaca. Later he became blind and penniless and died on the island of Ios.

At the time Homer is thought to have lived there was considerable trading activity from Asia Minor with the Phocaeans from near Izmir leading the way establishing colonies as far away as Marseille (in 600 BC) and doubtless voyaging much further and also bringing back stories from other ships they encountered. We know too little about the Phocaeans except that they were excellent seamen and carried out astounding voyages around the Mediterranean. From them a geography could easily be absorbed and implanted in an epic poem.

There are a couple of practical points to consider when mulling over the theories about the *Odyssey* and the geography contained in it.

The first I have touched upon and relates to the details on navigation in the epic. Homer was obviously acquainted with the prevailing winds and the stars to sail by. When Calypso tells Odysseus to keep the Great Bear or the Plough on his left to reach Greece from her island (Malta?) this is exactly what a sailor can do today to maintain an easterly course from Malta or Sicily to get to Greece. The *meltemi* in the Aegean, the wind that still blows, is accurately described by Homer. When distances, directions, and weather matters can be so verified, then it is only reasonable to take Homer at his word for many other matters as well.

The second point concerns the power of existing place names. The erratic Heinrich Schliemann made his discoveries of ancient sites by taking Homer literally and digging where the bard said events had taken place. Much to the consternation of professional archaeologists he discovered many of the ancient sites mentioned in the *Iliad* and the *Odyssey*. We should not underestimate the names that have survived through the centuries to this day: Scylla and Charybdis in the Messina Strait, Circeo (Circe's island) south of Rome, the Aeolian islands north of Sicily, Cape Malea at the bottom of the

Peloponnese, and of course Ithaca in the Ionian. The question of Ithaca and the King of the Kefallenes remains an enduring one and perhaps it is best to leave it at that and accept that the island that bears the name today is the island of the *Odyssey*.

Language

It should be remembered that the Greek spoken today, demotic Greek, is not ancient Greek though it is largely derived from it. Anyone who speaks ancient Greek will be able to pick up a little over 50 per cent of the Greek spoken today, though the pronunciation may not be what you expect. In rendering Greek from the Cyrillic into the Roman alphabet there are very real difficulties and there are no absolutes, just guidelines.

Greek is difficult to master because right from the start you come up against the Greek alphabet which for most people may as well be hieroglyphics. Yet the alphabet can be conquered with a little persistence and common words and phrases to get you by in the tavernas and bars and on the street can be picked up by ear. One of the obstacles to learning Greek is that you so often come across someone speaking English that the need to learn Greek evaporates. However if you can only learn a few phrases, a 'hello' and 'goodbye' and 'how are you?', the effort will be repaid, especially in out of the way places. In Appendix I a few useful phrases will be found.

The Greek Orthodox church

For someone from the west, from the world of Roman Catholicism and Protestantism, the churches and the black-robed priests of the Greek Orthodox church constitute another religious world, and so it is. Up until the last meeting of the Council of Nicaea in 787, the western and eastern branches of the church had stumbled along together, growing apart but outwardly united. Post Nicaea the churches grew apart, partly on doctrinal issues, but mostly one suspects because of the geographical and cultural isolation between Rome and Constantinople. In Rome they spoke mostly Latin, in Constantinople Greek. In the west priests were celibate, in the east they married. In Rome the Pope was infallible, in

Constantinople articles of faith were decided by a council of bishops. In the west the spirit of God came from the Father and the Son, in the east from the Father.

The overthrow of Constantinople by the Turks in 1453 scattered the church as far afield as Russia and today the Orthodox church is still spread widely across the Balkans and into the steppes. The church was allowed to continue under the Turks and it became a focus for rebellion against the occupiers of Greece.

Today the church, although much weakened in this secular age, still permeates Greek life. For the Greeks the big event of the year is not Christmas, but Easter, *Pasca*. The date of Easter is reckoned in a different way to that in the west, and the celebration is focussed on the Resurrection rather than the Crucifixion. On Good Friday a service marks the Descent from the Cross and the *Epitafion* containing the body of Christ is paraded through the streets. In some places an effigy of Judas Iscariot is burnt or blown up. This latter can be a spectacular event as all Greek men love playing with dynamite and the effigy is inevitably stuffed with it. All Greek homes brew up a soup from the offal of the lamb which is to be eaten on the Resurrection and depending on your

Cave-like interior of a small orthodox chapel. Unfortunately more and more are being locked because of theft of the icons and ornaments

inclination, the soup may be tasty or you may have problems sampling even a spoonful of assorted tripe and other organs.

Late Saturday night there is the *Anestisi* mass to celebrate Christ's return. In the church all the lights are turned out and then from behind the altar screen the priest appears with a lighted candle and proceeds to light the candles of those in the church. Everyone responds with *Kristos Anesti* (Christ is risen) and there is a procession with the lighted candles through the streets to the sound of fire-crackers and sky-rockets, or any other explosive devices that are to hand. This is not a good time to be in trouble at sea as a lot of out-of-date flares are used up – though don't be tempted yourself as it is against the law to do so and there have been prosecutions. The traditional greeting everyone utters at this time is *Kronia Polla* (Many years or Long life). In the home boiled eggs, traditionally dyed red, are dished out and the normal sport is to bet your egg against the others, in the manner of conkers, or to surprise your friends with a solid rap on the head with the egg to crack the shell.

There are many local saints' days in the villages and towns and the whole place will often close down for them even if they are not on the list of state holidays. Greeks normally celebrate not their birthday, but the day of the saint they are named after – their name-day. In some churches there are icons to a saint reckoned to provide an above average service and these will have numerous votive offerings. Many of these are simple affairs, a pressed metal disc showing what blessing is required, whether for an afflicted limb, safety at sea, a new-born baby or a family house. Some of the older votive offerings are more ornate and elaborate, sometimes a painting or a model of a ship where thanks are given for survival at sea, or a valuable brooch or piece of jewellery for some other blessing. Greek churches are wonderful places, the *iconostasis* always elaborate and adorned, and the interior a dark and mystical place. It constantly amazes me that even in the most out-of-the-way places, on a rocky islet or a remote headland, that every church and chapel and shrine will be newly whitewashed and cleaned and will have an oil lamp burning or ready to burn in it.

Octopus drying in the sun for charcoal grilling in the evening

Food

Greek food is not for the gourmet, rather it is plain wholesome cooking that goes with the climate and the Greek idea that a meal is as much a social occasion as a culinary experience. This is not, emphatically not, to say that Greek food is not enjoyable. I love the unadulterated flavours of charcoal-grilled fish with a squeeze of lemon over it, or a *salata horiatiki*, the ubiquitous mixed salad swimming in olive oil and peppered with *feta* and black olives – the simplicity of the combination of ingredients brings out the best in them. In some restaurants and in Greek family cooking you will come across dishes that have been lost in the tourist areas where either the lethargy of taverna owners or the whingeing of visitors for a bland 'international' cuisine revolving around steak and chips has removed them from the menu. Some of the island tavernas still have a dish or two specific to the island or region such as Cephalonian meat pie on Cephalonia, but for the majority the dishes on the menu are those which are simply prepared and cooked and a few favourites such as *moussaka* and *stifadho*.

The principal meal in Greece is the midday meal and most oven-cooked dishes are prepared in the morning for this meal. In the evening these dishes will simply be partially reheated and served up as an overcooked lukewarm mess. Restaurants in Greece are categorised as either an *estiatorio* (a restaurant), a taverna (a simple tavern), or a *psistaria* (a restaurant specialising in fresh prepared food, mostly grilled meat), but the distinctions between these have now become so blurred that most restaurants call themselves a taverna.

The menu in a taverna will have two sets of prices, one with service and one without, and since all food comes with service you pay the higher price. In fact waiters are paid on results and the difference between the two prices goes to them which explains why some waiters work their butts off and others, often family who are not paid on results, loaf about ignoring your frantic pleas for a drink. In most Greek tavernas you will be invited into the kitchen or to a counter displaying the food to make your choice, a handy convention that gets over the problem of knowing what it is you are ordering from the menu. Only in the flasher restaurants will you be requested to order from the menu and there will normally be an English translation on the menu or on a board on the wall to help you out in most places.

A typical Greek meal will be a starter and main course with other side dishes ordered at random. Dessert is not normally served in a taverna although you may get fresh fruit or yoghurt. When ordering don't order everything at the same time as it will all arrive at once or sometimes you will get the main course first and the starter second. Often the food will be just warm, it having been set aside to cool as Greeks believe hot food is bad for you, a belief that has some backing from the medical community. If you get everything in order and hot, and things have improved in recent years, you are on a winner. If you don't, just order another bottle of wine and settle yourself in for the evening like the other Greeks around you – after all, what have you got to do that's so important after dinner.

Below there is a list of the common dishes you will come across though obviously they vary in finesse and taste from taverna to taverna according to the skills of the cook.

Soups, salads and starters

Avgolemono	Egg and lemon soup, often with a chicken and rice broth
Fakes	Lentil soup
Fasolada	Bean soup
Hortosoupa	Vegetable soup
Psarossoupa	Fish soup
Tzatziki	Yoghurt and chopped cucumber dip
Taramasalata	Fish roe dip
Melitzanasalata	Aubergine dip
Patatasalata	Potato salad
Skordhalia	Potato and garlic dip, sometimes accompanies other dishes as a piquant sauce
Salata horiatiki	Mixed salad, usually tomatoes, cucumber, onion, green pepper, black olives, and *feta*
Domatasalata	Tomato salad
Salata marouli	Green salad, usually lettuce
Horta	Spring greens, often including rocket and spinach
Rizospanaki	Rice mixed with spinach
Piperies psites	Baked peppers
Melitzanes tiganites	Fried aubergines, delicious if freshly fried
Kolokithakia tiganites	Fried courgettes
Fasolia yigandes plaki	Giant or butter beans in a tomato sauce
Tiropita	Cheese wrapped in *filo* pastry, mini-versions of the large snack *tiropitas*

Some of the above can accompany the main course.

Main courses

Brizola khirino	Pork chop, normally charcoal-grilled
Brizola mouskhari	Beef chop, normally charcoal-grilled
Paidhakia	Lamb chop, normally charcoal-grilled
Souvlaki	Kebab, usually lamb or beef
Keftedhes	Meatballs in a sauce, usually tomato but may be an egg and lemon sauce
Bifteki	A burger, but usually homemade
Kotopoulo	Chicken, may be oven-roasted or spit-roasted

Astakos usually = crayfish as here and not lobster proper

Kokoretsi	An offal (liver, kidneys, heart, tripe) kebab charcoal-grilled. Can be excellent
Moussaka	Aubergine and mince with a bechamel sauce not unlike a Greek version of shepherds pie
Stifadho	A meat (usually lamb) and tomato stew
Pastitsio	Pasta with a mince and cheese sauce, baked in the oven
Makaronia	Spaghetti, may be with a meat or tomato sauce
Domates yemistes	Stuffed tomatoes
Piperies yemiste	Stuffed peppers
Kolokithia yemiste	Stuffed courgettes
Melitzanes imam bayaldi	Aubergines baked with tomatoes – a dish left over from the Turkish occupation that literally means: 'the imam fainted'

Fish and seafood

Ohtapodhi	Octopus, may be charcoal-grilled or cooked in a wine or ink sauce
Kalamaria	Squid, normally coated in a light batter and deep fried
Soupia	Cuttlefish, normally deep fried
Psaria	Fish, normally fried or grilled
Barbouni	Red mullet
Fangri	Bream
Sfiritha	Grouper
Tonnos	Tuna
Xsifia	Swordfish
Marithes	Whitebait normally deep fried, you eat them head and all
Garidhes	Prawns, normally fried or grilled
Astakos	Crayfish

Desserts

Normally desserts and sticky sweets are found in a *Zakhoroplasteia* (patisserie) and in some of the up-market cafés.

Baklava	Honey and nut mixture in *filo* pastry
Kataifi	Honey and nut mixture in a sort of shredded wheat
Rizogalo	Rice pudding
Galaktobouriko	Custard pie
Loukoumadhes	Small doughnuts in honey
Pagota	Ice-cream

There will also be assorted sticky cakes though I personally find most of them too sugary.

Fish and chips and chicken-in-a-basket

Wine-making the old fashioned way in Vassiliki – this vintage contained significant quantities of dead wasps and a bit of cigarette ash to give that certain Greek cachet

Wine

Greek wine is a source of mystery to most western oenophiles. There are grape varieties in Greece few have ever encountered before. The production is so inconsistent that wines vary radically from year to year. Most of the wines are oxidised or maderised. Storing wine properly is virtually unknown and most wine is new wine. Until 1969 there was no real government control of wines of a specific origin. To compound all of this wine will often be sitting in a shop window where it gets a dose of sunlight every day. Given all these problems it is amazing that some Greek wine is as good as it is. On the plus side Greek oenology is slowly on the mend and given the climatic conditions, the interesting grape varieties, and the excellent results of a few wine producers who have imported new wine-making technology and nurtured their product, the portent for the future is good. We may well see a renaissance in Greek oenology that will return it to its ancient elevated status.

Vines for wine-making were growing in Greece before anyone in France or Spain had ever seen or heard of the plant or its product. Estimates vary, but probably sometime around the 13th to the 12th centuries BC Greek viticulture was well established. The mythic origins of the introduction of the vine are associated with Dionysis and trace the route of the vine from India and/or Asia to Greece. Dionysis was said to be the son of Zeus and Semele (daughter of Cadmus, King of Thebes) who was brought up in India by the nymphs and taught the lore of the vine and wine-making by Silenus and the satyrs – sounds a wonderful childhood to me. He journeyed from India across Asia Minor to Greece bringing the vine and accompanied by a band of followers.

One can imagine a religious cult growing up around wine, the visions and hallucinations from imbibing it could only have been supernatural, and the introduction of it to Greece would have been unstoppable, hence its incorporation into the mythic universe of the ancients. The Homeric *Hymn to Dionysis* tells of his journey around the islands distributing the vine and describes vine leaves sprouting from the masthead of his ship. Nor is it surprising that the cult of Dionysis was associated with the release of mass emotion, was a fertility cult, and that the Dionysian Festival included wild uninhibited dancing and at times violence and sacrifice – all things associated in one way or another with alcohol today.

There is no way we can know what ancient wine was like. It was referred to by its place of origin, thus Pramnian, Maronean, Khian, Thasian, and Koan wine were mentioned by name much as we mention a Bordeaux or Côte du Rhône today. Whether or not it was all resinated as in the ubiquitous *retsina* surviving today is unknown. Most likely amphoras of wine were sealed with a resin mixture to prevent oxidation and this imparted a flavour to the wine. Over time it was assumed that the resin itself, and not the exclusion of oxygen, prevented wine going off and oxidizing and so resin was added directly to the wine to produce *retsina*. It is unfortunate that many people only get to drink bottled *retsina* today as the stuff from the barrel is superior and should be drunk as a new wine. Much of the bottled *retsina* and some of the barrel *retsina* is simply bad wine that can only be made to taste palatable by resinating it.

Of the general wines on the market, many are made by co-operatives and the preparation, production, storage and bottling is at best sloppy. Some of the better wines to look out for are:

Agioritikos From Mt Athos. The red (Cabernet Sauvignon) and white (Sauvignon blanc) are good value.
Domaine Carras (Côtes de Meliton) Good young reds and whites.
Naoussa Good reds.
Lion de Nemea Good red (Agiorgitiko).
Lemnos AO Good whites.
Paros AO Whites and reds, though not always consistent.
Santorini AO Good whites though variable.

There are also a number of Muscats that are considered to be good quality though they are not to my taste. The *Samos Muscat* from the island is considered the best although *Muscat of Cephalonia* and *Muscat of Patras* produced by *Achaia Clauss* also get a mention. Sweet red liqueur wine vaguely resembling port is produced from the Mavrodaphne grape and *Mavrodaphne of Patras* produced by *Achaia Clauss* and *Mavrodaphne of Cephalonia* are passable port-type wines. Many of the local wine shops have a local Mavrodaphne in stock and this is often acceptable.

In the Ionian there are a number of wines that deserve mention, though they are not all easily obtainable.

Mainland
Zitsa AO Good white from Ioannina. Made from the Debina grape by the local co-operative, drink it young.

Corfu
Theotoki Roppa Excellent reds and whites from Kakotriyis, Petrokorintho, Robola, and Sauvignon blanc made near Roppa. Almost impossible to find, but try.
Santa Domenica Good reds and whites from Kakotriyis grapes made near Levkimmi.
Grovino Good red made near Roppa.

Levkas
Santa Maura Red made by the local TAOL co-operative in Levkas.

Cephalonia
Robola of Cephalonia AO Good white produced in Cephalonia as its name indicates. Made from Robola grapes and variable in quality.
Gentilini Excellent whites produced in Argostoli. Made from Chardonnay, Tssaoussi, Robola, and Sauvignon blanc varieties by a small vineyard under Nikolaos Kosmetatos. Difficult to find but worth the effort.
Calliga Good reds and a rosé.
Manzavino Reds and a rosé.
Laguna Good white though variable.

Zakinthos
Verdea A dry astringent white famous in Zakinthos and produced by a number of wine-makers. It is not consistent and should be drunk early.

Greek wine is not helped by a dose of sunlight everyday

Background basics

Getting there

There are good land, sea and air communications to Greece and to the Ionian islands and mainland.

By air
The area is well served by airports and there are numerous scheduled and charter flights to all of them.

Corfu Has scheduled and charter flights every day from many European destinations. Internal flights to Athens.

Aktion near Preveza and Levkas Has charter flights, mostly from the UK. Internal flights to Athens.

Cephalonia Has charter flights, mostly from the UK and Germany. Internal flights to Athens.

Zakinthos Has charter flights from the UK and other European countries. Internal flights to Athens.

Apart from these airports you can fly into Athens and get a connecting flight to one of the regional airports, though as they are often full it pays to book the flight in advance. There are also regular buses to Patras (about 2½ hours) and four buses a day to Levkas (about 4½ hours).

By sea
Ferries run from Trieste, Venice, Ancona, Bari, Otranto and Brindisi. The two places most people aim for are Ancona and Brindisi.

Trieste One company operating a weekly service to Patras in the summer.

Venice One company operating a weekly service to Katakolon on the Peloponnese. It is really more of a cruise and consequently expensive.

Ancona Four companies operate bi-weekly trips to Patras. The extra cost compared to more southerly ports is offset by the reduction in distance you have to travel by land to Brindisi or Otranto.

Bari One company operating a bi-weekly service to Patras though it seems to be intermittent.

Otranto One company operating three sailings weekly to Corfu and Igoumenitsa.

Brindisi Has traditionally been the main ferry terminal for western Greece and according to the demand has between four and eight companies operating services. Prices are keen with all the competition and there will always be several services on any one day. Depending on the company the ferries usually stop at several ports in the Ionian, among them: Corfu, Igoumenitsa, Paxos, Vathi (Ithaca), Sami (Cephalonia) and Patras.

Prices for any of the crossings are seasonal with peak prices in July, August and part of September. In the winter and spring the number of crossings is reduced and in some cases ferries may be switched to another service altogether. Out of season it is probably best to make for Ancona or Brindisi.

By land
It is a long haul down to Greece from northern Europe. From Calais you can get to Ancona in two days though three is more relaxed. From Ancona and Brindisi there are ferries to Corfu, Igoumenitsa and Patras. It is also possible to drive down through Germany, Austria and Yugoslavia to northern Greece and then across Greece to the Ionian, but this is something of a marathon taking at least three to four days hard driving and the trip through Yugoslavia has nothing to recommend it. Until the Yugoslavs sort themselves out the trip through the civil war zone is at present hazardous to say the least.

You can keep a car in Greece for six months renewable for another six months if you take it out and bring it in again – after that you will have to pay duty on it, in spite of EU regulations.

Getting around

By local ferry
From Corfu there is a good service to Igoumenitsa and Paxos. Although there is an improved service in the Inland sea S of Levkas, you will have to plan connections carefully. The ferry services are most easily seen on the accompanying map, but I have outlined them briefly below.

Corfu Regular daily connections to Igoumenitsa and Paxos. Local tripper boats run to Errikousa.

Levkas Daily connections from Nidri to Meganisi and from Vassiliki to Fiskardho on Cephalonia.

Ithaca Daily connections from Vathi to Patras, Astakos, Sami on Cephalonia, and from Frikes to Vassiliki on Levkas.

Hire motorbikes are the cheapest way to get around and can be found on the major islands – just keep your wits about you when dealing with local traffic

Cephalonia Daily connections from Sami to Patras and Ithaca, from Poros to Killini and some connections to Zakinthos, from Fiskardho to Vassiliki on Levkas, some connections from Pessades to Ay Nikolaos on Zakinthos, and some connections from Argostoli to Zakinthos.

Zakinthos Daily connections to Killini and some connections to Pessades and Argostoli on Cephalonia.

Some of these routes operate only in the summer and some may disappear altogether if they prove unprofitable. Likewise new services appear if an operator feels he can make a profit.

Water-taxis and tripper boats

In the more touristy areas like Corfu and Paxos water-taxis run trips to nearby beaches or villages. Tripper boats also run from anywhere there is a sizeable concentration of tourists and it is possible to get a one-way trip on one of these. Local *caiques* can also be hired to do short trips across or between islands – there is no standard rate and it is up to you and the boatman to come to a mutually agreeable price.

Buses

Local bus services vary widely between the islands, but even the best of the services are infrequent. To get about by bus you will need to check departure times the day before and to exercise a little and sometimes a lot of patience. The larger islands, Corfu, Levkas, Cephalonia and Zakinthos have the best services while smaller islands like Ithaca have an intermittent service. On the mainland opposite bus services are also infrequent and you will have to budget a whole day to get to most places and back.

Taxis

Most of the islands and the mainland towns and larger villages have taxis or you can phone for one. Fares are reasonable as long as there is a meter and it works or the price is roughly agreed upon first. In some of the more touristy spots like Corfu or Argostoli on Cephalonia, tourists are fleeced by drivers, but on the whole little of this goes on.

Hire cars and bikes

In many of the tourist resorts you can hire a car or jeep, or more commonly a motorbike of some description. Hire cars and jeeps are expensive in Greece and if there are not four people it is not really worth it unless you are feeling frivolous.

Hire motorbikes come in all shapes and sizes from battered Honda 50's to 500cc brutes. It is rare to be asked for a licence, but the operator will normally hold your passport. It is also rare to be offered a helmet. The reliability of hire bikes varies considerably with some bikes only a year or so old and others still struggling along after years of battering by would-be TT riders. On the whole I have found the Honda/Suzuki/Yamaha step-through 50's to be the most reliable even when getting on in years and the larger tyres compared to scooters like *Vespas* make them safer on gravel roads.

All of the operators charge you for insurance, but read the small print as it doesn't seem to cover you for very much. You are expected to return the bike if it breaks down and to pay for any damage to the bike if you have an accident. Bear in mind that Greece has the highest accident rate in Europe after Portugal and that on a bike you are vulnerable to injury. Even coming off on a gravel road at relatively low speed can cause serious gravel burns, so despite the heat it is best to wear long trousers and solid footwear. Roads on the islands are usually tarmac for the major routes and gravel for the others. Despite all these warnings a hire bike is the best way to get inland and with care you can see all sorts of places it would be difficult for a car to get to.

Walking

There are some fine walks around the islands and on the mainland coast. The main problem is finding a good map as most locally produced maps should be treated with a healthy scepticism. Tracks which have long since disappeared will be shown and new tracks will be omitted. The best policy is to set out with the spirit of exploration uppermost and not plan to necessarily arrive somewhere, rather to dawdle along the away. This mode of walking is encouraged by the energy-sapping heat of the summer. Take stout footwear, a good sun-hat, sunglasses, sun-bloc cream, and most importantly a bottle of water.

Shopping and other facilities

Provisioning

In all but the smallest village you will find you can obtain basic provisions and in the larger villages and tourist areas there will be a variety of shops catering for your needs. Greece now has a lot more imported goods from the other EU countries and you will be able to find familiar items, peanut butter, bacon, breakfast cereals, even baked beans in the larger supermarkets and specialist shops. Imported items are of course more expensive than locally produced goods. Shopping hours are roughly 0800 to 1300 and 1630 to 2000, though shops will often remain open for longer hours in the summer if there are customers around, especially in tourist spots.

Meat Is usually not hung for long and is butchered in a peculiarly eastern Mediterranean way – if you ask for a chicken to be quartered the butcher picks up his cleaver and neatly chops the chicken into four lumps. Salami and bacon are widely available in mini-markets.

Fish Except for smaller fish is generally expensive. Some fish, like red snapper and grouper, are very expensive and prawns and crayfish have a hefty price tag except off the beaten track.

In Greece a supermarket is really a mini-market and a mini-market is very 'mini'

The ubiquitous *periptero*, a covered stall selling cigarettes, sweets, ice-cream and cold drinks, aspirin and sun-tan oil, useless beach toys, newspapers, indeed anything which can be squeezed into or around a couple of square metres and it will likely have a metered telephone as well

Fruit and vegetables Fresh produce used to be seasonal, but now EU imports mean more is available longer. It is prudent to wash fruit and vegetables before eating them raw.

Bread Greek bread straight out of the oven is delicious, but it doesn't keep well. Small milk loaves called *tspureki* keep longer than the normal bread and in some places brown or rye bread can be found and this also keeps better than your average white loaf.

Staples Many items are often sold loose. Some staples, loose or packaged, may have weevils.

Cheese Imported cheeses such as Dutch *edam* or *gruyère* are now widely available courtesy of the EU. Local hard cheeses can also be found and *feta* is available everywhere.

Yoghurt Greek yoghurt is the best in the world as far as I am concerned. Use it instead of salad dressing or cream.

Canned goods Local canned goods are good and cheap, particularly canned fruit. Canned meat is usually imported and expensive.

Coffee and tea Instant coffee is comparatively expensive. Local coffee is ground very fine for 'Greek coffee' and tends to clog filters. Imported ground coffee is available.

Wines, beer and spirits Bottled wine varies from good to terrible and is not consistent, usually because it is not stored properly. Wine can be bought direct from the barrel in larger villages and towns and at least you get to taste before you buy. *Retsina* is also available bottled or from the barrel. Beer is brewed under license (*Amstel* and *Henninger* are the most common), is a light lager type and eminently palatable. Local spirits, *ouzo* not dissimilar to *pastis*, and Greek brandy often referred to by the most common brand name as just *Metaxa*, are good value and can be bought bottled or from the barrel.

Banks

Eurocheques, postcheques, travellers cheques, the major credit cards (*Access* and *Visa*) and charge cards (*American Express* and *Diners Club*) are accepted in the larger towns and tourist resorts. You will need your passport for identification. Many of the larger places now have an ATM, (automatic teller machine) or 'hole-in-the-wall machine', which will give you cash in drachmae from the major credit cards with a pin number. *Visa* or *Mastercard* generally do the trick and the benefit of this transaction is that you will be getting drachmae at the UK rate which is generally better than the rate in Greece.

For smaller places carry cash. Banks are open from 0800–1300 Monday to Friday. Most post offices and some travel agents will change travellers cheques and Eurocheques.

Post

Post offices can be found in larger villages and towns. Mail can be sent to them c/o Poste Restante and the service is reliable. One tip: get the assistant to look under your first name, Esq., and the boats name as well as your surname. You will need your passport for identification.

Telephones

You can direct dial from almost anywhere in Greece. The telephone system is not too bad although it is not unusual to get a crackly line and sometimes to be cut off or find someone else talking on your line. Telephone calls can be made from a kiosk with an orange top to it, a blue-top kiosk is for domestic calls only. In the towns there will be an OTE (Overseas Telephone Exchange) where you can make a metered call and pay the clerk on completion. Telephone calls can also be made from metered telephones in a *periptero* although the charge will be higher than at the OTE.

Telephone cards are now widely available and can be purchased from grocery and other shops, even from the *periptero* that have metered telephones.

Mobile digital phones using the GSM system can be used in Greece as long as your service provider has an agreement with one of the Greek mobile phone companies. You may be required to leave a deposit with your service provider before you leave. In most places the phones automatically lock into the system and coverage in the Ionian is good with this exception: if you are in a bay with high land blocking out the signal then you may not be able to use the phone.

Paradoxically the system often works better when you are out sailing around.

IDD code for Greece 30. IDD code for the UK 44.

Public Holidays

Jan 1	New Year's Day
Jan 6	Epiphany
Mar 25	Independence Day
May 1	May Day
Aug 15	Assumption
Oct 28	Ochi ('No') Day
Dec 25	Christmas Day
Dec 26	St Stephens Day

Movable
First Day of Lent
Good Friday
Easter Monday
Ascension

In addition many of the islands or regions have local Saints days when a holiday may be declared and some shops and offices will close.

Sailing information

Navigation

Navigation around the islands and along the coast is predominantly of the eyeball variety. The ancients navigated from island to island and prominent features on the coast quite happily and this is basically what yachtsmen still do in Greece. Eyeball navigation is a much maligned art, especially now that electronic position finding equipment has arrived on the scene, but for the reasons outlined below, it is still essential to hone your pilotage skills.

For good eyeball navigation you need the facility to translate the two-dimensional world of the chart into the three-dimensional world around you. Pick out conspicuous features like a cape, an isolated house, a knoll, an islet, and visualise what these will look like in reality. Any dangers to navigation such as a reef or shoal water may need clearing bearings to ensure you stay well clear of them. Any eyeball navigation must always be backed up by dead reckoning and a few position fixes along the way.

Anyone with electronic position finding should exercise caution using it close to land or dangers to navigation. The paradox of the new equipment is that while you may know your position, often to an accuracy of 100m or less, the chart you are plotting your position on is not accurate in terms of its latitude and longitude. Most of the charts were surveyed in the 19th century using astronomical sights and the position of a cape or a danger to navigation, while proportionally correct in relation to the land mass, may be incorrect in terms of its latitude and longitude. Some of the charts carry a warning, and corrections for latitude and longitude, usually the latter, of up to 1M! Consequently you are in the anomalous position of knowing your position to perhaps within 200m, but in possession of a chart which may have inaccuracies of a mile in its longitude. Blind acceptance of the position from electronic position finding equipment can and has lead to disaster.

Navigation and piloting hazards

The comparatively tideless waters of the Mediterranean, a magnetic variation of just over 2° east, and the comparatively settled summer patterns remove many of the problems associated with sailing in other areas of the world. Just having no tidal streams of any consequence to worry about enhances your sailing a hundredfold. Despite this there are hazards to navigation which while not specific to the Mediterranean, should be mentioned here.

Haze
In the summer a heat haze can reduce visibility to a mile or two which makes identification of a distant island or feature difficult until you are closer to it. Sailing from Paxos down to Preveza or Levkas you may not be able to positively identify features until you are two miles or so off. Heavy rain cleanses the air and dramatically improves visibility.

Sea mist
In parts of the Ionian, especially around the north of Corfu and in the Corfu channel, there may be a dense radiation fog in the morning which can sometimes reduce visibility to half a mile or less. The mist will gradually be burned off by the sun and by afternoon should have disappeared.

Reefs and rocks
The Ionian has only a few isolated dangerous rocks and reefs and with care these are normally

Fickle winds in the Meganisi channel

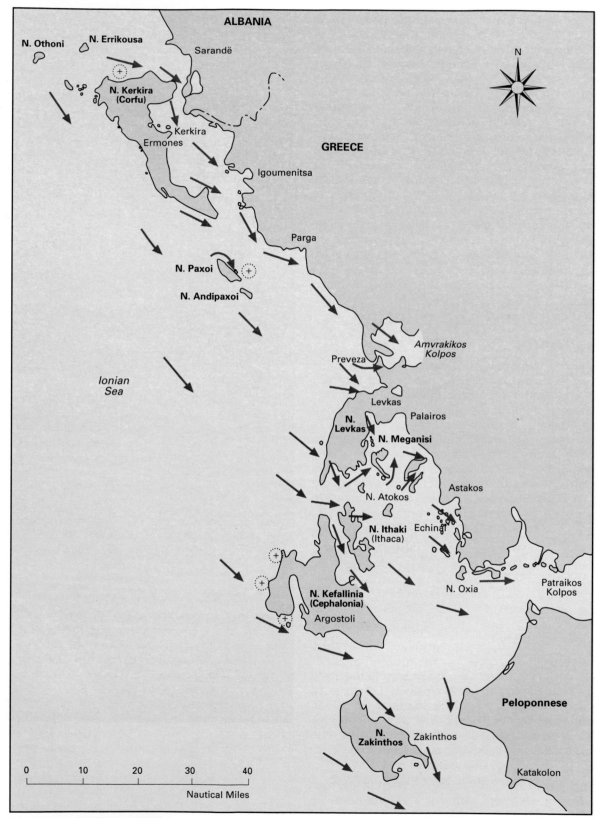

ALBANIA

N. Othoni   N. Errikousa

Sarandë

N. Kerkira
(Corfu)

Kerkira
Ermones

GREECE

Igoumenitsa

N
N

Parga

N. Paxoi

N. Andipaxoi

Amvrakikos
Kolpos

Preveza

Ionian
Sea

Levkas

Palairos

N.
Levkas

N. Meganisi

Astakos

N. Atokos

N. Ithaki
(Ithaca)

Echinal

N. Kefallinia
(Cephalonia)

Argostoli

N. Oxia

Patraikos
Kolpos

Peloponnese

N.
Zakinthos

Zakinthos

Katakolon

0   10   20   30   40

Nautical Miles

PREVAILING SUMMER WINDS

easily spotted. However this absence of large areas of shoal water or extensive reefs can make the navigator lazy in his craft. The clarity of the water in the Mediterranean means you can easily spot rocks and shallows from the colour of the water. Basically deep blue is good, deep green means its getting shallow, lighter green means watch out, and brown lets you identify species of molluscs at first hand. However with a chop of any sort the whitecaps on the water can make identification of shallow water and reefs difficult and you should give any potential dangers a wide berth.

Fishing nets

Care is needed around local fishing boats or in isolated bays where there may be surface nets laid. Vigilance is needed not to run over a net and incur not just the wrath of a fisherman, but most likely the net wrapped tightly around the propeller.

Lights

Although the islands and coast are quite well lit, the sheer extent of them means that it is impossible to light any but the most common routes used by ships and commercial fisherman. Navigation at night out of the common routes should be avoided unless you are familiar with the area.

Winds

The winds in the Ionian are remarkably consistent in the summer. From June until the end of September the wind blows down onto the Ionian from the NW to WNW. Generally it arrives around noon, blows between Force 3 to 6 (10 to 25kt), and dies down at sunset. It is a proper gentleman's wind that allows you to motor northwards in the morning calm should you so desire and leaves the evenings calm so you can enjoy an anchorage in comfort. The prevailing wind is channelled and funnelled by the land masses in its way so that it can blow off the land and down channels from anywhere between N and SW. Off the high land there can be strong gusts on the leeward side such as on the E side of Ithaca and Zakinthos. In July and August the wind is at its strongest and the presence of dense clouds hugging the summits of the islands, particularly Cephalonia, Ithaca and Zakinthos, tells you it is going to be fairly strong that day.

A strong *maistro* is often signalled by dense cloud hugging the summits of the islands

In the evening there may be a katabatic wind off the high mainland mountains generally blowing from the NE. This usually gets up around 2000 and can blow up to Force 6 (25kt), but usually less, and normally dies down after 2 or 3 hours.

In the spring and autumn there may be gales from the south when a depression passes over. Sometimes a moderate to strong southerly will quickly turn to the north and increase in strength, so care is needed when sheltering from southerlies. Thunderstorms, usually with an associated squall (winds can be up to 40+kt), also occur in the spring and autumn, but are generally over within 2 to 3 hours. A *scirocco* may also blow from the south, usually in the spring, bringing a sickly humid heat and the red sand of the Sahara from whence it comes.

Berthing

Berthing Mediterranean-style with the stern or bows to the quay can give rise to immense problems for those doing it for the first time, or even the second or third time. Describing the technique is easy: the boat is berthed with the stern or bows to the quay with an anchor out from the bows or stern respectively to hold the boat off the quay. It is carrying out the manoeuvre which causes problems and here a few words of advice may be useful, but will not replace actually doing it.

Everything should be ready before you actually start the manoeuvre. Have all the fenders tied on, have two warps coiled and ready to throw ashore with one end cleated off, and have the anchor ready to run, in the case of a stern anchor have the warp flaked out so it does not tie itself into knots as you are berthing. The manoeuvre should be carried out slowly using the anchor to brake the way of the boat about half a boat length off the quay. The anchor should be dropped about three or four boat lengths from the quay and ensure you have sufficient chain or warp beforehand to actually get there.

Many boats have a permanent set-up for going bows-to so there is not too much scrabbling around in lockers to extract an anchor, chain and warp. This can be quite simple: a bucket tied to the pushpit to hold the chain and warp and an arrangement for stowing the anchor on the pushpit. Boats going stern-to must have someone who knows what they are doing letting the anchor chain go. It should run freely until the boat is half a boat length off the quay. When leaving a berth haul yourself out with the chain or warp using the engine only sparingly until the anchor is up – it is all too easy to get the anchor warp caught around the propeller otherwise.

Berthing bows-to: kedge out the back, fenders out, mooring warps ready

The good tourist

However much you hate being tagged with the label, we all are tourists, some longer term than others. If you like you can be the good holiday-maker, visitor, yachtsman, or whatever name that doesn't offend you. What is required of those of us who travel upon the water around the Ionian islands, or anywhere else in the world for that matter, is that we do not stain the waters we travel upon or the land we come to. Some tourists regrettably seem not to have any understanding of the delicate relationship between tourist and locals and are so boorish and spend so much time whining about the faults of the country they have come to that I wonder why on earth they bothered – possibly because nobody in their own country could stand them. Which is not to say that the locals are angels, they can manage to emulate the worst of American and British excesses and can be as boorish as the worst of us, but then this is their country and so I suppose they have more license to do so. Local interaction aside, there are a number of substantive local complaints about us.

Rubbish

Many of the smaller islands are just not geared up to disposing of the rubbish brought in by tourists and on the water you will be visiting some small villages or deserted bays where there are literally no facilities at all. You should take your rubbish with you to a larger island and dispose of it there. Even the larger islands have questionable methods of disposing of rubbish and there is nothing wrong in trying to keep the number of convenience wrapped goods you buy to a minimum. My particular *béte noire* is bottled drinking water as the discarded plastic containers can be found everywhere and when burnt, (the normal way rubbish is disposed of on the islands) produce noxious gases and dangerous compounds.

It hardly needs to be said, you would think, that non-biodegradable rubbish should not be thrown into the sea. Even biodegradable rubbish such as vegetable peelings or melon rind should not be thrown into the water, except when you are five or more miles from land, or it ends up blowing back onto the shore before it has decayed or been eaten by scavengers. Toilets should not be used in harbour if there is one ashore, or they should be used with a holding tank. Holding tanks should not be emptied until you are well offshore.

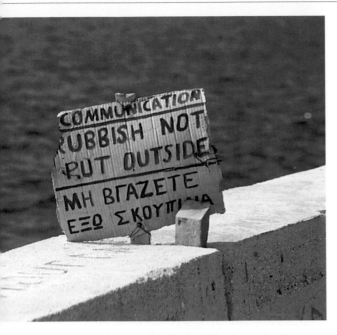

Many of the smaller islands just cannot cope with piles of rubbish from summer-time tourists who apparently cannot read – close by this sign on Kalamos were bags of rubbish left by visiting yachts

I don't think most people can quarrel with the above, but sometimes I hear the argument that because the locals pollute the sea and the land, then why bother yourself. It is true that the locals are often the worst offenders, but consciousness of pollution and individual responsibility for it is spreading through the villages and towns and as tourists we have a responsibility to keep the wilder parts of Europe free from pollution when we have made such a tip of our own backyard. Moreover many of the sources of pollution are there to service the tourist trade and if there were no tourists then there would be less pollution.

Noise pollution
This comes in various forms from the simple banality of making your presence known in an anchorage with the tape or CD player turned up full blast to inconsiderate motorboat owners with loud exhausts. Those who play loud music in deserted bays should reflect as to whether they would not be more comfortable in a noisy urban disco, preferably in their own country. Another annoying noise in an anchorage is the puttering of generators and those who need to run their generator all day and night might consider whether they may not be more comfortable in a marina where they can hook up to shore-power –

there are a lot of nice marinas along the French and Italian Riviera. Motorboaters with noisy outboards and inboards, and water-bikes which somehow always contrive to have the most irritating whine in their exhaust note as well as the most irritating people driving them, should keep well clear of boats at anchor and keep noise levels to a minimum when they do come into an anchorage or harbour, or anywhere for that matter where they intrude on the peace and quiet most people, themselves included, come for.

Safety and seamanship
In some places small powerboats and inflatables roar around an anchorage without regard for those swimming in the water. This is not just irritating but potentially lethal. If you have ever seen the injuries sustained by someone who has been hit by a propeller, you will immediately understand my concern. Accidents such as these frequently result in death or for the lucky, horrible mutilation. Those on large craft should also keep a good lookout when entering an anchorage where people are in the water or when their own crew is swimming off the back of the boat.

Remember when picking up someone who has fallen overboard to engage neutral or you may replace death by drowning with death by propeller injuries. Although water-bikes do not have a propeller they are just as lethal if they hit someone at speed and injure them – it doesn't take long to drown.

In many bays swimming areas are now cordoned off with a line of small yellow conical (usually) buoys. Although this restricts the area you can anchor in, the swimming areas should be avoided and in fact you can be fined for anchoring in one of these areas. Certainly the locals will let you know in no uncertain terms that you should not be there.

Conservation
Under the aegis of organisations like the World Wildlife Fund, Greenpeace, and Friends of the Earth, conservation is coming of age in Greece. Amongst the campaigns being waged two are of especial importance in the Ionian.

The first is the Monk Seal Project. The Mediterranean monk seal, *Monachus monachus*, is numbered amongst the twelve most endangered animals in the world and is the rarest species of seal left. It is specific to the warm waters of the Mediterranean although small numbers are found on the Atlantic coast of Morocco. There are estimated to be only 500 to 800 of these animals left with approximately half the population in Greece.

The Ionian is one of the places where the seal is found and in Fiskardho the Monk Seal Project funded by the World Wildlife Fund is attempting to educate local fishermen and tourists about the species and its habitat. One of the big problems is the encroachment of tourism into the habitat occupied by the seals. Illegal spear-fishing using sub-aqua equipment is eroding the food supply – Italian visitors have been cited as the chief culprits and there have been several convictions, but the blame does not lie solely here. Small powerboats and inflatables with powerful outboards exploit quiet places and the coastal caves where these retiring animals live. Those on the water and the land can help by keeping away from coastal caves and rocky coastlines and at all times should avoid making too much noise – the seals are easily frightened. Any illegal fishing whether by sub-aqua divers or dynamiting should be reported to the port police or any other authority. If you want further information or can help with the project contact Alibi Panou, Fiskardho, Cephalonia, Greece.

The second is the Sea Turtle Project on Zakinthos. The loggerhead turtle, *Caretta caretta*, needs a fine, sandy, south-facing beach to lay its eggs in. Unfortunately one of the principal breeding sites at Laguna on Zakinthos is also a popular tourist beach and unrestricted development along it has made it more difficult for the beleaguered turtles to use the site. The waters around Kolpos Laguna have now been made a restricted zone for any craft on the water and the zone is enforced by the coastguard and local police. (For details on the restricted zones see the relevant section under Zakinthos in Chapter 3.) The restricted zone should give the turtles a bit more of a chance to breed successfully in this area and those on the water should endeavour to stay away from the area during the breeding season.

For more information contact the Sea Turtle Protection Society of Greece, PO Box 511, 54 Kifissia, 14510 Greece.

Weather forecasts

Because of the high and large landmasses in Greece it is extremely difficult to predict what local winds and wind strengths will be. The Greek meteorological service does its best but nonetheless it faces an almost impossible task. Fortunately the wind direction and strength in the Ionian is remarkably consistent in the summer. For those who really want to listen to a weather forecast try the following sources, but remember to interpret them leniently.

In the few marinas and at a number of other places like Contract Yacht Services in Levkas a marine forecast will be posted or available.

VHF Ch 27. Forecast in Greek and English at 0900 local. Cannot be received everywher.

Weather forecasts are transmitted on the National Programme. All transmissions are in Greek only.

Local times

0630 (winter 0650)	Athens	729kHz	412m
1310–1325	Corfu	1008kHz	298m
2145–2200	Patras	1485kHz	202m

On Greek Public Television a weather forecast in Greek (but with synoptic charts and wind direction and force) is shown after the news at 2100 and 2200 local time on both Channel 1 and 2. In many of the *cafeneion*s you will find a television you can watch over a beer or a coffee.

Yachts with Navtex or a weatherfax receiver will be able to get forecasts in the Ionian. Navtex has the advantage over weatherfax in that transmissions are more reliable and you don't need to hang around waiting for a viable fax transmission.

About the plans

The plans which accompany the text are designed to help those cruising in the area to get in and out of the various harbours and anchorages and to give an idea of where facilities are to be found. It is stressed that many of these plans are based on the authors sketches and therefore should only be used in conjunction with the official charts. They are not to be used for navigation.

Key to symbols

 3 2 : depths in METRES

<1 : shallow water with a depth of 1m or less

(++) : rocks with less than 2 metres' depth

(⚹) : rock just below or on the surface

(2) : a shoal or reef with the least depth shown

⊾ : wreck partially above water

◎ ◎ : eddies

(╫) : wreck

(4)Wk : dangerous wreck

▨ : rock ballasting on a mole or breakwater

⌒ : above-water rocks

⌒ : cliffs

⚓ : anchorage

⚓̸ : prohibited anchorage

⊹ : church

✳ : windmill

⌠ : chimney

⛫ : castle

✈ : airport

⌒ : ruins

▪▪▪ : houses

⚓ : port police

⊡ : fish farm

⊖ : customs

▣ : travel-hoist

⌐c : yacht club

⟙ : water

⬧ : fuel

✉ : post office

○.T.E : Telecommunications

i : Tourist information

⚡ : electricity

⚱ : pine

⚘ : trees other than pine

▲ : port of entry

○ : radiobeacon

⊕ : waypoint

⊶ : yacht berth

⌇ : Local boats (usually shallow or reserved)

⊙ : bn

⚑R : port hand buoy

⚑G : starboard hand buoy

⚑ : mooring buoy

Characteristics

✳ : Light

⊞ : Lighthouse

F : fixed

Fl. : flash

Fl(2) : group flash

Oc. : occulting

R : red

G : green

W : white

m : miles

s : sand

m : mud

w : weed

w : rock

Quick reference guide

At the beginning of each chapter there is a summary of the information relating to the harbours and anchorages described. Compressing information into such a fixed framework is difficult and somewhat clumsy, but the list may be useful to some for route planning and as an instant memory aid to what a place offers.

Key

Shelter
A   Excellent all-round
B   Good with prevailing winds
C   Reasonable shelter but sometimes dangerous
O   Calm weather only

Mooring
A   Stern- or bows-to
B   Alongside
C   Anchored off

Fuel
A   On the quay
B   In the town
O   None

Water
A   On the quay
B   In the town
O   None

Provisions
A   Excellent
B   Most provisions available
C   Meagre supplies
O   None

Tavernas
A   Good choice
B   Some choice
C   One or two
O   None

Plan
•   Harbour plan

Note The taverna key applies to quantity not quality

I. Corfu and nearby islands

	Shelter	Mooring	Fuel	Water	Provisions	Tavernas	Plan
Corfu							
Limin Kerkira (Corfu)	A	AB	A	A	A	A	•
Nisis Vidho	C	C	O	O	O	O	
Ormos Garitsas	B	C	O	O	A	A	•
NAOK Yacht Club	A	A	O	B	A	A	
Gouvia Marina	A	A	A	A	A	A	•
Sidhari	O	C	O	B	C	C	
Rodha	O	C	O	O	C	B	
Ormos Imerola	C	C	O	O	O	C	•
Kassiopi	C	A	B	B	B	B	•
Ormos Vroulias	C	C	O	O	O	O	
North Corfu Channel							
Ay Stefanos (E coast)	B	C	O	B	C	B	•
Ormos Kouloura	C	C	O	O	O	C	•
Ormos Kalami	C	C	O	O	C	C	•
Ormos Agni	C	C	O	O	O	C	•
Benitses	O	C	B	B	B	B	•
Boukari	O	C	O	O	C	C	•
Petriti	B	AC	O	B	C	C	•
Ak Levkimmi	O	C	O	O	O	O	
Kavos	C	A	O	O	O	O	•
Ormos Ay Yeoryiou	C	C	O	O	O	C	
Ay Stefanos (W coast)	B	AB	B	B	B	B	•
Palaeokastrita	B	AC	B	B	C	A	•
Othoni							
Ormos Ammou	B	C	O	B	C	C	•
Ormos Fiki	O	C	O	O	O	O	
Errikousa							
South Bay	B	C	O	O	C	C	•
Paxoi and Andipaxoi							
Getting around inland							
Lakka	B	AC	O	A	C	C	•
Longos	C	AC	O	O	C	C	•
Limin Gaios	A	A	B	A	B	A	•
Mongonisi	A	AC	O	O	O	C	•
Andipaxoi	C	C	O	O	O	C	

Opposite: Gaios. Step ashore into the town square – that is if you can get a berth here

Corfu
(Nisos Kerkira)

Ask anyone to name three Greek islands and Corfu will invariably be one of them – Mikonos and Rhodes will probably be the other two. It is famous and infamous as a resort island. Aircraft are continually landing and taking off at the small airport, ferries churn in and out of Corfu harbour from Italy and Patras, landing-craft type car ferries shuttle back and forth from Igoumenitsa, all helping to swell the population from its normal 100,000 to over half a million in the summer months. It is impossible to ignore this congestion, parts of the island have wall-to-wall concrete hotels as awful as any in the Mediterranean, but surprisingly enough it is possible to escape the crowds – though it takes a little effort.

Corfu's popularity is derived largely from its geography. The sickle-shaped island lying just off the mainland coast of Greece and Albania has three times the rainfall of the islands in the central Aegean and consequently is a verdant green place even through the hot summer months. It has good beaches and a typically sunny Mediterranean climate, the necessary ingredients along with the green and shaded interior for an idyllic holiday island. Couple this with a recent history of comparatively benign English administration leaving familiar architecture and natives used to English peculiarities, and it was inevitable that the crowds would flock here.

Numerous invaders throughout the known history of the island have probably prepared the Greeks for the invasion of sun-starved northerners at the end of the 20th century. The name of the island that most people know it by is not even the official one. Properly it is Kerkira after the ancient name Corcyra, but this was changed during the Byzantine occupation to Corypho (peaks) after the twin peaks in the town, which was then bastardised by the Venetians to Corfo or Corfu.

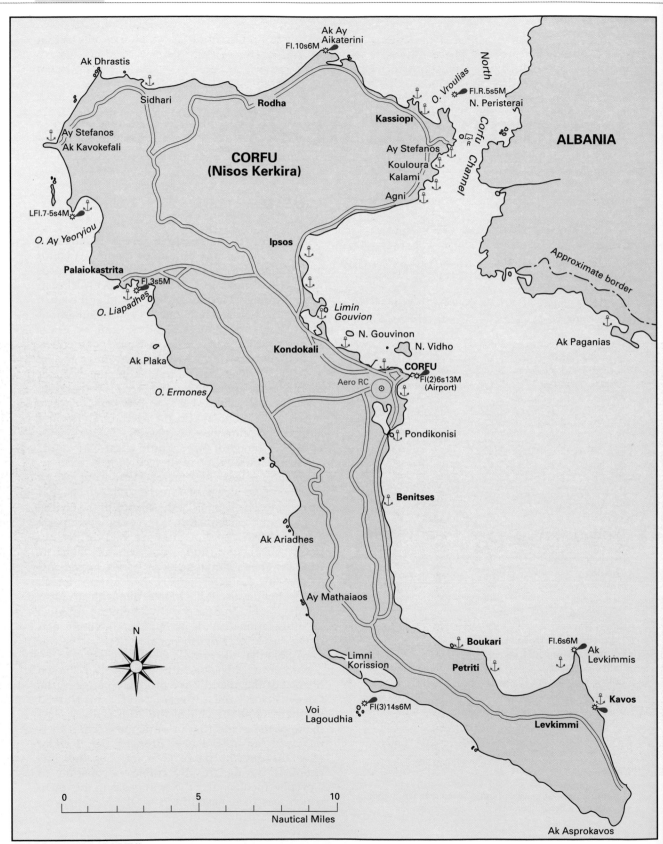

NISOS KERKIRA (CORFU)

Myth

Corfu is traditionally identified as Skheria, the island of the Phaeacians, where Odysseus was washed ashore naked and exhausted after his raft broke up on voyage from the island of Calypso to his home on Ithaca. Homer does not mention Corfu in the *Odyssey*, but it has been identified as Skheria since commentaries on Homer began.

There are some silly traditions, many of them recent inventions or reinventions for tripper boat commentaries, associated with the story. The Phaeacians provided a ship to take Odysseus to Ithaca and on its return Poseidon, angry at Odysseus for blinding his son the Cyclops, turned the ship and crew to stone. The stone ship is usually identified as Pondikonisi, the small island off the lagoon to the S of Corfu town, and sometimes as the islet off Ormos Liapadhes at Palaeokastrita.

Palaeokastrita is often identified as the site of the capital of the island under the Phaeacians, a marvellous steep-to site perfect for an acropolis, with a natural harbour below. Homer tells us that Odysseus was washed ashore at the foot of steep cliffs and only escaped being dashed against them by swimming into a river mouth. Such a site exists at Ermones just over 4M down the coast and is popularly identified as the place mentioned in the *Odyssey*. Here Naoussa, daughter of the king, arrived with her handmaidens to do the family washing in the river and discovered Odysseus. It's a touching story but you have to wonder why Naoussa struggled all the way from Palaeokastrita to Ermones to do the washing. And if the capital of Skheria was sited around present day Corfu town then it seems unlikely Odysseus would have been rescued from Ermones at all.

Mysteriously the Phaeacians disappeared without trace, no pre-Greek city has been discovered, and the verifiable history of the island begins with a colony from Corinth.

Corfu old harbour – picturesque but smelly

History

In 734 BC Corinth established a colony called Corcyra with the main site just south of present-day Corfu town. In the same year a sister-colony was established at Syracuse on Sicily and trade from the south of Italy flowed into Greece via Corcyra, virtually guaranteeing its prosperity. A few remains of the ancient city can be found south of present day Corfu. The ancient harbour was most likely the lagoon next to the airport. It is now very shallow, probably due to silting.

In 665 BC the upstart colony rebelled against Corinth and defeated the Corinthian fleet sent to quell it in what Thucydides recorded as the first naval battle in Greek history. In 433 BC Corinth and Corcyra again clashed and when the Corcyrans asked Athens for help, they indirectly sparked off the Peloponnesian War between Sparta and Athens.

In 200 BC the Romans occupied Corcyra, their first conquest in Greece, and retained it until the decline of the empire. Byzantium inherited it as part of the territory of the Eastern Roman Empire, but being so far away from the centre of power it was neglected and became easy prey for invaders from the north.

Like much of Greece, Corfu was trampled underfoot by invaders for the next 800 years. The Vandals, the Ostrogoths, Slavs and the Normans were the significant invaders until finally the Venetians arrived and claimed Corfu as part of their prize after they had sacked Constantinople. They did nothing for almost 200 years, but in 1386, after a request for help by the Corfiotes, they established a garrison at Corfu town that was the start of more than four centuries of occupation. Venetian control of Corfu and of the other Ionian islands was essential for the protection of their trading fleets bringing spices, especially pepper, and precious goods like silk and ivory, from the east.

When the Turks swept through Greece in the 15th century they left Corfu alone, but in 1537 they turned their attention to the island and landed a large force backed up by cannon. The Turks failed to take the citadel, but sacked the other villages on the island and took nearly half of the population captive. After the siege the Venetians decided the west of Corfu needed extra defences and built the fort above the old harbour which became known as the 'new castle' as opposed to the 'old castle' on the peninsula terminating in Ak Sidhero.

In 1716 the Turks tried again, landing 30,000 troops to take Corfu town. After six weeks of bloody assault on the two forts, the Turks mysteriously gave up and sailed away when it seemed all was lost for the defenders and the capital would fall. The Greeks attributed the miracle to the island's patron saint, St Spiridon, he is also credited with saving the island from famine and the plague, so not surprisingly Spiros is the most popular male name on Corfu to this day.

Venetian rule came to an end in 1797 when the republic fell to Napoleon. French rule brought

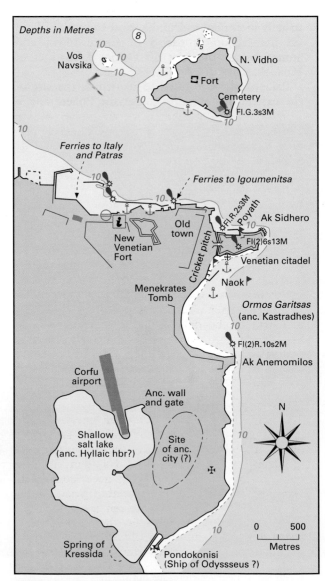

CORFU TOWN AND ENVIRONS

with it much democratic reform and a good deal of building and re-building around the island. Corfu town was turned into a lookalike French provincial town with the building of the Liston, Corfu's version of the Rue de Rivoli, and a rationalised street plan and construction for the rest.

After the defeat of Napoleon in 1813 Corfu passed to the British and a year later all of the Ionian islands were incorporated into a protectorate under their control. British control was by turns benevolent and repressive. The Corfiotes got good roads, a hospital and university, and importantly religious freedom so they could practice Greek Orthodoxy again. But when Commissioner Maitland refused to let the Corfiotes go to help in the struggle for independence on the mainland in the 1820's, local feelings were embittered against the English and a nationalist movement was formed to agitate for union (*enosis*) with the Greek mainland.

In 1863 Corfu and the other six Ionian islands became part of the newly reborn Greece. The British left behind them not only roads and buildings, but a fondness for cricket and ginger beer amongst the local population. Ginger beer is still brewed and cricket is played on the Esplanade (*Spianada*) every Wednesday and on weekends. During the Second World War Corfu was occupied by the Italians, though it was a benign occupation as acts of war go. When the Germans attempted to move in the Italian forces fought off their erstwhile allies though they were doomed against the superior German forces. In 1944 the Germans left and the British were back in Corfu to the delight of the Corfiotes. They have been there ever since, an army of tourists that occupy the beaches and bars, though now the Corfiotes are paid handsomely for being occupied.

Getting around inland

There is an intermittent bus service to the major villages on the island, but generally you are better off hiring a motorbike or a car. One of the legacies of the British was a good road system and the major roads are tarmac and in good condition. Hire motorbikes are a reasonable price, there being some competition between the numerous hire-shops, so check out a few before you hire. Car hire is expensive and really only worthwhile if you have four people to cram into the car or jeep.

Unless you want to mingle with the crowds I suggest you head south towards Ay Mat Theos, Aryirades, and Levkimmi, villages that have more to do with things Greek than things British or German and are also near some of the best and least crowded sandy beaches.

Limin Kerkira

(Corfu Harbour)

Corfu Harbour is the port for Corfu town, the principal town on the island and with a resident population of 30,000, the largest town in the Ionian islands. Nearly all of the ferries running between Patras and Italy stop here so travellers can get quickly onto Patras or jump across the Adriatic to Brindisi or Ancona. The airport is one of the busiest outside of Athens (and also ranks as one of Europe's top five most dangerous airports) with charter and scheduled flights all over Europe and internal flights to Athens. The car ferries from Igoumenitsa bring in land travellers. And many of the yachts arriving in Greece clear in here after crossing from Italy or coming down from the

Dalmatian coast. Not surprisingly therefore, Corfu town is many peoples first introduction to the Ionian islands.

Pilotage

Approach From the north Nisis Vidho obscures most of the buildings in the town. Closer in the huddle of buildings of the old town, the 'old castle' and the lighthouse on Ak Sidhero, and the urban sprawl of Greater Corfu to the west, will be seen. There is a safe passage between Nisis Vidho and Vos Navsika, the rock above water approximately 750m west of Vidho. From the south the 'old castle' on Ak Sidhero stands out well. Normally the large ferries in the commercial port and the car ferries from Igoumenitsa will be seen arriving or leaving.

Mooring If you have to clear in (non-EU yachts only) make for the customs quay inside the western breakwater. The shelter here is not always good with a strong NW breeze (the prevailing wind) so it is best to arrive in the morning and aim to be off the quay by midday. Yachts normally go alongside in the E basin and despite the fact that it is very smelly in here, (it is literally a running sewer), it is crowded in the summer. Shelter inside is good.

Yachts wanting to escape the unsavoury E basin can anchor in Ormos Garitsas or berth at the NAOK Yacht Club.

Facilities

Services Fuel and water on the quay in the W basin of the old harbour.

Provisions Ashore there are all the facilities you would expect in a big town. Good shopping for all provisions once you have found your way to the shops and markets behind the 'new castle' out of the touristy part of the town.

Eating out Restaurants and bars everywhere. The *Averoff* behind the E basin is as good as any or for a quiet and slightly more up-market meal try *The Old Venetian Well* in a courtyard in the old quarter.

Other Internal and international flights. Ferries to Patras and Brindisi. Banks. PO. Hospital. Dentists. Hire cars and motorbikes.

General

Corfu town is a place to wander around rather than one in which to visit monuments though it has some of those. The streets of the old quarter running off the Esplanade are mostly given over to tourist boutiques selling bad onyx chess sets, T-shirts from China and Korea emblazoned with

The unmistakable outline of the old citadel on Ak Sidhero, Corfu

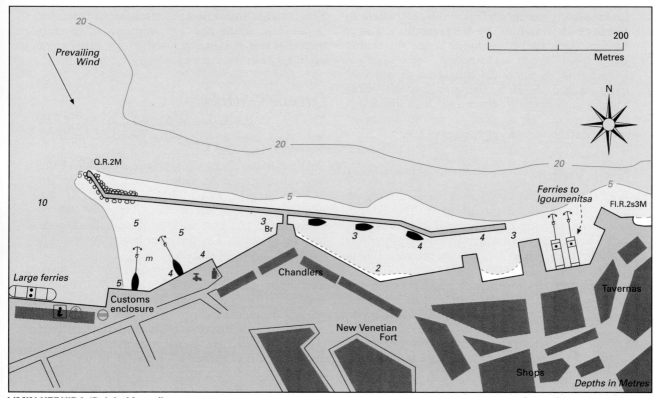

LIMIN KERKIRA (Palaio Limani)

something along the lines of *I love Corfu* or worse, and tacky local pottery. There are no bargains to be had in the tourist boutiques, but bowls turned from olive wood and gold and silver are worth looking at.

Away from the tourist alleys the old quarter is a warren of alleys between the Italianate houses and here the sights and sounds approach something closer to everyday Corfiote life. There are a few restaurants and bars tucked away from the mainstream that are worth exploring. On a Wednesday or on weekends an hour or two can be pleasantly wasted sitting in one of the bars on the Esplanade watching a cricket match on the green.

If you feel in need of a little edification about the history and life of Corfu there are several interesting museums.

Archaeological Museum Is situated just south of the Esplanade at Vraila St 5. There are numerous interesting finds from the island, but two stand out. The Gorgon Pediment dating from around 500 BC is a Medusa head with wings on her back and serpents at her head and waist. It is a brilliant piece of Corinthian sculpture that needs no ancient pedigree to vouchsafe it. In an adjacent room is the sculpture of a lion from the same period, probably from the tomb of a warrior.

Museum of Far Eastern Art Situated in the Palace of St Michael and St George on the north side of the Esplanade. Not the sort of museum you might expect to find on a Greek island, but this extensive eclectic collection by a Greek diplomat, Grigorios Manos, was bequeathed to Corfu, and well repays a visit.

Paper Money Museum Situated in the Ionian Bank building on N. Theotoki St. Again not the sort of museum you might expect to find here, but well worth a visit to look at a history of the stuff we all use and are constantly short of.

Museum of Byzantine Art Situated in the Church of the Virgin Mary Andivouniotissa just off Arseniou St which runs around the coast on the N side of the old quarter. Contains a small collection of icons from churches around the island.

The Achillion Not actually in Corfu, but 16km S near the village of Gastouri. However Corfu is the easiest place to arrange a trip to this monument to bad taste. It was built by Empress Elizabeth of Austria, dedicated to Achilles hence the name, and like much Germanic neo-classical architecture, is an awful amalgam of different styles hedged about by bad statuary, the whole being a monument to kitsch that is so awful it is almost good. It is now a casino operated appropriately by a German consortium.

Nisis Vidho

With the prevailing NW winds the anchorage on the S side of Vidho can be used. The bottom comes up very quickly so you will have to anchor in 5–15m where convenient. In calm weather it is possible to anchor in the cove on the west side in 2–10m.

The island was fortified by the Venetians and then by the British. Before the British forces left in 1864 they blew up most of the defensive works on the island to the anger of Corfiotes. Later it became a prison island and then a borstal. Tripper boats run excursions across to the island in the summer and usually include a tour around the eroded rock of Vos Navsika to the west.

Poyath Yacht Club
(Corfu Offshore YC)

The Corfu Offshore Yacht Club harbour near the tip of Ak Sidhero on the north side is private and visiting yachts are not usually accommodated.

You may be able to find a berth here, but enquire in advance from the old harbour. The club organises sail training activities and a number of yacht races in the summer.

Ormos Garitsas

The bay on the S side of Ak Siderho. Anchor in 5–12m on mud, good holding. Good shelter from the prevailing wind but open to S.

The NAOK Yacht Club on the west side of the bay offers berths to visiting yachts. There are 2–3·5m depths along the outer half of the breakwater. Go stern- or bows-to where convenient. The bottom is mud and weed, poor holding in places. Good shelter inside. A charge is made by the yacht club.

Ashore there are restaurants and bars and there are shops for provisions nearby. Water and showers at the yacht club. The Esplanade is just above the anchorage.

Garitsas or Kastradhes is assumed to have been the Harbour of Alkinoos for ancient Corcyra. The ancient city is scattered over the hill to the south and although the remains of the city wall, several temples, and the possible site of the *agora* have been identified, there is little to see since most of the ancient stone has been 'quarried' over time by the Corfiotes for building materials.

Pondikonisi

S of Garitsas off the end of the shallow lagoon is one of the most photographed places in Corfu,

Pondikonisi before the age of instant hotels and jet engines. Old postcard

the twin islets of Vlacherna and Pondikonisi. Pondikonisi is the outermost islet and is traditionally said to be the Phaeacian ship that ferried Odysseus home and was turned to rock by Poseidon. Vlacherna is connected to Kanoni on Corfu by a causeway and has the Monastery of Vlachernas on it.

What most guide books neglect to mention is that the peninsula of Kanoni is now irrevocably scarred with some of the worst modern architecture on Corfu and that planes thunder in overhead continually throughout the day – Kanoni and the islets are begrimed with spent aviation fuel and you can't hear yourself speak most of the time. Why anyone would want to come on holiday here is difficult to understand and after looking at the twin islets from seawards I recommend anyone on the water to desert the flight path and head N or S.

Limin Gouvion and Gouvia Marina

This large landlocked bay lies just over 3M WNW of Limin Kerkira and Corfu town. At the S end of the bay Gouvia Marina has been established and this has become the yachting hub of Corfu. Around the slopes to the N there is a string of hotels of varying architectural merit.

Pilotage

Approach Nisis Gouvion in the southern approaches and Ak Kommeno and Vrakhos Foustanopidhima on the N side of the entrance are readily identified. In the entrance itself the buoys marking the channel will be seen. Care is needed to avoid the mud bank spreading out over half of the channel on the S side and of the shoal water and rocks on the N side. A course of 231° from the S tip of Foustanopidhima bearing towards the hotel above the old galley sheds shows the way in, though with the buoys in place there is little room for confusion.

Mooring Gouvia Marina can be contacted on VHF Ch 69. Berth where directed in the marina where you will usually be assisted by marina staff on the quay. There are laid moorings tailed to the quay.

Shelter in the marina is now much improved with the construction of new piers and is generally good. However some berths are still uncomfortable with the prevailing wind, especially those on the far west quay, and in

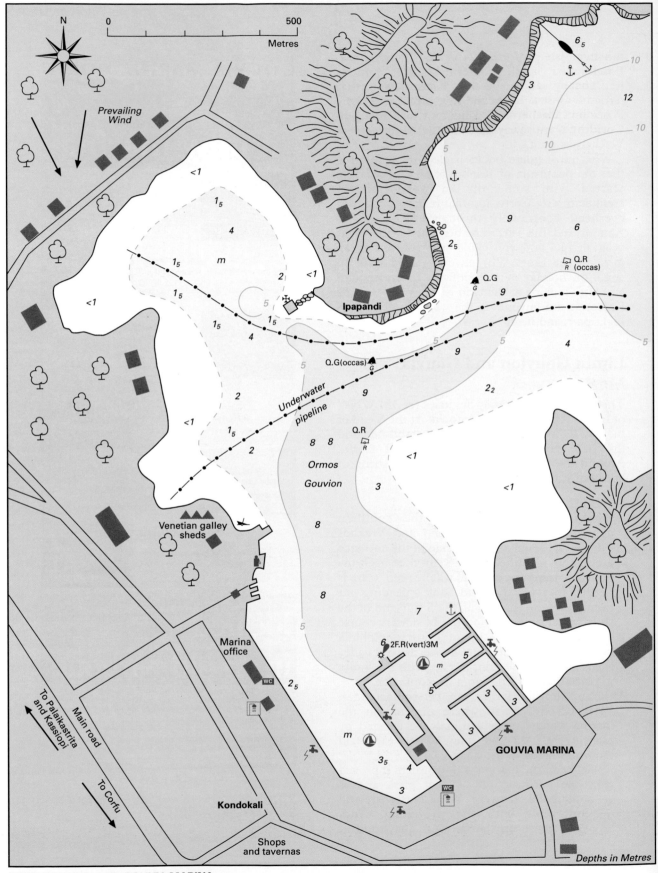

LIMIN GOUVION AND GOUVIA MARINA

some cases berths may become untenable on here.

There is now really no room to anchor in Limin Gouvion. Anchoring is prohibited in the north of the bay and the south is now taken up with the new marina berths.

Facilities

Services Water and electricity at all berths. Shower and toilet blocks. Laundry. Fuel dock. Sewage pumpout. 65-ton travel-hoist. Chandlers and yacht repair facilities.

Provisions There is a supermarket in the marina and others in Kondokali high street.

Eating out Restaurant and café at the marina. Others in Kondokali.

Other Banks and PO. Hire cars and motorbikes. Intermittent bus to Corfu town.

General

Gouvia is a bit like a giant Butlins transported to Corfu. This stretch of coast with Kondokali, Gouvia, Dasia, and Ipsos along it has little to do with things Corfiote or even things Greek apart from its geographical location. This area is mostly devoted to cheap package holidays and the means of making those here feel they never left home – English breakfasts, English roasts on Sunday, English pubs, English newspapers and magazines – most of the signs are in English and most of the people you meet will be English apart from a few Continentals who inadvertently booked a holiday

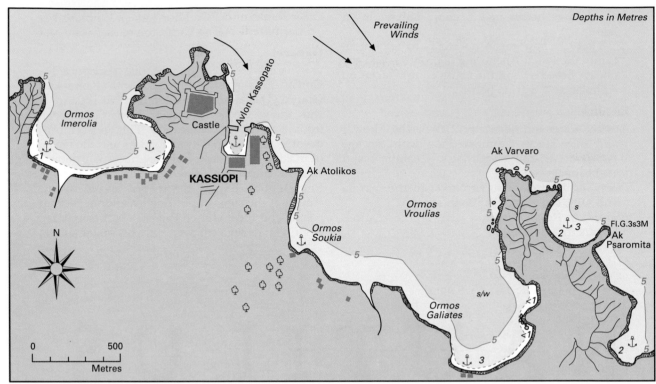

ORMOS IMEROLIA TO AK PSAROMITA

here. Many of the buildings are new and nearly all are villas or small hotels and pensions built in the last ten years for the trade in tourists.

Kondokali and Gouvia, small villages as recently as fifteen years ago supported by a little fishing and local agriculture, have disappeared under the onslaught of reinforced concrete. There are still a few spots where things Greek can be found, but its a hard slog finding them.

The old Venetian galley sheds at the N end of the marina are worth a walk though they have not been restored or even protected from the elements. In the shallows off the sheds there are a few wrecks from more recent seafarers who were engaged in cigarette smuggling to Italy – though the authorities keep threatening to remove them. Corfu along with Levkas further S was previously a centre for cigarette smuggling with conspicuous high-powered motorboats berthed in the town centres, but the smuggling days are over and the ex-smugglers are captains of tripper boats or prop up the counters in bars telling stories of derring-do.

Nisos Gouvinon

In calm weather or when the prevailing wind is not blowing strongly you can anchor off the S side of Gouvinon. Care needs to be taken of a shallow patch off the middle of the island and another off the small pier on the SW corner.

Akra Kommeno

The bay on the S side of Ak Kommeno sheltered from the E by Vrakhos Foustanopidhima provides good shelter from the prevailing northwesterlies. Anchor in 5–12m on mud and weed and take a long line ashore if possible. There are several hotels with associated restaurants and bars scattered around the headland.

North coast of Corfu

There are few sheltered places for a yacht to go along the N coast until past Ak Ay Aikaterini.

Note

The advent of new fast ferries running between Greece and Italy has brought with it the problem of massive ferry wash. At speed these ferries push a massive wall of water that crashes into what were otherwise protected anchorages and harbours causing damage to yachts and other small craft. When the ferries first began running they caused a lot of damage and there were thousands of claims against the ferry companies involved. This has caused the ferries to slow down in coastal waters with the exception of the northern approaches to Corfu. What this means is that places like Kassiopi and some of the northern and northeastern bays will experience the wash from these ferries.

If you do experience damage from one of these ferries document the time, damage, etc and make a claim. If possible take photographs and if you get no satisfaction, get in touch with the Greek Tourist Board. Eventually the ferry operators will get the message that speeding in coastal waters is not only environmentally damaging, but it also going to cost them.

Sidhari

There is a good beach at Sidhari and a short mole where local *caiques* berth, but the anchorage off the beach can only be used in calm weather or light southerlies. Care is needed of rocks and reefs and shoal water bordering the coast. Restaurants and bars ashore.

Rodha

A good sandy beach, but like Sidhari the anchorage can only be used in calm weather. Restaurants and bars ashore.

Ormos Imerola

A bay with two sandy beaches close west of Kassiopi. Some shelter from the prevailing westerlies can be found on the W side of the bay. Anchor in 3–5m on mud, sand and weed. In strong westerlies the bay may become untenable. The overspill of buildings from Kassiopi comes across the isthmus to the bay. Restaurants and bars ashore.

Kassiopi

(Avlon Kassopeto)

A small harbour tucked under the headland with a Venetian castle on the summit. The best place under the short mole is invariably crowded and you will be lucky to get a secure berth here.

Kassiopi

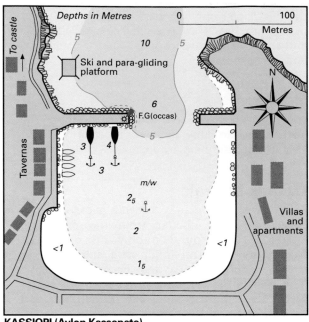

KASSIOPI (Avlon Kassopeto)

Depths in Metres

Ski and para-gliding platform

To castle

Tavernas

F.G (occas)

m/w

Villas and apartments

Pilotage

Approach From the W the castle on the headland and the buildings around Ormos Imerola are readily identified. From the E the houses of Kassiopi will be seen.

Mooring Go bows-to behind the short mole if you can find room. The only alternative is to anchor in the middle of the harbour where it can be uncomfortable and sometimes untenable with the prevailing winds.

Also don't forget the note on ferry wash which significantly affects Kassiopi and can make the harbour positively dangerous.

Facilities

Services Water ashore and a petrol station on the outskirts of the village.

Provisions Good shopping for provisions nearby.

Eating out Restaurants and bars around the waterfront.

Other Bank. PO. Hire motorbikes. Tripper boats run around the coast.

Ay Stefanos in the North Corfu Channel

General

The original small fishing village here has been pretty much swamped by the new buildings, mostly self-catering villas and apartments and small hotels. The place still has a sympathetic feel to it outside of July and August and it is possible to get away on some pleasant walks.

The castle on the hill has Byzantine foundations with Venetian top works. There has been a castle or fort here since Hellenic times. At the end of the 11th century the Norman fleet under Robert Guiscard based themselves at Kassiopi while they sacked the island, though they failed to take the capital. When the Venetians retaliated and the island was retaken they destroyed the fort at Kassiopi so it could not be used by hostile forces again. The inhabitants dispersed throughout the island and the once prosperous town dwindled in size to a small village.

Ormos Vroulias

The large bay immediately E of Kassiopi. In light westerlies a yacht can anchor tucked into Ormos Soukia, a cove halfway down on the W side, or at the head of Ormos Vroulias itself. The bottom is mostly sand and weed. In strong westerlies and northerlies the bay can be untenable.

Just around the E side of Ak Varvaro a yacht can shelter under Ak Psaromita or in the cove just S of it. The latter anchorage is the best and can be used in moderate to light westerlies – wonderful deserted surroundings and clear water.

North Corfu Channel

This channel between Corfu and the mainland opposite divides Greece from Albania. Albania is just one mile away from Corfu and in the channel it is less than a mile to this sad, battered country attempting to shrug off its communist legacy.

In the approach from the W Nisis Peristerai with a small lighthouse on it is easily identified. The passage between Peristerai and Corfu is clear of dangers in the freeway. The danger in the channel is Ifalos Serpa, a reef extending E from a headland just above Ay Stefanos. The reef is marked by a stone cairn in the middle and by a platform and light structure (Q.3s7M) near the end of the reef.

A number of yachts have ripped their bottoms out on the reef including *Carinthia V*, a super

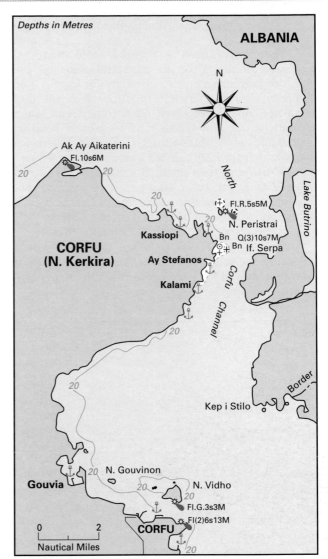

CORFU: NORTH CHANNEL

yacht built for Helmut Horten, a German department store tycoon. On her maiden voyage the yacht went from Cannes to Athens where the owner and his wife left, ordering the yacht back to Cannes. Speeding up the Corfu channel the yacht hit Serpa and went to the bottom, taking the John Bannenberg interior with it but fortunately not the crew. Herr Horten promptly commissioned *Carinthia VI* though the skipper now tends to avoid Corfu.

On the other side of the channel Albania poses a problem of another sort. Many stories circulate about the dastardly deeds of the Albanian authorities, but these are mostly from people who aren't even sure where Albania is. At present the confused situation in Albania means it should be avoided.

There have been a number of incidents of piracy off the Albanian coast and some off the nearby Greek mainland coast and in Corfu. The present state of anarchy in Albania means that yachts should keep well off the coast and when approaching the North Corfu Channel keep as close as practicable to the Greek coast. Yachts on passage from Italy can head around the south end of Corfu and then up to Gouvia if there is a real need to get there or alternatively it makes more sense to head for Paxos, Preveza or Levkas. Given the prevailing winds are NW in the summer this presents few problems. At present there is a strong Greek Naval presence and this should ensure the safety of craft in the area. However it would pay to keep an eye on developments and act accordingly.

Charter yachts should listen to advice from the area manager or flotilla leader. Generally the advice has been to avoid the area around the North Corfu Channel from Kassiopi down to Gouvia. The latter is generally reckoned to be safe despite incidents there in the past. The anchorages on the mainland coast at Pagania and the harbour at Sayiadha should also be avoided. Anywhere south of Corfu is safe and there are no problems chartering a yacht out of Gouvia and heading south.

For the future it is necessary to keep an eye on developments here. One thing that is for sure is that predicting the political path of a newly emerging country such as Albania is next to impossible. After the demise of communism in Albania it was thought the country would soon open up to yachts and tourism to help out the ailing economy. How wrong we were.

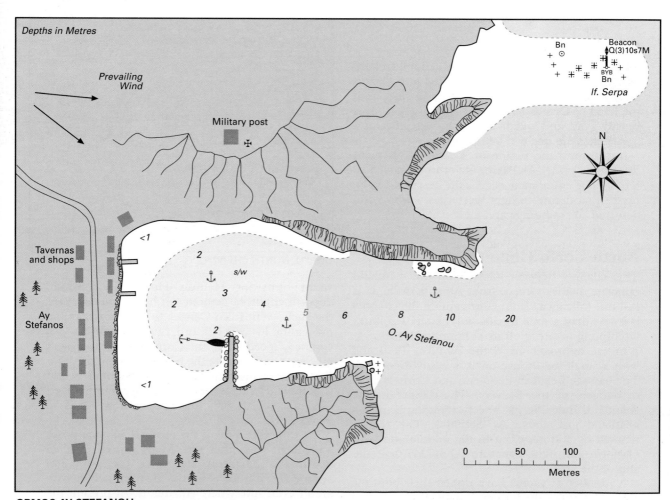

ORMOS AY STEFANOU

The miniature harbour at Ormos Kouloura – only accessible to craft drawing less than a metre

Ay Stefanos

A small inlet tucked in S of Ifalos Serpa. Once into the entrance the buildings around the head of the inlet will be seen. Anchor in 2–7m where convenient on mud, sand and weed. Although there are sufficient depths for a small yacht to go bows-to the outer half of the small mole inside, there is rarely room in the summer and anyway you are better off anchored out. This is especially true now because of the wake from the fast ferries which can penetrate the bay. Good shelter from the prevailing winds.

There are numerous restaurants and bars ashore and some provisions can be obtained. Around the slopes are villas built for the more discerning self-catering visitors. The bay retains a relaxed and uncrowded feel to it despite the number of restaurants which attract customers from as far away as Corfu who seem undeterred by the winding road down to the village.

Ormos Kouloura

A small bay S of Ay Stefanos. It is immediately recognisable from the small church perched on the edge of a miniature harbour, though from the S you won't see it until close-to. Only very small boats can get into the harbour, there is just over a metre in the entrance and about 1·5m in the middle. Even if you get in there is little room to berth. Care should be taken of the shoal water and reef with less than a metre over it bordering the breakwater for nearly 100m to the N and E.

Yachts can anchor to the W of the entrance to the harbour and take a long line ashore. Alternatively anchor in 8–15m in the bay. Good shelter from the prevailing winds.

There is a taverna immediately above the harbour which is popular in the day, but by evening the bay is a peaceful place. The surroundings are simply enchanting.

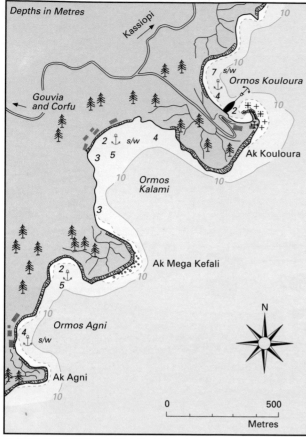

Depths in Metres

Kassiopi →

Ormos Kouloura

← Gouvia and Corfu

Ak Kouloura

Ormos Kalami

Ak Mega Kefali

Ormos Agni

Ak Agni

N

0   500
          Metres

ORMOI KOULOURA, KALAMI AND AGNI

Ormos Kalami

A large bay immediately S of Kouloura. Anchor in 4–10m where convenient. The bottom is sand and weed, good holding. This bay is subject to gusts off the hills with the prevailing northwesterlies so make sure your anchor is well in. Some provisions and tavernas ashore.

Ormos Agni

The last of the trio of bays from Kouloura. Agni is a two headed bay. Yachts normally anchor in the S end in 4–10m on mud and weed. However there is no reason why a yacht cannot anchor at the N end. Tavernas ashore at the S end. Off the tavernas here there are wooden jetties where it is possible to go stern-to. Because of the wash from the high speed ferries it is really better to anchor off. If you do go on a jetty make sure you go stern-to and keep the yacht pulled well off the jetty to avoid damage from the wash.

The slopes around Kalami and Agni are steep-to but cultivated with olives though there are the tall silhouettes of cypress and pine in places. The coast road largely misses these two places and they are peaceful spots punctuated by the whirr of *cicadas* and the puttering of *caiques* rather than the whine and dust of cars and motorbikes.

South of Corfu town

Benitses

Benitses was once a small fishing village, but that was long ago. Now it resounds to the sound of amplified *bouzouki* and disco music and is host to considerable numbers of tourists in the summer.

A large white hotel complex is conspicuous immediately N of the resort proper. There is a small harbour, but it is occupied by resident tripper boats and you will be lucky to find a berth. Anchor off in 3–10m. This can only really be a lunch stop (should you desire it) as the prevailing wind makes it very uncomfortable and usually untenable here. Tavernas and bars ashore everywhere.

Boukari

A small village situated approximately 1½M W of Ak Voukari. Like Benitses the prevailing wind sets in from the N here so it can only be used as a lunch stop. Tavernas ashore.

Petriti

A bay with a small shallow harbour where reasonable shelter from the prevailing wind can be found.

Pilotage

Approach Immediately S of Ak Voukari an eroded escarpment is easily identified. Closer in the mole of the small harbour and the buildings of the hamlet will be seen. From the E care needs to be taken when rounding Ak Levkimmi. The cape itself is very low-lying and shoal water extends up to ½M off.

Mooring Enter the bay of Petriti slowly as it is quite shallow. Anchor off in 2–3m on mud, sand and weed. Alternatively go bows-to the quay on the west side taking care of irregular depths in places. The mole on the E is used by

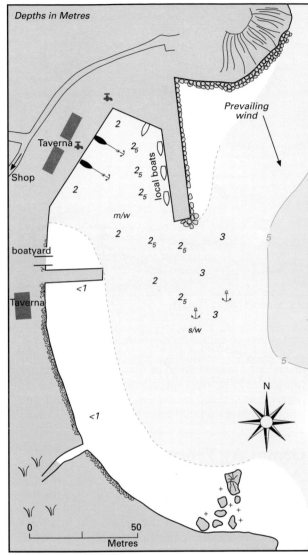

PETRITI

Depths in Metres · Taverna · Shop · boatyard · Taverna · local boats · Prevailing wind · m/w · s/w · N · 0 50 Metres

much a sleepy hollow. The bay is attractive, a shaded green place with a stream running down through reed beds to the sea, a group of wind-sculpted knobbly rocks in the sea at the S end of the bay, and shallow water near the beach providing a safe swimming area in translucent water.

Ak Levkimmi

The low-lying cape on the W side of the southern Corfu channel. The cape is difficult to pick out from the distance and the first thing you are likely to see is the light structure hovering in the haze above the sea. Shoal water extends for up to ¾M N of the cape and ½M E. Although the shallows are readily identified in calm weather, with the prevailing wind kicking up a chop the shoal water can be difficult to spot. Keep a good distance off the light structure and if in doubt over how far off to go, head even further out. One of the flotilla operators calls it the Venus flytrap of the Ionian and that is a pretty fair description.

In calm weather yachts sometimes anchor on the W side of the cape in 4–10m, but with the prevailing northerlies this anchorage is not tenable except in the morning calm.

Kavos

A new harbour constructed for the ferries from the mainland. The ferries berth on the W quay and from here there is a rough gravel road to Levkimmi. There appear to be good depths in

the local fishing boats and care is needed to avoid their permanent ground tackle when going bows-to the village side of the harbour. Reasonable shelter from the prevailing wind at anchor and good shelter in the harbour.

Facilities
Several tavernas and bars ashore. *Stumates Taverna* on the waterfront is a popular haunt for flotilla boats stopping here. Some provisions.

General
The hamlet has a few visitors by land, a few tripper boats call briefly for lunch, and a few yachts stop here, but otherwise Petriti is pretty

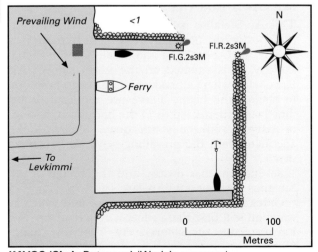

KAVOS (Skala Potamou) (Work in progress)

Prevailing Wind · <1 · N · Fl.R.2s3M · Fl.G.2s3M · Ferry · To Levkimmi · 0 100 Metres

most of the harbour and several yachts have used it as a refuge when they tired of beating northwards to Corfu. The only place for yachts to go is on the S quay. Shelter here is mediocre only as the prevailing northerlies blow in through the entrance and set up a surge. With strong northerlies it may become untenable and if you have to leave there are few places nearby where it is safe to enter at night. Strong southerlies cause a surge in the harbour.

Ashore the area is being developed as a resort area and there are some tacky hotels, tavernas and bars, and of course a disco.

In the vicinity of Ak Levkimmi is the entrance to the canal leading to Levkimmi village. Only very small boats drawing less than a metre should attempt to enter the canal. The village of Levkimmi is an attractive place and the only person I know who has been up the canal to the village speaks of it in glowing terms.

Ak Koundouris and Ak Asprokavos

Off these two capes at the S end of Corfu an area of shoal water extends for more than ½M in places and a yacht should keep well off.

West coast of Corfu

There are few safe anchorages on the W coast as the prevailing wind sets directly down onto it and the only really secure shelter is at Ay Stefanos and Palaeokastrita.

Ay Stefanos (W coast)

This Ay Stefanos is not to be confused with Ay Stefanos on the northeast coast. The harbour has only recently been built and details are somewhat sketchy. It is situated on the north side of Ak Kavokefali where a breakwater has been built out to shelter the bight. There are reported to be mostly 2-3 metre depths in the harbour. Go stern or bows-to on the south quay. Shelter looks adequate from the prevailing northwest to west winds.

Several tavernas nearby and the village of Ay Stefanos is about a mile away.

Greek place names are often repeated which is why you will find Vathi (deep), Ay Nikolaos (the Patron Saint of Sailors), Ay Yeoryios (Saint George, the same one as our dragon slayer), used for different geographical places, even places

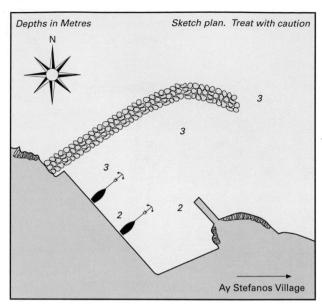

AY STEFANOS (WEST COAST)

quite close to each other as here with Ay Stefanos.

St Stephen (Stefanos) was the first Christian martyr who was accused of blasphemy and stoned to death. Why this protomartyr should be so popular in Greece is a bit of a mystery, but you will find places named after him all over Greece.

Ormos Ay Yeoryiou

(Ag Georgiou)

A large bay situated under Ak Arilla. Reasonable shelter from light westerlies can be found tucked up into the N corner off the beach, but in a brisk onshore breeze it becomes untenable. The beach is marvellous and tavernas and bars open in the summer.

Palaeokastrita

(Ormos Liapadhes, Limin Alipa)

Pilotage

Approach With the prevailing wind setting onto the coast there can be big seas in the approaches and care is needed. If possible make the approach in the morning before the prevailing wind gets up. The village of Lakones on the hill above can be identified and closer in the monastery on Khersonisos Monis Palaeokastrita, the headland to the W of Ormos Liapadhes, will be seen.

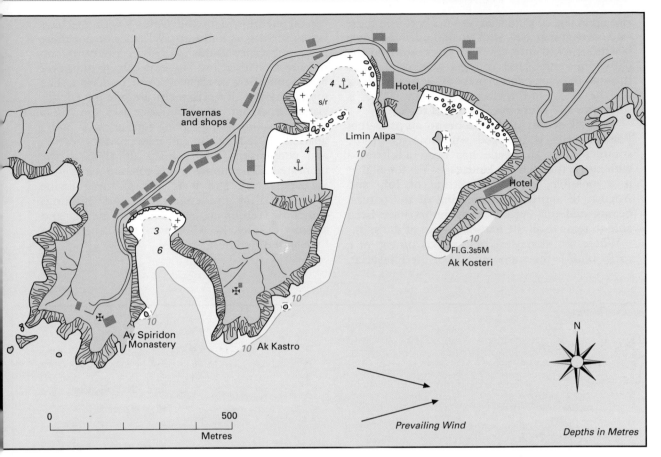

APPROACHES TO LIMIN ALIPA (PALAEOKASTRITA)

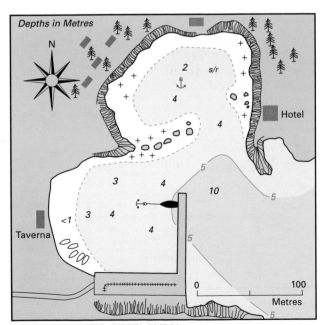

PALAEOKASTRITA (LIMIN ALIPA)

Once into the bay some of the hotels around the slopes will be seen and the harbour mole on the W of the bay is easily identified. Care is needed of the above- and below-water rocks across the entrance to the N cove and also partially obstructing the entrance to the harbour.

Mooring Go stern or bows-to in the harbour if there is room or anchor in the N cove. The bottom is mud and sand, good holding. Good shelter in the harbour from the prevailing winds but dangerous in southerly gales.

Facilities

Water ashore. Most provisions can be found. Restaurants and bars nearby. Intermittent bus to Corfu town.

General

The site is without doubt one of the most spectacular in the Ionian. From seaward the cliffs rise up in jagged pinnacles, eroded here and there into caves and arches, with small sand and shingle beaches tucked into coves at the bottom of the cliffs. From the land you get wonderful views through the olives and cypress of the sea crashing on the cliffs and rocks below. The water is turquoise and azure over sand and rock.

With all of this it should be no surprise that Palaeokastrita is besieged with tourists in the summer. The landscape has been adulterated with hotels that mar the landscape. Yet for all that it is possible, especially outside of July and August, to appreciate something of the natural beauty and not even tour operators have been able to remove all the natural charm of the spot.

Where the monastery now stands on top of a rocky bluff is the supposed site of the Phaeacian capital mentioned in the *Odyssey* with the bays below serving as harbours. Whether or not there is any substance to this assertion is doubtful – no trace of a civilised pre-Hellenic culture have ever been found here or anywhere else on Corfu. The monastery is well worth a visit despite the crowds visiting it. A sign at the entrance asks you *Not to enter the monastery in bathing suits or shorts* and a gnarled old lady at the entrance provides scarves and wrap-around skirts for a donation to the monastery. The monks inside tolerate the visitors amazingly well and it is one of those divine mysteries that the courtyards and buildings somehow retain a semblance of peace and serenity despite the whirring video cameras and babble of different languages.

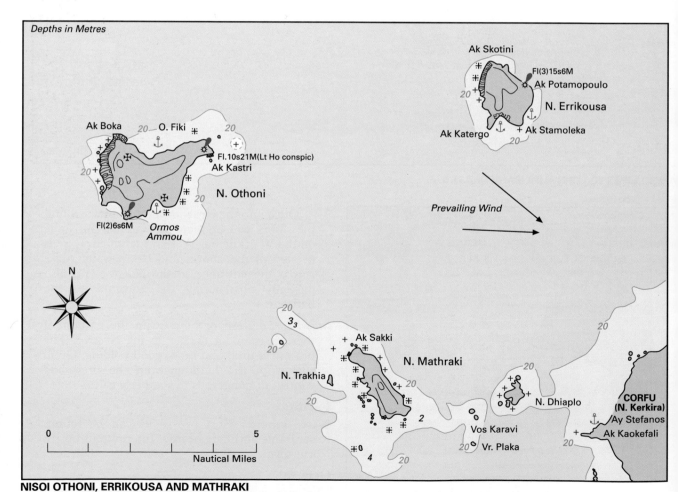

NISOI OTHONI, ERRIKOUSA AND MATHRAKI
Note: The shoals and reefs around the islands, especially N. Mathraki, are not all shown and reference should be made to a large scale chart.

Othoni, Errikousa and Mathraki

Nisos Othoni

Othoni is the precipitous outer island of the group of islands lying to the N of Corfu. At one time when sea levels were lower it would have been joined via Nisos Mathraki to Corfu by a narrow land bridge that can be traced on the depth contours of a chart. Although Othoni is a high bold island, some 393m (1289ft) in the SW corner, it is often obscured by haze and sea mist in the summer, so much so that yachts crossing from Italy to Corfu will often not see it until a mile or two off. The island is much used by yachts as a stepping stone en route to or from Italy and no doubt has been so used since antiquity.

The Italian name for the island is Fano, probably a corruption of *faro*, 'lighthouse'. The name indicates it had a lighthouse in Venetian times. There is a Medieval fort on the top of Kastri, in the NE, where the present lighthouse stands, and it is likely a lighthouse existed here in the Middle Ages. As well as the fort there is reported to be an acropolis on the island certifying its importance as a stepping stone in ancient times. Othoni is sometimes mentioned as Homer's *Ogygia*, the island where Calypso seduced Odysseus and he, not surprisingly, tarried for seven years. Though one should never dismiss local folklore out of hand, it is probable that Malta or one of the islands around Sicily is more likely to be Homer's *Ogygia*.

In this century Othoni has served as a stepping stone for a more nefarious trade, cigarette smuggling to Italy. On several occasions when on passage between Italy and Othoni I have seen high speed motorboats scudding across the horizon and in Ammou on Othoni there used to be a variety of exotically powered craft, the sort that have three 300 HP outboards on a 12m light planing hull. Its not something you enquire about, but presumably the boats couldn't get back to the Italian base port because of the *guardia di finanza* or bad weather, and Othoni provided the nearest convenient port of refuge. Although the Greek authorities know what is going on, they rarely intervene to assist the Italian authorities unless the smuggling boats break Greek laws.

Ormos Ammou

The only village on the island is scattered around the shores of a bay on the S side. A ferry runs irregularly from Corfu in the summer and *caiques* carrying the islands needs run from Corfu and Sidhari. Most visitors to the island arrive by yacht, usually en route from or to Santa Maria di Leuca in Italy.

Pilotage

Approach Though Nisos Othoni is high and bold, it is difficult to pick out in the summer haze until 1½–2M off. The lighthouse on the NE corner is conspicuous and the light tower on the SW corner can be identified closer in. In the approach to the bay care needs to be taken of Ifalos Aspri Petra, a rock with less than 2m over it, lying directly in the southern approaches. Care is also needed in the approach from the SE of rocks and shoal water extending off the coast. The fishing harbour on the E side of the bay is rock bound and should not be approached.

Mooring Anchor in 2–10m where convenient keeping clear of the ferry turning area off the end of the breakwater. The bottom is sand outside the 5m line and sand and rock inside it – care is needed of the rocks which can snag an anchor. A yacht can also anchor off the outer end of the harbour breakwater with a long line

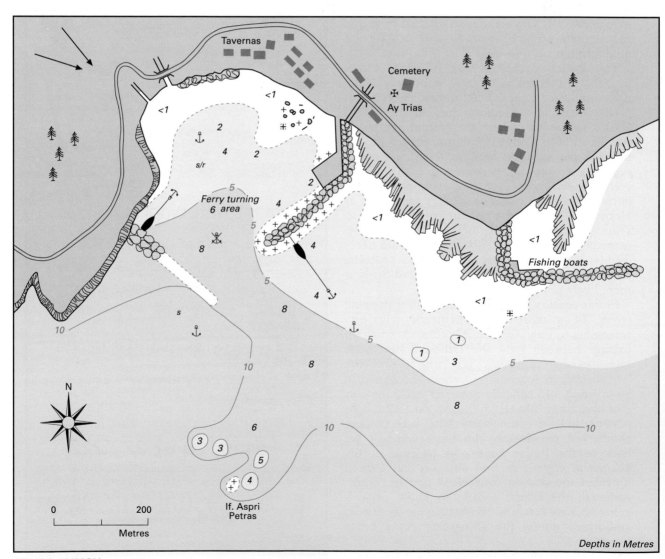

Depths in Metres

to it. Small yachts can berth on the W side of the quay when the ferry or supply *caique* are not due, but most yachts will be better off anchored out. In the summer the prevailing wind blows out of the bay and shelter is good, though some swell works around into the anchorage making it a bit rolly. The bay is open to the S.

Facilities

Limited provisions from a shop attached to one of the tavernas where small amounts of money can be changed and there is a metered telephone. Several tavernas open in the summer and locally caught fish is often available. A small hotel and village rooms available.

General

Everything on Othoni revolves around the small village of Ammou and its harbour. Communication is mostly by *caique* although there is a rough road used by tractors and the few motorbikes. The rough interior offers some interesting cross-island trekking though it would be wise to let someone in the village know where you are setting off for.

Ormos Fiki

The bay on the N side can be used to shelter from southerlies or explored in calm weather. It is untenable with the prevailing northwesterlies. From the W the approach is free of dangers, but from the E there are several underwater rocks off Ak Kastri. In the bay there are above- and below-water rocks off the beach, though these are easily spotted. Anchor in 4–10m on sand and rock.

The bay is a wild forlorn place, stunted *maquis*, a few shepherds' shelters, and a messy pebble beach dotted with tar washed down onto it from the Adriatic.

Nisos Errikousa

Nisos Errikousa, also called by its old name, Merikha, lies 7M due E of Othoni and 6M off the NW tip of Corfu. It is a lower island than Othoni, less craggy and bold. The only village, really a hamlet, is in the large bay on the S side of the island. The long sandy beach around the bay and its proximity to Corfu attracts tripper boats which charge over here in the summer, drop their queasy-looking cargo off on the beach, and a few hours later charge back to Corfu town with them.

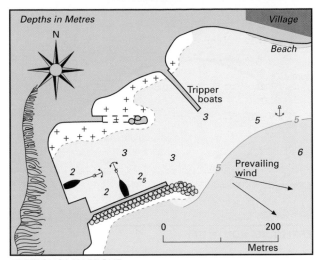

ERRIKOUSA HARBOUR

South Bay

The large bay in the S between Ak Katergo and Ak Stamoleka on the SE tip of the island.

Pilotage

Approach The approach is free of dangers except for above- and below-water rocks off Ak Katergo and Ak Stamoleka. The white cliffs of Ak Katergo are conspicuous and closer in the small electricity generating plant at the E end of the beach will be seen as well as the houses around the W end.

Mooring The bottom slopes gradually to the beach. Anchor in 3–6m where convenient, although care must be taken of a cable, presumably for electricity or telephones, lying approximately 150m off the shore. The bottom is sand, good holding.

A yacht can enter the harbour on the W side of the bay although care is needed of the remains of the mole on the north side. Go stern or bows-to the south or west quays taking care of depths close to the quay where the bottom is irregular in places. Shelter in the harbour is good from the prevailing northwesterlies and the harbour should also afford some protection from southerlies. If there is room you may find a place on the pier running out from the shore closer to the village although it is much used during the day by the tripper boats. Good shelter in the bay from the prevailing NW winds.

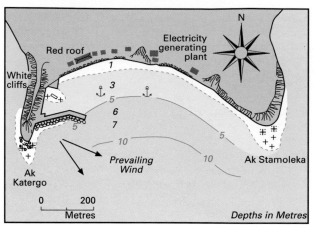

ERRIKOUSA SOUTH BAY

Facilities

Limited provisions. Several restaurants ashore where locally caught fresh fish is available. Village rooms available. Communications mostly seems to be by the tripper boats from Corfu and Gouvia which also carry goods over to the island.

General

From midday until the mid-afternoon the bay buzzes with trippers from Corfu, but by four o'clock they have all departed and quiet descends. On the E side of the island a yacht can find shelter from the prevailing winds in some idyllic coves and bights with excellent snorkelling in the clear water. Inland, like Othoni, the island promises some good trekking.

Nisos Mathraki

The jagged island lying S of Othoni and Errikousa and 5M W of the NW tip of Corfu. It is surrounded by above- and below-water rocks, islets, and shoal water. The small island of Dhiapolo lies nearly midway between Mathraki and Corfu on a bridge of shoal water.

Few yachts visit here, there is no anchorage protected from the prevailing winds, and the reefs and shoal water make navigation tricky. There are safe channels on either side of Dhiapolo, but attention must be paid to the chart to avoid several reefs. Local fishermen after crayfish and rock-dwelling fish like grouper are the only craft to frequent the waters around the islands.

Nisos Paxoi and Andipaxoi

(Paxos and Anti-Paxos)

Paxos and its diminutive Anti-Paxos lie some 7M S of Corfu, two small islands offering refuge between Corfu and Levkas further S. Paxos itself is only 5M long by 2½M wide and has a permanent population of around 2,000, including some eccentric British residents who discovered the tiny island years ago. Anti-Paxos lying just over a mile S is 2½M long and 1M wide with a permanent population of just 50.

The two islands are still idyllic places despite the large numbers of waterborne visitors who descend on them in July and August. The water here is that almost unbelievable blue and green of picture postcards set off by the dull sheen of cultivated olive groves. In fact until the invasion of the last decade olives were the only thing that kept Paxos going – local folklore has it that Harrods sells only Paxiot olive oil.

Paxos has few claims to fame in the ancient world except for a melancholy one, of little consequence in our rigidly monotheistic universe, but of shattering importance in ancient times when a panoply of gods inhabited the world. It was off Paxos that it was announced Pan was dead, the only god to have died in our time

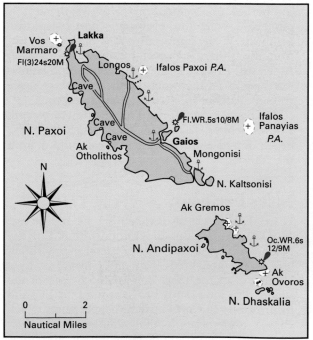

NISOI PAXOI AND ANDIPAXOI

according to Robert Graves. Plutarch gives this account in his sadly titled *Why the Oracles Cease to Give Answers*.

'Epitherses told me that, designing a voyage to Italy, he embarked himself on a vessel well laden both with goods and passengers. About the evening the vessel was becalmed about the Isles Echinades, whereupon their ship drove with the tide till it was carried near the Isles of Paxi; when immediately a voice was heard by most of the passengers (who were then awake, and taking a cup after supper) calling unto one Thamus, and that with so loud a voice as made all the company amazed; which Thamus was a mariner of Egypt, whose name was scarcely known in the ship. He returned no answer to the first calls; but at the third he replied, Here! here! I am the man. Then the voice said aloud to him, When you are arrived at Palodes, take care to make it known that the great God Pan is dead. Epirtheses told us, this voice did much astonish all that heard it, and caused much arguing whether this voice was to be obeyed or slighted... Being come to Palodes, there was no wind stirring, and the sea was as smooth as glass. Whereupon Thamus standing on the deck, with his face towards the land, uttered with a loud voice his message, saying, The great God Pan is dead.'

Plutarch *The Moralia* transl. by R. Midgley 1870

Apart from the muddled navigation details – it would be almost impossible for the ship to travel under sail or oar from the Echinades to Paxos in a single evening and there is virtually no tide in this area – and despite Plutarch's account, when Pausanias visited Greece a century later he found Pan still actively worshipped, so there may be life after death for pantheists after all.

Getting around inland

Motorbikes can be hired in Gaios and from there the islands only road runs up to Lakka, branching off in the middle of the island to Longos. Although there is just one road, it is worth an excursion inland through the old olive groves set amongst grey eroded rocks. There are pleasant walks everywhere from any of the harbours around the island.

Lakka

A large bay on the N end of Paxos much inhabited by tripper boats, dinghy sailors, wind surfers, and yachts.

Pilotage

Approach The exact location of the bay is difficult to determine despite its size. From the W the lighthouse on the NW side of the island is easily

Lakka on Paxoi

53

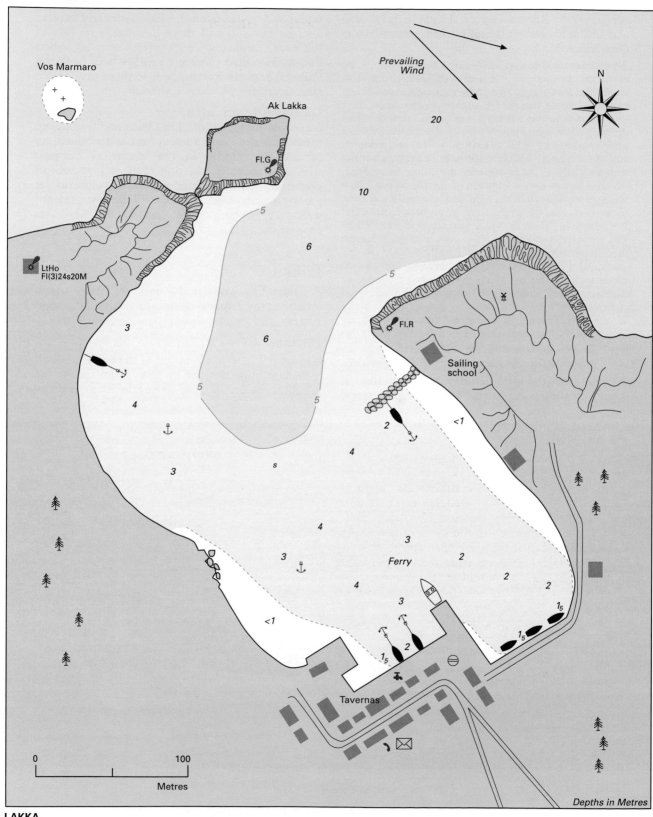

Vos Marmaro

Ak Lakka

Fl.G

LtHo
Fl(3)24s20M

Prevailing
Wind

N

20

10

5

6

5

3

6

5

Fl.R

Sailing
school

4

<1

5

5

s

2

3

4

4

3

2

2

4

Ferry

2

2

3

1₅

3

1₅

4

3

1₅

2

1₅

<1

Tavernas

0   100

Metres

Depths in Metres

LAKKA

identified, but it will not be seen from the E and SE. Closer in the light structures at the entrance will be seen. In the summer boats are constantly coming and going, showing the entrance. There are no dangers in the approaches except Vos Marmaro off the W side of the entrance and Ifalos Paxoi off Longos.

Mooring Anchor where convenient in the middle or anchor and take a long line ashore in the NW corner. There is some room on the quay for small and medium-sized yachts, though do not obstruct the ferry berth or berths for local boats. With care parts of the quayed area E of the town quay can be used though it is best to go bows-to. The bottom is sand and weed, good holding. Good shelter from the prevailing winds but prolonged N–NE winds cause a very uncomfortable swell.

Facilities

Limited water on the quay although it may be turned off altogether in the summer. Most provisions ashore. Tavernas and bars. PO.

General

The bay is picturesque. The slopes about are covered with the dull green of olives with the occasional tall cypress sticking up. The hamlet huddles at the head of the bay, a collection of earthy brown tile roofs and faded pastel walls. The water, mostly just four or five metres over a sandy bottom, is a patchwork quilt of blues and greens. Inevitably this combination attracts considerable numbers of people to it. In the summer the quayside is a noisy bustling place quite out of proportion to the size of the hamlet. The bay is churned up by speedboats, sailing dinghies, wind surfers, and the odd tripper boat coming and going, a cocktail of colour and chaos.

In the morning it is worth going around the W side of the island where there are several impressive sea caves eroded into the equally impressive cliffs. At one time a small colony of monk seals lived here, but no more – these shy animals have moved elsewhere since the tourist presence increased. Local myth also has it that a Greek submarine sheltered in one of the caves during the Second World War, but this is a common bit of Homeric myth-making throughout Greece and in the Ionian alone there are two other caves where submarines sheltered according to local folklore.

Limin Longos

(Logos)

A miniature harbour a third of the way down the E coast from Lakka.

Pilotage

Approach Care is needed of Ifalos Paxoi, a reef approximately ½M E of Longos. It can be identified in calm weather as a small patch of turquoise water, but is difficult to see otherwise. The line of rocks running out from the coast S of Longos are easily identified and close in the houses of the hamlet and a chimney of the old soap factory will be seen.

Mooring There are no really comfortable berths here. The small harbour is reserved for local boats and tripper boats. Go stern-to the outside of the mole with a long line to it or anchor and take a long line ashore to the N side of the bay. With the prevailing wind you roll around most uncomfortably with the ground swell.

Just under a mile S of Longos, S of the conspicuous line of rocks running out from the coast, there is a quiet anchorage off a sandy beach suitable in calm weather or light northwesterlies.

Facilities

Some provisions ashore and tavernas and bars.

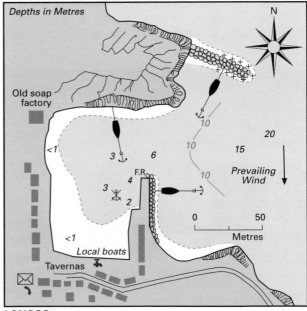

LONGOS

Disused soap factory at Longos on Paxoi

General

The little fishing port is a beautiful spot, a huddle of houses around the miniature harbour. Formerly it relied on fishing and olives for its livelihood. It still has a small fishing fleet though much of the catch now goes to Corfu. The old soap factory on the shore that turned the leftovers from olive oil production into soap has been disused for years. Now the inhabitants have a thriving trade in tourists though it is all quite sympathetic and the village retains a pleasant feel to it.

Ifalos Panayias

A reef just under the water lying approximately 2½M E of Nisis Panayia, the islet at the entrance to Limin Gaios. Some dispute the charted position and say it should be closer to the mainland, but it looks about right to me. An area of shoal water lies to the E and S of the reef. It is difficult to see with the prevailing winds which whip up chop over it, so it should be given a wide berth. Unfortunately the reef lies very close to the course between Gaios and Parga so care is needed and a dogleg course should be made to keep well clear of it.

Limin Gaios

(Port Gayo, Limin Paxoi)

The main harbour on the island tucked in and completely hidden behind the islet of Ay Nikolaos. This is where all ferries and tripper boats arrive or leave and in the summer there are a large number of them testifying to the tiny islands popularity. Ferries and excursion boats run from Corfu and Parga on a daily basis and some of the large ferries from Italy also stop here.

Pilotage

Approach It is difficult to see the entrance to the harbour from the N although closer in the small lighthouse on Nisis Panayia will be seen. Care is needed in the N entrance as tripper boats and small ferries charge in and out of here and it is impossible to see if anyone is coming in the opposite direction where the channel curves abruptly to the S.

Gaios looking in through the south entrance. If you draw anything close to 2 metres use the north entrance

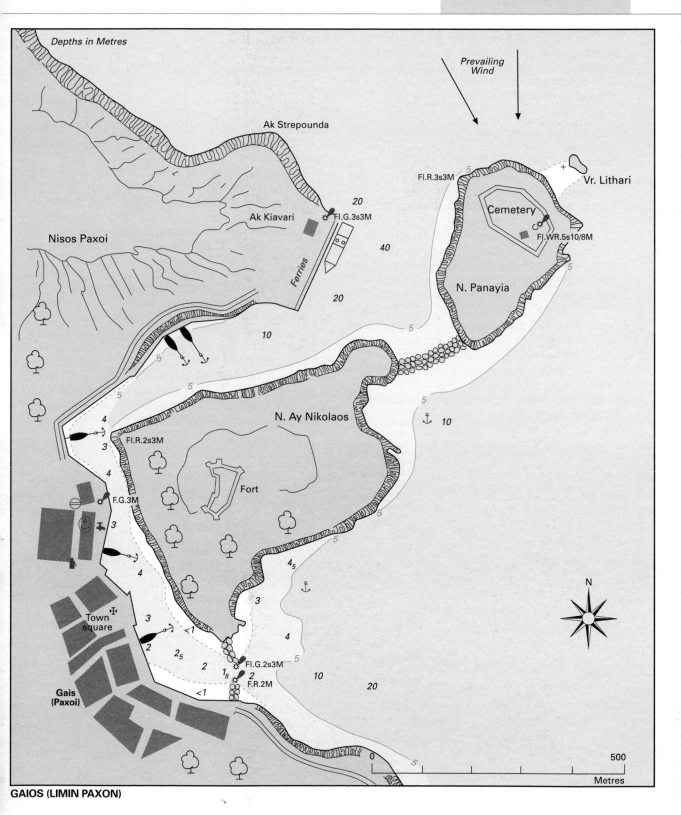

Depths in Metres

Ak Strepounda

Prevailing Wind

Fl.R.3s3M

Vr. Lithari

Ak Kiavari

Fl.G.3s3M

20

Cemetery

Nisos Paxoi

40

Fl.WR.5s10/8M

Ferries

20

N. Panayia

10

5

5

5

5

N. Ay Nikolaos

10

4

3

Fl.R.2s3M

4

F.G.3M

Fort

3

4

5

4

3

4

3

Town square

4

3

2

5

2

5

2

Fl.G.2s3M

Gais (Paxoi)

1₈

2

F.R.2M

<1

10

20

N

0

500

Metres

GAIOS (LIMIN PAXON)

From the S it is easier to identify where the harbour is as some of the buildings of Gaios can be seen. In the S entrance there are barely 2m depths in the middle and no room to manoeuvre out of the channel, so wait until the way is clear.

Mooring The harbour is so crowded in the height of summer that anyone arriving after two or three o'clock is unlikely to find a berth on the town quay. Go stern- or bows-to wherever you can find or negotiate a berth keeping well clear of the ferry quay. Crossed anchors are a fact of life here and something you will just have to live with. The new quay in the north channel doesn't have the cache of being on the town quay, but does have some peace and quiet and even better, you can usually find a berth here. Go stern or bows-to where there is room, but remember you will be dropping your anchor in quite deep water in the channel. Larger yachts can anchor off under the breakwater between Ay Nikolaos and Panayia. Shelter in Gaios is good from the prevailing summer westerlies, but not as good as it looks from strong southerlies when there can be a considerable surge in the harbour.

Facilities

Services Water near the quay though it can be in short supply in the summer. Water can also be obtained by mini-tanker. Contact the *Kirki Bar* near the southern entrance. Fuel near the quay.

Provisions Provisions available in the town though things here are a little more expensive than elsewhere as nearly everything is brought in by ferry.

Eating out Tavernas and bars in the town. There are several good tavernas on the road out of town well away from the hubbub of the centre. The *Three Brothers Restaurant* on a rooftop in town has also been recommended.

Other Bank. PO. Hire motorbikes.

General

Gaios is chaos in the summer. Yachts and their owners are running around in circles searching for berths, those already berthed are defending their patch against newcomers, water-taxis carve up the water going about their business, and landlubbers sit in cafes on the square and watch bemused. The square itself, hedged in by buildings on three sides and by the harbour on the other, is always buzzing with conversation and waiters shouted orders. Despite all this, or

Gaios looking up the south channel

perhaps because of it, Gaios is a beguiling spot where once you have gone to so much trouble to secure a berth, it seems a pity to move on too quickly.

There is nothing here you must go to see for your education. On the island of Ay Nikolaos that shelters the harbour a medieval fort and a chapel sits on the summit. In the town there is some pleasing architecture from the 19th century. And there are pleasant walks out of town through the ubiquitous olive groves of Paxos. Like Corfu, many of the olive groves were planted under Venetian occupation and some of the old gnarled trees on the island are said to be four or five hundred years old and still bearing.

One other inhabitant of Gaios has to be commented on and that is the taverna cat. At every taverna there are as many cats as there are tourists, hordes of cats, some attractive and some battle-scarred with minor bits of anatomy like an eye or an ear missing, but all intent on sharing your meal with you.

Mongonisi

(Spuzzo)

Just over a mile SE of Gaios is the enclosed bay of Mongonisi. The approach is straightforward although it can be difficult to determine exactly where the bay is until close-to.

Go bows-to on the N or E if there is room. Alternatively anchor off where convenient. The bottom is mud and weed, good holding once through the weed. Good all-round shelter.

Ashore there is Theo's taverna and bar set amongst gnarled old olives. Depending on the night it can be low-key and relaxed in here or a riotous and rowdy party. You can walk around the rough road to Gaios or in the summer water-taxis run back and forth. Mongonisi is actually the name of the small islet forming the E side of the bay joined to Paxos only by a rough causeway.

Nisis Kaltsonisi

A small islet just off Nisis Mongonisi. In the narrow gap between the two islands a yacht can anchor with care. It is mostly very deep shelving quickly. Clear water and an oasis of peace on this crowded island.

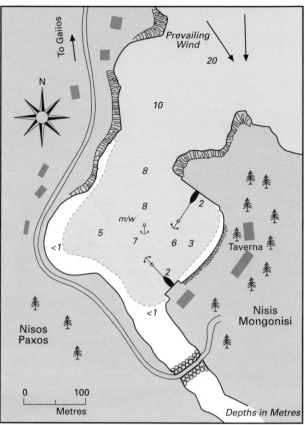

MONGONISI (ORMOS SPUZZO)

Nisos Andipaxoi

(Anti-Paxos)

The small island lying to the S of Paxos. It is popular with yachts and tripper boats who charge over here to the sandy beaches (Paxos doesn't have many good sandy beaches) and the wonderful clear water.

Anchor off where convenient on the NE side of the island. Care is needed of above- and below-water rocks fringing the coast. When the prevailing wind blows strongly a swell is pushed down the E coast making it uncomfortable, though there are a few places you can tuck in to stay overnight with care.

In the daytime it is crowded with yachts and tripper boats, but if you stay for the night it is peaceful. Ashore there is a taverna. Numerous farms are dotted about the island linked by stone-walled lanes through well kept vineyards. The island is said to produce a good wine, but I must say I have never sampled any of it.

59

2. The mainland coast from Pagania to Preveza

	Shelter	Mooring	Fuel	Water	Provisions	Tavernas	Plan
Pagania	A	C	O	O	O	O	•
Sayiadha	B	A	O	B	C	C	•
Igoumenitsa	B	AB	B	B	B	B	•
Ormiskos Valtou	A	C	O	O	O	O	•
Platarias	B	A	B	A	B	C	•
Mourtos and nearby islands	A	AC	B	B	B	B	•
Ormos Paramithas	C	C	O	O	O	C	
Parga	B	AC	B	A	B	A	•
Ormos Ay Athanasiou	C	C	O	O	B	B	•
Ormos Ay Kiriakis	C	C	O	O	O	O	
Ormos Ay Ioannou	C	C	O	O	O	O	•
Ormos Fanari	O	C	O	O	O	O	
Two Rock Bay	C	C	O	O	O	O	
Ligia	B	A	O	B	C	C	•
Preveza	B	AB	A	A	A	B	•
Ormos Vathi	A	C	O	B	O	C	•
Amvrakikos Kolpos (Gulf of Amvrakia)							
Vonitsa	B	AC	B	B	C	C	•
Loutraki	C	C	O	O	O	O	
Amfilokhia	O	AC	B	B	C	C	•
Menidhion	B	AC	B	B	C	B	•
Nisoi Vouvalo and Korako	C	C	O	O	O	O	
Salaora	C	C	O	O	C	C	

This stretch of coast forms the western edge of Northern Greece with the Epirus and the start of the Pindus mountains, towering, ragged sheets of rock, arching across mainland Greece to the northern Aegean. For the most part the mountains drop abruptly into the sea except where a river mouth has deposited silt to create a coastal plain as at Igoumenitsa and around Preveza. The Epirus has always exercised a

Opposite: Fishing boat with reed net. Menidhion

powerful hold on those who have visited it. The Pindus are the mountains that Homers 'rosy fingered dawn' touches. Eccentric travellers as diverse as John Morrit on his 'Grand Tour', Lord Byron looking for Ali Pasha, and a melancholy Edward Lear tramping the mountains to record them in watercolours and in his *Diary of a Landscape Painter in Greece and Albania*, all came this way. Recently the region was highlighted in Nicholas Gage's *Eleni*, the tale of terror in the mountains during the Second World War and the bloody civil war that followed.

Yet despite this sort of eminent reporting over the years, it remains very much an out of the way region compared to the islands across the water. Any trips inland will be repaid tenfold. It may surprise many to know that this mainland region was Turkish right up until the end of the Second Baltic War when the Greek Army finally captured Ioannina in February 1913. There are still old folk alive who were born under Turkish occupation and memories are long in the mountains – so bide your tongue.

Note

The warning regarding the situation for anchorages close to Albania mentioned in Chapter 1 applies to mainland anchorages and harbours close to Albania. It bears repeating here. There have been a number of incidents of piracy off the Albanian coast and some off the nearby Greek mainland coast and in Corfu. The present state of anarchy in Albania means that yachts should keep well off the coast and when approaching the North Corfu Channel keep as close as practicable to the Greek coast. Yachts on passage from Italy can head around the south end of Corfu and then up to Gouvia if there is a real need to get there or alternatively it makes more sense to head for Paxos, Preveza or Levkas. Given the prevailing winds are NW in the summer this

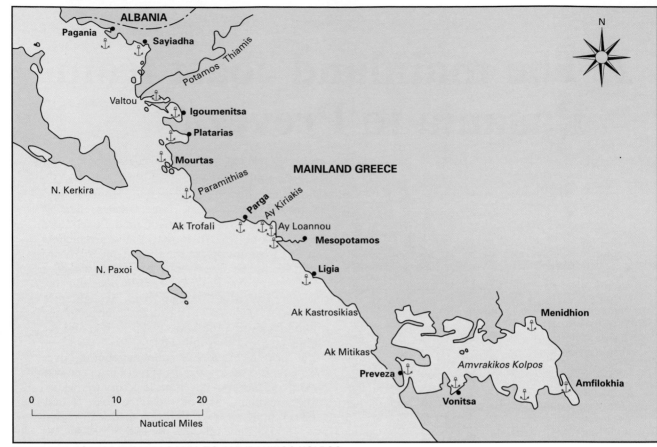

MAINLAND GREECE FROM PAGANIA TO AMVRAKIKOS KOLPOS

presents few problems. At present there is a strong Greek Naval presence and this should ensure the safety of craft in the area. However it would pay to keep an eye on developments and act accordingly.

Charter yachts should listen to advice from the area manager or flotilla leader. Generally the advice has been to avoid the area around the North Corfu Channel from Kassiopi down to Gouvia. The latter is generally reckoned to be safe despite incidents there in the past. The anchorages on the mainland coast at Pagania and the harbour at Sayiadha should also be avoided. Anywhere south of Corfu is safe and there are no problems chartering a yacht out of Gouvia and heading south.

I have chosen to leave the plans and pilotage details for Pagania and Sayiadha in the book as it may be that sometime in the future things will get better, some order and sanity will appear in Albania and we will once again be able to sail around close to the border without an accompanying gunboat.

Pagania

There have been a number of incidents concerning yachts and Albanians at or near Pagania and even a gun battle between the Greek navy and some stray Albanians. For the time being keep well clear of it.

An enclosed bay sitting right under the Albanian border. The rough road running around the coast appears to disappear where the headland, Ak Pagonias, sheltering Pagania behind, obscures it, as it metaphorically might close to the wastelands of Albania. Care needs to be taken of the fish farm just inside the entrance to the bay. A yacht can anchor in the SW or SE corner in 3–6m on mud and weed. Good all-round shelter.

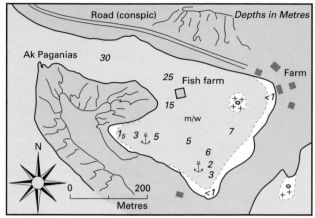

PAGANIA (See caution note)

This remote corner of Greece is about as close to Albania as you can get, the border is just over ½km away so don't stray too far.

Sayiadha

Like Pagania, Sayiadha is not far from the Albanian border, so for the time being it is best to avoid the area.

A small harbour off the hamlet of Sayiadha. The harbour has been modified from its former shape making it almost impossible for all but small yachts to get inside. There is 1·4m or perhaps slightly more in the narrow entrance on the E side of the breakwater, but care is needed of rubble at the sides.

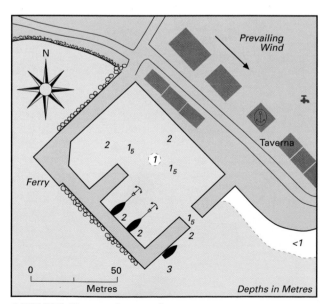

SAYIADHA (See caution note)

A yacht can go alongside the quay on the outside of the mole near the entrance though it can get bumpy here with brisk westerlies. Shelter inside the harbour is excellent if you are small enough to get in. The hamlet ashore is a little visited place where the tavernas serve simple but good fare, including good fresh fish caught locally.

Like Pagania, Sayiadha sits close to the border with Albania. It is also quite close to the tiny village of Lia up in the mountains which would have remained entirely unknown but for the success of Nicholas Gage's *Eleni*, the semi-autobiographical account of his search for the murderer of his mother in the bitter civil war following the Second World War. This region, close to communist Albania, was a stronghold of the Greek communists who committed the sort of awful atrocities described in *Eleni*. The book is a fascinating read, describing the sort of hand-to-mouth existence that was the lot of many of these remote villages, and the awfulness of family set against family and brother against brother as sides were taken for communist or nationalist.

Note

Care must be taken of the shoal water extending out from the coast S of Sayiadha. There are reports that this area is greater than that shown on the charts.

Igoumenitsa

The large enclosed bay lying under the flat marshy land, the river delta built up by the Potamos Thiamis, opposite the middle skinny part of Corfu. Igoumenitsa is the mainland ferry port for Corfu and at all times of the day and night there are ferries churning to and from Corfu town.

Pilotage

Approach In the approach, Nisadhi Pasoudhi, although only 50m high, stands out well against the flat river delta to the N. Closer in the buildings of Igoumenitsa will be seen and the light buoys marking the channel into Ormos Igoumenitsa show the channel into the bay. In practice the numerous ferries coming and going pinpoint where the harbour is.

Igoumenitsa looking out to the entrance channel from the south side of the bay

Mooring Go stern- or bows-to in the basin where convenient. The shelter here is reasonable from the prevailing northwesterlies, but it can get a bit bumpy – as much from the wash of craft in the harbour as from the wind.

A yacht can also anchor in the NW corner of the bay where the bottom shelves gently to the shore. In calm weather there is a quite enchanting anchorage in the S corner of the bay, but the prevailing wind blows in here making it untenable in the summer. There is also reported to be a good lee under Nisis Ay Dhionisios in attractive surroundings, but I have no other details on the anchorage. The bottom around Igoumenitsa is mostly mud, good holding.

Facilities

Services Water on the quay and fuel in the town.
Provisions Good shopping for provisions.
Eating out Tavernas in the town although many of them are awful places catering for the itinerant population passing through.
Other Banks. PO. Irregular buses to Preveza.

General

Igoumenitsa was a small fishing village and sometime ferry harbour before the Second World War, rebuilt afterwards as a modern town and the ferry port for Corfu and ferries from Italy. It has

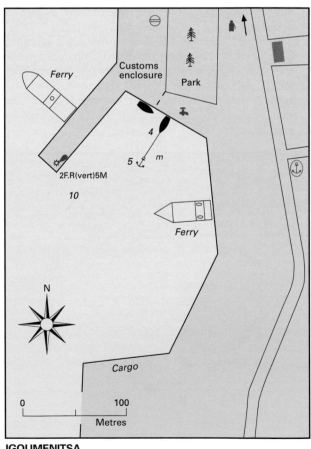

IGOUMENITSA

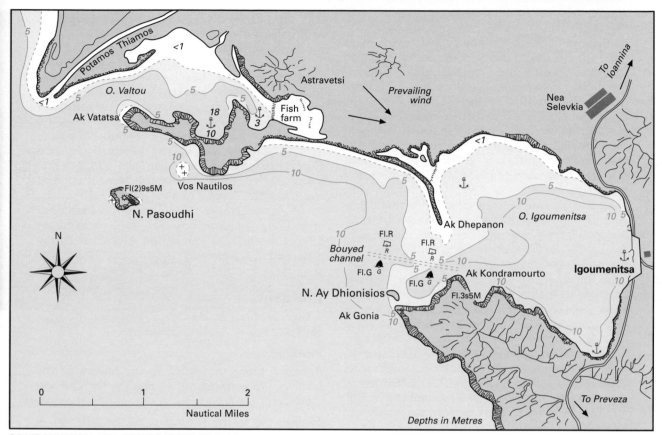

ORMOS VALTOU AND ORMOS IGOUMENITSA

the feel of a town where everyone is passing through, billboards point you to ticket agents, fast-food places let you grab a hamburger before you catch the ferry, and bars let you sit down to wait for the ferry. The town seems to have no purpose other than as a ferry port and it looks like it, though to be fair in recent years the waterfront has been tidied up and now has a pleasant seaside park.

Igoumenitsa is the place to make an excursion to Ioannina and to Dodona. Ioannina is one of the better preserved old Greek towns with the new quarter built next to the old quarter rather than on top of it. The old town next to the lake has an oriental feel to it with several mosques and minarets and a bazaar dating from the Turkish occupation. Ioannina was the stronghold of Ali Pasha, 'the lion of Ioannina', and he is buried on the island in the lake – boats run regular trips across in the summer.

Dodona is 21km from Ioannina along a good if winding road. The sanctuary of Dodona is one of the oldest in Greece, if not the oldest. Homer mentions 'wintry Dodona' and calls the servants of the oracle *selloi* or *helloi*, from where it is said, *Hellas*, the word for Greece and things Greek is derived. It was famous for its oracle long before Delphi arrived on the scene. It is likely that the sanctuary was established by Dorians moving down from the north and the oracle was said to come from the rustling of the leaves of a giant oak tree. One of the largest theatres in Greece was built here in the 3rd century BC, ten metres wider than Epidavros, and it is still largely intact today even if some of it has been stitched together with concrete. Other buildings have been excavated, but it is the theatre which is the star of the site, and the annual theatre festival held in August must be spectacular.

Ali Pasha

At the end of the 18th century and beginning of the 19th Ali Pasha was a name feared by all in Ioannina and the surrounding district. Depending on what he could wring out of them, Ali allied himself with the Turkish Porte, the British, or the French to further his ambition and greed for power and wealth. He rose to power in the Ottoman war against the Austrians and was made Pasha of Trikala in 1788. In the same year he seized Ioannina and made it his base to control the Epirus.

Ali Pasha's rule was associated with cruelties of all kinds. He used ingenious methods of torture for his victims: roasting on a spit, crucifixion, flaying to death, grid-iron, drowning, any and every method was tested. In 1801 it is said that Kyra Phrosyne, the mistress of his oldest son was drowned in the lake along with seventeen others. Kyra had refused his advances whereupon he raped her, had her bound live into a weighted sack and thrown into the lake. In 1803 sixty Souliot women, trapped in Zalongo Monastery by Ali's men, jumped to their death over a cliff rather than submit to the tyrant and his violent sexual practices. His harem was said to number over 500 and his lifestyle became a byword for luxury and hedonism.

In 1809 Lord Byron with Hobhouse visited Ali Pasha and marvelled at his luxurious lifestyle, something Byron was much accustomed to. In *Childe Harold's Pilgrimage* he describes Ali as a man under whose 'aged venerable face' are deeds that 'stain him with disgrace'. In a letter to his mother he goes further and calls Ali '. . . a remorseless tyrant, guilty of the most horrible cruelties. . . as barbarous as he is successful, roasting rebels, etc.' Ali Pasha met his end when the patience of the Sultan ran out and Turkish troops were sent to kill him. Ali escaped to the island in the middle of the lake where he was finally killed by a bullet fired up through the floor of the Monastery of Pantaleimon. A small museum preserves the place and it, as well as the island village itself, deserves a visit.

Ormiskos Valtou

The somewhat bleak anchorage, sometimes known as Igoumenitsa Creek, is on the N side of the entrance to Igoumenitsa. Make for the innermost cove on the S side where the fish farm cuts off further access to the inlet. Anchor in 3–5m on mud and weed, good holding. Good all-round shelter in splendid isolation.

From the inlet there is a pleasant walk over the sand dunes and beach to the N side of Igoumenitsa Bay. The land around the river mouth was formerly a group of small islands until river silt fused them into the mainland. They are believed to be the ancient Sybota (demotic Sivota) Islands where the Corinthians and Corcyrans fought a naval battle in 433 BC that indirectly led to the Peloponnesian War. The name has now passed to a group of islands to the S of Igoumenitsa (see below) which has interesting implications for the theories of Dörpfeld and his quest for Homer's Ithaca discussed in Chapter 3.

Platarias

A small harbour inside Ormos Platarias, the large bay lying under Ak Kondramourto.

Pilotage

Approach Once into the bay the houses of the village are easily identified and the harbour will be seen.

Mooring Go stern- or bows-to in the inner basin where there are mostly 2m depths off the quay. Good shelter from the prevailing wind.

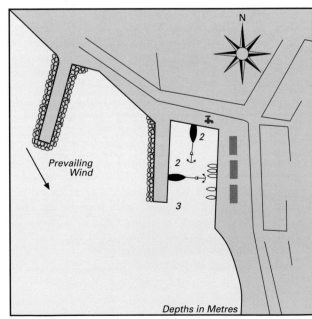

PLATARIAS

Facilities

Water on the quay. Good shopping for provisions and tavernas on the waterfront.

General

The village has a modest tourist trade on the strength of its sandy beach stretching around the head of the bay and is popular with flotillas.

Mourtos and nearby islands

Just over 5M S of Ak Kondramourto, the S entrance to Igoumenitsa, lie the Sivota Islands and on the mainland shore opposite the village of Mourtos. The high bold islands: Nisis Ay Nikolaos, Nisis Sivota, and Nisis Mavros Noros, are easily identified from the N or S.

Pilotage

Approach The lighthouse on the N end of Nisis Sivota is conspicuous and from the N a ruined three-storeyed house on the coast is easily identified. The entrance from the N or S is straightforward, but a yacht should not attempt to pass between Nisis Ay Nikolaos and Nisis Sivota where a reef obstructs the passage.

Mooring There are several anchorages around the mainland and islands.

1. **Mourtos village**. The quayed area off Mourtos village is tenable in the prevailing winds although it is not always comfortable. Go stern or bows-to the village quay on the SE taking care of the depths. For the section of quay not protected by the stubby mole it is best to go stern-to so the bows are pointed into the chop that enters the bay with the prevailing winds, not to mention any ferry wash that rolls in as well. Generally good protection, although the further you are to the north along the quay the better the protection.

The pontoon under the stubby mole is for *Sailing Holidays* flotilla boats and you may be able to get a berth on it if no boats are due in – but do enquire in advance.

2. **Monastery Bay**. In the cove NW of Mourtos village off a restaurant. Anchor and take a line to the shore or to the short jetty if possible. There are mostly 1·5–2 metre depths off the outside of the jetty. Shelter here is better than it looks if you are tucked into the N corner.

3. In the cove immediately S of Mourtos. This is one of the best places to be with good all-round shelter. Anchor where convenient and

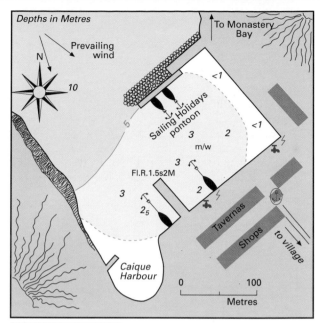

MOURTOS HARBOUR

take a long line ashore or anchor in the channel though it is quite deep. The bottom is mud and weed, generally good holding. In the summer there can be a strong S-going current, strong enough so that boats lie to the current rather than to moderate winds.

4. The small cove on the E side of Ay Nikolaos Island is mostly fairly shallow so most craft anchor just inside the entrance. Shallow draught craft can get further inside. Care needs to be taken of a reef a short distance into the cove.

Note Depths in the channel between Nisis Ay Nikolaos and the mainland decrease abruptly to a 2m bar opposite the entrance to the next cove on the mainland. With care most craft drawing 1·8m or less can get through here, but it should be negotiated slowly. It is an eerie feeling coming up to 2m depths in crystal clear water from depths of 10m on either side.

5. **Sand-bar Bay**. At the S end of the channel there is an enclosed cove sheltered by Nisis Mavros Noros with a sand bar blocking off the E end. Much of the bay is taken up with the moorings for dinghies of the hotel above, but a space can sometimes be found. Good shelter inside. Anchor in 2–3m on sand.

6. **End Bay** or **Fourth Bay**. If you circumnavigate Nisis Mavros Noros there is an attractive anchorage on the E side off the sand bar mentioned above. Good shelter in light to

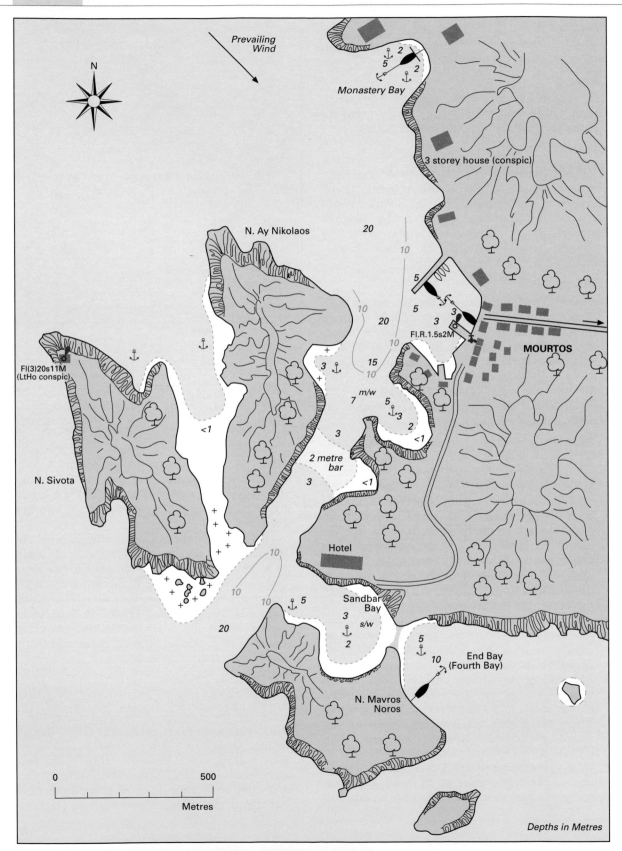

Prevailing Wind

N

Monastery Bay

3 storey house (conspic)

N. Ay Nikolaos

20

10

10

20

10

5

5

3

Fl.R.1.5s2M

15

10

MOURTOS

Fl(3)20s11M
(LtHo conspic)

3

7 m/w

5 3

2

<1

N. Sivota

<1

2 metre bar

3

<1

3

Hotel

10

10

10

5

Sandbar Bay

3 s/w

2

5

End Bay
(Fourth Bay)

10

20

N. Mavros Noros

0   500

Metres

Depths in Metres

MOURTOS AND NISOI AY NIKOLAOS, SIVOTA AND MAVROS NOROS

moderate northwesterlies, but strong westerlies send an uncomfortable swell in. Anchor in 4–10m with a long line ashore. The bottom is sand and weed, mostly good holding once the anchor is dug in.

7. In calm weather there are several attractive anchorages off the N end of the gap between Nisis Sivota and Nisis Ay Nikolaos. Once the prevailing wind gets up it blows straight into here so the anchorages must be vacated – until then they are enchanting places under the wild slopes of the islands. When you vacate the anchorage do not attempt to head south down between the islands as there is a reef and shoal water between them.

Facilities

Most facilities are in Mourtos village. For provisions or a meal you can walk from Monastery Bay (about 20 minutes) or from the anchorage in the channel. Better still take the dinghy around to the village. Water and electricity on the quay. Fuel in the town. Most provisions can be found. Tavernas and bars on the waterfront or in the village proper. At Monastery Bay there is *Perri's Taverna* overlooking the bay which has good food and a wonderful view. The hotel above Sand Bar Bay does not welcome passing trade and in any case is an 'all-inclusive' tourist ghetto well worth avoiding.

General

The rugged islands close to the steep-to coast make Mourtos an attractive place and inevitably a developer spotted its attractions and built a hotel overlooking what has become known as 'Sand-bar Bay'. This disturbs the tranquillity of the place, especially at night when the disco booms its monotonous beat out over the anchorage. In Mourtos village the atmosphere is more convivial and there are several good tavernas that will repay the dinghy trip from any of the anchorages.

Ormos Paramithias

Just under 5M SSE of Sivota Island there is a long sandy beach around Ormos Paramithias. It is easily recognised by the large hotel on the slopes above the bay. Ormos Paramithias can only be used in calm weather as the prevailing wind blows straight into it.

Immediately N of the bay there is an inlet which offers good shelter in light to moderate westerlies and can be used overnight. The steep-to coast all

the way along here has some wonderful isolated sandy beaches, notably Ormos Perdhika, Ormos Arillas, Ormos Paramithias, the bay under Ak Varlaam, and the bay above Ak Trofali.

Parga

Parga is the village tucked under the castle to the E of Ormos Valtou, the bay that is most used by yachts and sand and sea lovers. Parga harbour is not really for yachts and most make for Ormos Valtou and the small harbour on its W side.

Pilotage

Approach From the W the massive remains of Kastelli near the village of Ayia is easily identified. From the S the small islet of Ay Nikolaos with a white chapel and the houses of Parga village will be seen.

Mooring Yachts normally make for the small harbour on the W side of Ormos Valtou. In the approach to Ormos Valtou care needs to be taken of Voi Spiridhonia, a reef lying approximately 100m off Ak Ay Spiridhonia. In calm weather it is easy to spot the reef, but

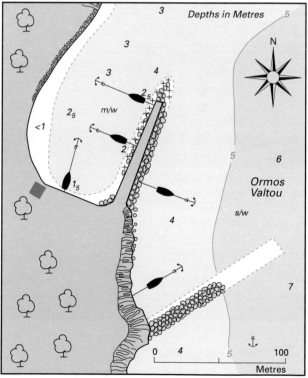

ORMOS VALTOU (PARGA)

The Venetian castle at Parga

with the whitecaps whipped up by the prevailing wind it can be difficult to see and it pays to round the cape a good distance off to avoid it. There is another rock with less than 2m about 100m N of the reef.

Go bows-to where possible behind the mole. Care is needed as the rock ballasting projects some distance out in places.

The new mole being built to the S of the old one is not yet complete, but a yacht can anchor under it with a long line ashore or to the mole. Yachts can also anchor off to the S of the old mole though the ski and para-gliding boats operating off the beach don't like you anchoring anywhere too far E of the old mole. The bottom is sand and weed, good holding. Good shelter behind the old mole and reasonable shelter from the prevailing winds when anchored off in the bay.

A yacht can go stern- or bows-to the jetty in Ormos Ay Athanasiou at Parga village itself, but there is usually little space amongst the tripper boats and the ferry. Shelter in Ormos Ay Athanasiou is not as good as it looks on the plan and with the prevailing wind some swell works its way into it.

Facilities

In Ormos Valtou there are bars and tavernas on the beach that open in the summer, but little else. To get provisions you must walk into Parga village around the beach and up around past the Venetian castle – it is some distance but to compensate the walk is a pleasant one. In Parga there is good shopping for provisions and numerous restaurants and bars. The *Castello Taverna* in Parga village is much recommended and *Kosta's Taverna* near the castle also has good food and wonderful views out over the bay. PO. Bank. Irregular buses to Igoumenitsa and Preveza. Ferry and tripper boats to Paxos.

General

Parga is one of the most attractive places along this coast with the old castle and the village straggling up the hillside – it is sometimes called the 'pine-cone' referring to its ellipsoid position with the houses looking like the seeds of the cone – and two picturesque bays on either side of the fortified summit. Justifiably it attracts considerable numbers of tourists in the summer and consequently when you approach it from the water you will find the beach on the W a sea of bodies and umbrellas and the water churned up

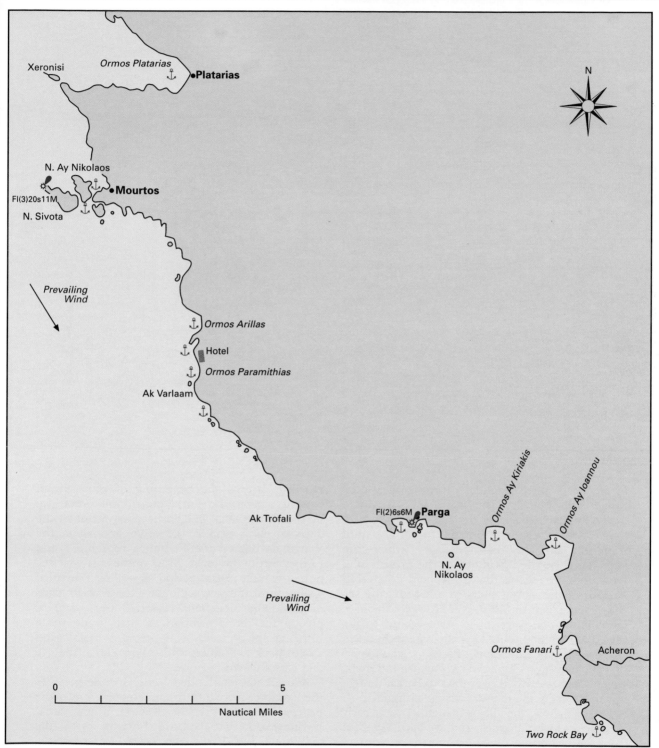

ORMOS PLATARIAS TO ORMOS FANARI

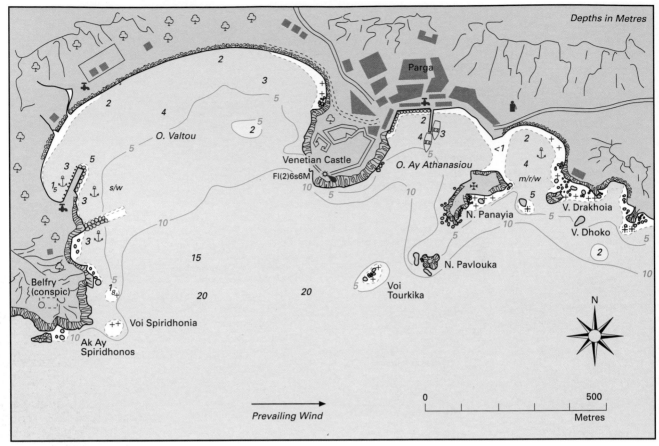

Depths in Metres

Parga

O. Valtou

Venetian Castle
Fl(2)6s6M

O. Ay Athanasiou

N. Panayia

V. Drakhoia

V. Dhoko

N. Pavlouka

Voi
Tourkika

Belfry
(conspic)

Ak Ay
Spiridhonos

Voi Spiridhonia

m/r/w

s/w

Prevailing Wind

N

0   500

Metres

ORMOS PARGAS

by ski boats and paragliders and the occasional tripper boat. Out of season it is more convivial.

The present village by the sea is actually new Parga. Old Parga was inland to the N until sometime in the 14th century when the inhabitants decided to move to the present site. Local folklore tells us that a shepherd discovered an icon of the Virgin Mary in a cave by the sea which was taken to old Parga. However the icon miraculously returned of its own accord to the cave, so the inhabitants took the hint and moved to new Parga. The name Parga is said to be derived from the Virgin Mary, *Panayia* in Greek, which was bastardised over time to Parga, though it is more likely the name is Slavic in origin.

The fort above the village is mentioned as early as 1337 and would appear to have been Venetian from the beginning though it may have Norman antecedents. The Turks resented this Venetian presence and in 1452 captured the town only to lose it two years later when the townspeople

rebelled. It was the beginning of centuries of battling against the Turks and ultimate betrayal by the British. In 1537 Barbarossa, terror of the Turkish navy, sacked the town and again the Venetians helped the Pargiotes to rebuild and further fortify the town. Most of the castle we see now was built in this period as well as a fortified wall around the town, though little now remains of this. The Venetians regarded the castle as pivotal for the protection of their trade route bringing spices, silks, and precious metals and stones back to Venice, and called Parga 'the eye and ear of Corfu'.

When Napoleon ended Venetian rule in 1797 the Pargiotes were quite happy to come under the protection of the French. However a new threat hovered on the Pargiote horizon with the ambitions of Ali Pasha who wanted to acquire the fortress at Parga and the surrounding region. In 1800 Ali Pasha besieged the fortress and the inhabitants cunningly hoisted the Russian flag, a ruse they hoped would convince Ali Pasha they were under the protection of a Russian fleet patrolling the Ionian islands. Later in the same year a treaty was signed between the Russians and the Turks recognising Parga as an autonomous town and region. In 1807 Ali Pasha again attempted to take Parga and again failed – the defensive position of the castle was well nigh impregnable from the sea or land and contained large cisterns and a freshwater spring close by. In 1814 the Pargiotes rebelled against their French masters in favour of the British, at the instigation of British agents it is said, and briefly the Union Jack was hoisted over the fortress.

What subsequently happened is a shameful episode in British colonial history. After holding Parga for two years the British negotiated to sell it to Ali Pasha in return for a guarantee of non-aggression towards their possessions in the Ionian islands. So it was that Ali Pasha finally got the fortress at Parga and 4,000 Pargiotes fled to Corfu on the 15th April 1816. It was not until 1913 that the town and region finally became a part of Greece.

Chapel on the islet off Parga town

The small harbour in Ormos Valtou. Parga

Ormos Ay Athanasiou

In the bay off Parga village there are numerous islets and rocks peppering the approaches and the bay itself. These are all easily identified and with care present no problems to navigation.

In the W half of the bay there are no useful places to anchor without getting in the way of the ferry and tripper boats. In calm weather a yacht can anchor in the E half of the bay. Care is needed when entering between Vos Kepa and Vos Drakhoia, two above-water rocks surrounded by reefs. Anchor in 4m on mud, rock, and weed, not everywhere good holding. The anchorage is attractive and it is worth a row across to Nisis Panayia where there is a chapel and a few remains of a small Venetian fort.

Ormos Ay Kiriakis

A large bay a mile E of Nisis Ay Kiriakis which is easily identified from the chapel on it. The distinctive red cliffs on the E side of the bay stand out clearly. A yacht can anchor in the NW corner where there is reasonable protection from the prevailing NW winds. Anchor in 3–10m on sand and weed, reasonable holding.

Ashore there is a hotel and villas around the beach. Several tavernas and bars open in the summer. The bay is thought to be the site of ancient Torine, a Greek and later Roman settlement, though little conclusive evidence has been unearthed and there are several other contenders for the site along the coast to the S.

Ormos Ay Ioannou

A large bay a mile E of Kiriakis. The approach and entrance are free of dangers and a yacht should head for the NW end of the bay and anchor in 4–10m on mud, rock, and weed, not everywhere good holding. The bay is subject to gusts off the hills with the prevailing winds so make sure your anchor is well in. Unfortunately the best place, the inlet Agnali Skouliki in the NW corner, is mostly obstructed by mussel beds.

The bay is rather a bleak place without a decent beach and because of this is relatively little populated by visitors from the land or the sea making it a quiet if desolate spot. On the W side of the bay off the inlet of Agnali Thoukidhikis a freshwater spring wells up from the sea bottom creating a murky whirlpool where the freshwater mixes with the salt. There is a considerable volume of freshwater escaping here some 30m below sea level and if you taste the water it is brackish rather than salt – not quite the pure freshwater that local folklore says was skimmed from the surface by ships of old to replenish their stocks.

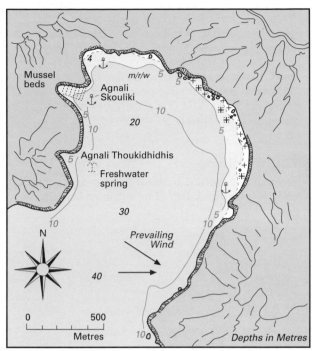

ORMOS AY IOANNOU

Ormos Fanari

A bay 2M S of Ay Ioannou. Unfortunately the bottom comes up quickly just inside the entrance and only shallow draught craft will be able to squeeze inside. There are depths of 8m just inside the entrance on the N side coming up quickly to 2m and less. The prevailing wind tends to blow straight into here, sending in a considerable swell making it virtually untenable except in the morning calm. It is a pity the bay cannot be easily used as there are interesting associations around and about.

Potamos Akheron, the river that flows into the bay and the sea here is the ancient Acheron where the souls of the dead were thought to descend into the underworld. The spot must have been known as early as the 9th century BC when Homer has Odysseus descend into the Acheron to consult Teiresias on his return – here Circe gives Odysseus his instructions for the journey.

'You will come to a wild coast and to Persephone's grove, where the hill poplars grow and the willows that so quickly shed their seeds. Beach your boat there by Ocean's swirling stream and march on into Hades' Kingdom of Decay. There the River of Flaming Fire and the River of Lamentation, which is a branch of the Waters of the Styx, unite around a pinnacle of rock to pour their thundering streams into Acheron.'

Near the village of Mesopotamo on a rocky pinnacle is the Necromanteion of Ephyra, the sanctuary to Hades and Persephone and source of an oracle of considerable fame in the ancient world. The Necromanteion is well preserved and a fascinating site to visit. Pilgrims to the site were guided along a labyrinthine passage to the sanctuary where some sources say that hallucinogenic vapours stupefied them before a terrifying descent by windlass to a chamber where the priests relayed the answers to the questions put to the oracle. In former times the Necromanteion of Ephyra was surrounded by a large lake or possibly a gulf of the Ionian extending inland from the coast which has now silted to become a swamp and has been partially reclaimed for farmland with the river Acheron meandering lazily through it. The remains of the site and its position still have an eerie feel to them, even in this monotheistic age.

Two Rock Bay

A small bay lying just over 2M S of Fanari. It can be recognised from the two above-water rocks lying in the immediate approaches. It is fairly shallow in here with 2m depths in the entrance and 1·5m depths further in. There is good shelter from the prevailing winds and no sea enters. A quiet place that could be a million miles from Parga and usually you will be the only one swimming in the clear waters of the bay. There used to be a lot of sand dollar starfish on the bottom at one time, but people forget that even if everyone takes 'just one', it doesn't take long for them all to disappear.

Ligia (Mitika)

A small rockbound harbour lying around 6 miles SSE of Two Rock Bay. The entrance is really very tricky and the approach should be made in calm weather only with someone up front conning the way in.

Pilotage

Approach The little cluster of houses above the harbour will be seen and closer in the rough stone breakwater can be made out against the steep slopes behind. The approach must be made from the SW heading between the two rock shelves either side of the entrance. Go very slowly and only make the approach in calm weather as the prevailing NW wind pushes a swell down onto the harbour and immediate

Ligia looking down onto the entrance. Note the rocks either side of the immediate approach

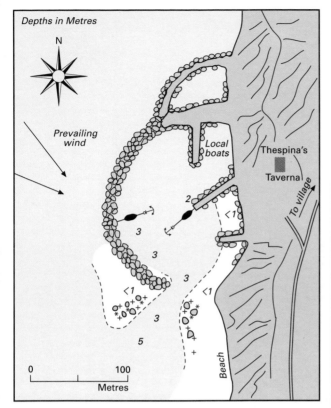

LIGIA

Preveza

The town of Preveza sits just inside the entrance to Amvrakikos Kolpos and NE of the island of Levkas that shelters the 'inland sea'. It is entered along a buoyed channel and if you are approaching it in the late afternoon with the prevailing wind pushing you in, there may be some apprehension until you pick up the buoys marking the entrance to the channel.

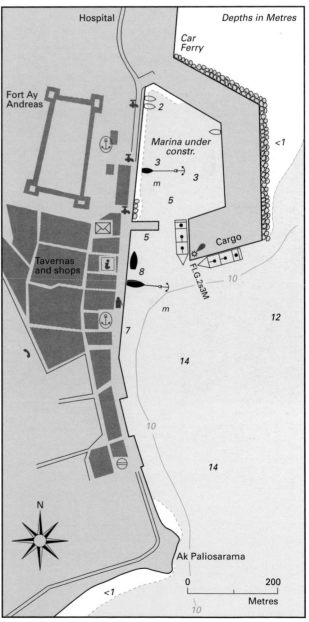

PREVEZA

approach. Once in the entrance you need to make a bit of a jink to starboard before turning into the harbour proper.

Mooring Berth stern or bows-to the outer rough stone breakwater with a long line ashore. There may be some space for a small yacht or two to go bows-to on the stubby pier, although berths here are usually occupied by the local fishing boats.

Facilities

You need to take the dinghy across to the short pier and from there there are a couple of tavernas up the hill. *Thespina's* near the harbour has been recommended. Limited provisions can be found and if you need anything else it is a hot taxi ride to Preveza or Parga – better to go without until you sail there.

General

It may be in this area that Ligia has some ancient associations, but although it is sometimes called Mitika it is not to be confused with Ak Mitikas further south where Octavius marshalled his forces prior to his defeat of Antony and Cleopatra off Aktion.

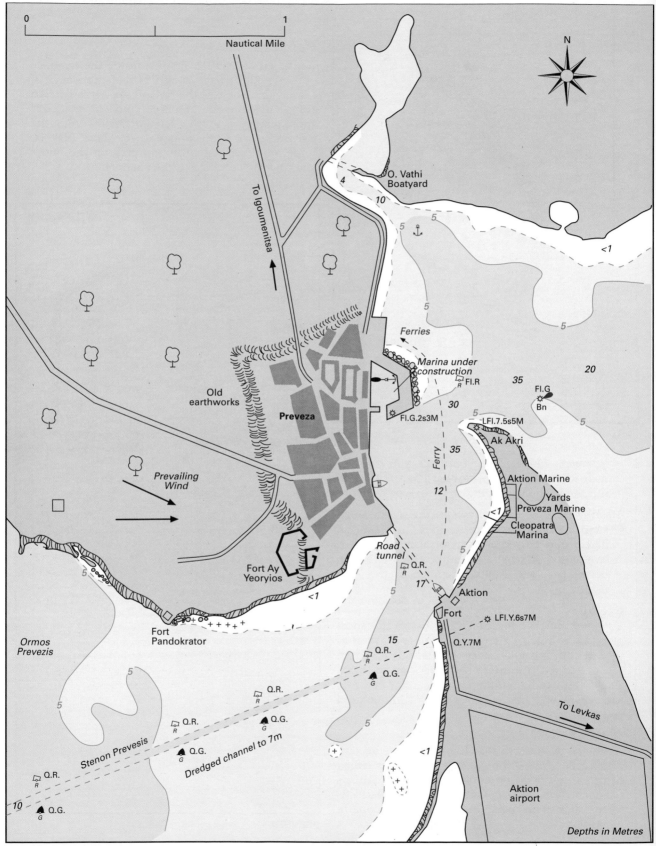

STENON PREVEZA

Pilotage

Approach In the approach from the NW a low thickly-wooded knoll to the N of Preveza stands out on the otherwise flat plain. Closer in Fort Ay Yeoryios will be seen. In the summer planes taking off and landing at Aktion airport are a handy guide to where things are. The buoys marking the channel can be difficult to see until quite close-to although they are big enough.

Once identified the approach through the channel is straightforward. There is often a current flowing out of the channel from Amvrakikos Kolpos and with the onshore swell pushed into it there can be a choppy confused sea in the outer part of the channel. Once into the lee of the land the sea will flatten. A tunnel has been burrowed under the sea from Aktion to Preveza town and although not yet finished, should be open in the near future. The ferries which currently run from Aktion to Preveza berth to the north of the basin, but it is likely they will be phased out once the tunnel is open.

Mooring Berth alongside or stern-to the long town quay where convenient. Shelter from the normal prevailing winds is good. Care is needed with SE gales which blow directly onto the quay – the best place is tucked up somewhere inside the mole.

Note A marina is now under construction in the basin and should be ready for use in the near future although it is likely not all facilities will be in place for some time. What will likely happen is that yachts will be directed not to berth on the town quay and will be 'requested' to berth in the marina. Protection in the basin should be good with the construction of the new mole at the entrance although a question mark will still stand over it when strong southerlies blow.

Facilities

Services Fuel in the town and water on the waterfront. When the marina is complete facilities should include water and electricity at berths and a shower and toilet block. At the time of writing these are still to be installed.

Provisions Good shopping for all provisions nearby in the town.

Eating out Tavernas and bars along the waterfront and in the town. The waterfront has now been pedestrianised and there are numerous new restaurants and bars. There is a very good

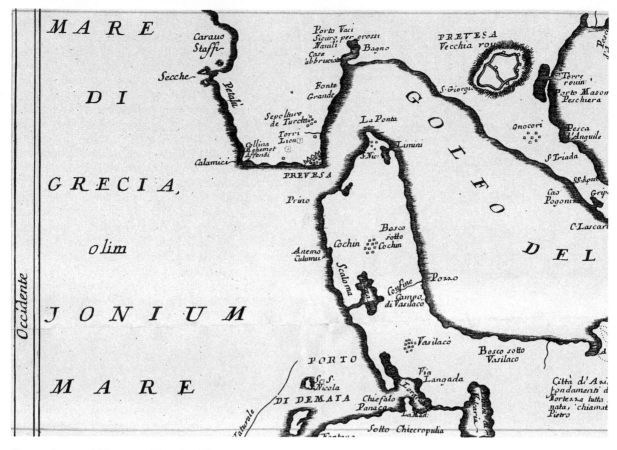

Preveza from an 18th-century Venetian Chart

grilled fish shop in the warren of streets around the clock tower which serves only grilled sardines and salad and good *retsina* from the barrel.

Other Banks. PO. Hospital. Dentist. Hire motorbikes. International and domestic flights leave from Aktion airport just across the channel.

General

Preveza comes in for a lot of stick from the guidebooks which call it dull, dreary, drab, insignificant, somewhere to pass through as quickly as possible on the way to somewhere else. In an earlier guidebook I described it in much the same vein, but now it has been cleaned up I like the place and its back streets at least give a hint of what an everyday working Greek town looks like. It has one of the most helpful tourist offices around and the pedestrianised waterfront is popular for that evening institution, the *volta*, where you stroll at a pace at the opposite end of

the spectrum to power-walking, stopping whenever you meet someone you know to say hello, exchange gossip, and have a drink if a café or bar is handy.

The town has an ancient pedigree dating from 290 BC when Pyrrhus, King of Epirus built a city here and named it Berenicia after his mother-in-law. Perhaps it did have disagreeable origins that blighted everyones view of it for evermore. When Augustus built Nikopolis the population migrated to the new city and Berenicia declined. Preveza was not heard of again until the end of the 13th century when it was mentioned as the southernmost city in Epirus. By 1499 the Venetians had occupied it and begun building the massive fortifications around the town that can only partially be seen today.

It was ceded to the Turks by the Treaty of Carlowitz in 1699, but retaken by the Venetians in 1717 in an ongoing struggle between the two super-powers of the time to control the coastal seaboard of the Ionian. Venetian rule ended with Napoleon's conquest of the Republic and Preveza was suddenly under the tricolour, though not for long. While Napoleon was occupied with his campaign in Egypt the cunning Ali Pasha attacked and overwhelmed the French force.

The 'Destruction of Preveza' lasted two days as the Turks sacked the city and murdered the inhabitants, French and Greek alike. Only one hundred Frenchmen were left alive, their compatriots were all beheaded, and local folk history tells us that these unfortunate hundred were forced to march to Constantinople carrying the heads of their comrades in sacks to present to the Sultan. The rape of Preveza was not complete. Ali Pasha then invited those who had fled the city to return, promising to restore their property and not to harm them further, indeed he swore on the Koran that none would be harmed, and dispatched ships to collect the scattered population. True to form Ali Pasha had the remainder of the duped population executed and it is said that on the tenth day the executioner died from his extensive labours. Like the rest of the region, Preveza only became Greek in 1912.

Much of the extensive fortifications erected by the Venetians around the city were dismantled in the 20th century though the remains can still be identified. The city itself was enclosed by walls and a deep ditch with earthworks outside it. Two forts within the defensive ring, Ay Andreas in the N by the new mole and Ay Yeoryios in the S by the channel, formed a strategic inner defence. On Ak Paliosarama there were further fortifications, called 'Punta' by the Venetians, with a battery that prevented ships entering or leaving Amvrakikos Kolpos. The triangular fort on the opposite shore at Aktion, where the car ferries now berth, was built by Ali Pasha. At the entrance to the Preveza Channel on the N side there remains Fort Pandokrator protecting the approaches to the channel. For walkers it is a pleasant ramble around to Fort Pandokrator and on to Ak Parginoskala, where there are also several pleasant coves and beaches popular with local bathers.

Nikopolis

Around six kilometres N of Preveza lie the remains of Nikopolis, the city Octavius built after his victory over Anthony off Aktion. This naval battle effectively resolved the civil war that had rent the Roman Empire and established Octavius as the one ruler, the legitimate Caesar of an Empire stretching from Spain to Egypt.

The story starts with the success of Julius Caesar during his campaigns in Gaul, against the Germans across the Rhine, and his triumphant return to Rome with Cleopatra on his arm. Although popular with his troops, he was not popular with the old aristocracy and it was they who arranged for his assignation in 44 BC, the 'Et tu Brute' scene in Shakespeare's *Julius Caesar*. Two figures emerged as successors: Octavius, Caesar's nephew, and Anthony, Caesar's best general. The two came to terms with each other and quickly defeated the aristocrats in the Battle of Phillipi. The Empire was divided between Octavius and Anthony, with Anthony taking the east and Octavius the western provinces.

The difference between the two rulers could not have been more marked. Octavius was a sickly youth, given to stammering, a methodical

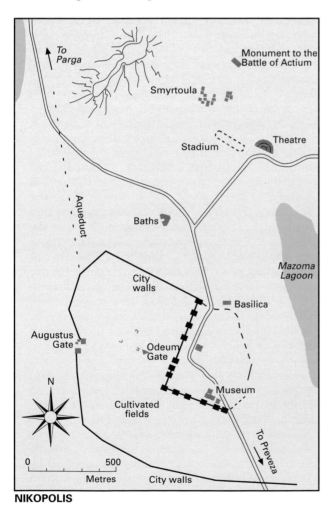

NIKOPOLIS

man who wanted a sensible solution to problems and worked slowly and meticulously to that end. Anthony was more in the mould of Julius Caesar, a brilliant general who was always in the thick of the fighting with his troops, a heavy drinker and notorious womaniser. Like Caesar he fell under the spell of Cleopatra whose powers of bewitching men seemed not to have dimmed. Anthony spent more and more time with his mistress, neglecting his men, the provinces, and his popularity in Rome. It was inevitable that a showdown with Octavius was in the offing. The two rulers marshalled their forces and met at Actium in the winter of 32/31 BC.

Anthony lost the battle before it started. His army and navy were based at Actium and suffered from supply problems and lack of preparation for the campaign. The troops and rowers for the galleys were badly quartered, badly fed, and decimated by disease. One by one Anthony's troops defected to Octavius and his rowers were replaced by farmers and shepherds from the local population. Octavius' fleet under the redoubtable Agrippa blockaded the supply routes to the S and cut off supplies to Anthony's army.

Numerically Anthony had the strongest and most experienced army, some 100,000 men against the 80,000 men of Octavius. Anthony's navy consisted of 500 ships including a large part of Cleopatra's Egyptian fleet, mostly heavy warships which had been covered in iron plate to withstand ramming, and appeared to be equipped for ferrying his numerically larger army to board the ships of Octavius. The opposing navy of Octavius was smaller, around 400 ships that were smaller and lighter and therefore more manoeuvrable. Anthony desperately wanted a land battle, but Octavius refused to confront him on the land and kept up the blockade of supplies, finally hemming Anthony in at Actium with a naval blockade right across the entrance to the narrow channel leading into Preveza.

Eventually Anthony realised he had to take on the navy and prepared his fleet. His orders were bizarre. He told his rowers to put all the sails on board, they were normally removed for battle, in case of an offshore wind. Anyone who sails in these waters knows the prevailing winds are invariably onshore, even in late winter and spring. His oarsmen interpreted this as an order to flee, especially when they saw all movable valuables being loaded on the ships of the Egyptian squadron. Octavius divided his fleet into three

and Anthony was forced to do the same. The slow ships of Anthony were surrounded and rammed by the smaller more manoeuvrable ships, but with his numerical advantage things were not going too badly until an entirely unexpected event. The Egyptian squadron suddenly appeared and sailed right through the naval battle and fled south. Anthony promptly abandoned his men and with a fast ship pursued his mistress. Shakespeare catches the shame and despair of it all in this passage:

She once being loofed
The noble ruin of her magic, Anthony,
Claps on his sea wing, and like a doting mallard,
Leaving the fight in height, flies after her.
I never saw such an action of shame.
Experience, manhood, honour, ne'Er before
Did violate so itself.

The army could not believe their general had deserted them and not until a week later, when they heard he had arrived in Egypt with Cleopatra, did they finally surrender to Octavius. The conclusion is well known. Anthony and Cleopatra committed suicide and Cleopatra's son by Caesar, a possible successor, was as one commentator put it, 'tidied away into a small box'.

Octavius, now rechristened Augustus Caesar, built Nikopolis to commemorate his victory. It was a city on a vast scale encompassed by great walls. To populate this city built in the middle of nowhere Augustus forcibly moved the populations from towns throughout the region and even further afield. When you look at the remains of the city it should be remembered that this is the later contracted version built under the Byzantine Emperor Justinian, occupying about one fifth the area of the original city. The city was embellished with fine buildings, a large theatre and an *odeum*, a fine stadium, an aqueduct to carry water from the Louros, and boasted three harbours including one on the Ionian side.

Octavius had a memorial built to the battle on the site, it is said, where his tent was pitched to survey the battle. Part of it survives above the theatre and the end of an inscription . . . TUNO is guessed to be a dedication to Neptune, no doubt in thanks for the fortuitous naval battle. The city prospered and it is thought to be the 'Nikopolis of Macedonia' where Paul spent a winter and wrote his Epistle to Titus. Towards the end of the 4th century AD it was attacked by Alaric the Goth and largely destroyed. Justinian

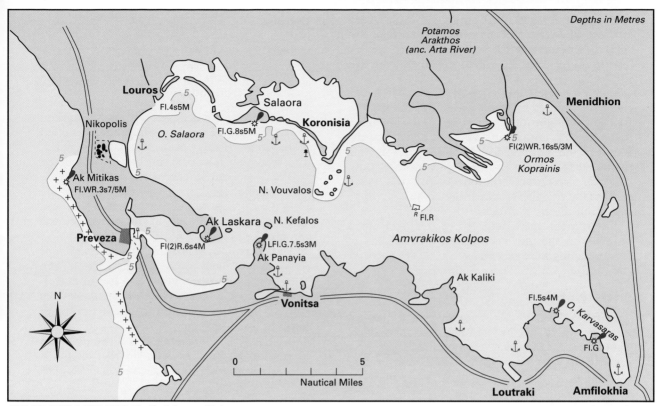

Depths in Metres

Potamos
Arakthos
(anc. Arta River)

Louros
Fl.4s5M
Salaora
Koronisia
Nikopolis
O. Salaora
Fl.G.8s5M
Menidhion
Fl(2)WR.16s5/3M
Ormos
Koprainis
Ak Mitikas
Fl.WR.3s7/5M
N. Vouvalos
Fl.R
Amvrakikos Kolpos
Ak Laskara
N. Kefalos
Preveza
Fl(2)R.6s4M
LFl.G.7.5s3M
Ak Panayia
Ak Kaliki
Fl.5s4M
O. Karvasaras
Vonitsa
Fl.G
N
0   5
Nautical Miles
Loutraki   Amfilokhia

AMVRAKIKOS KOLPOS (Gulf of Amvrakia)

rebuilt it, though the much smaller version that we see today. When the Slavs pushed south it was abandoned in favour of Navpaktos and it was never revived.

There is not really a lot to see at the site. The theatre, Augustus' monument, the baths, the odeum, and the walls built by Justinian remain in good condition. The old walls, the stadium, and the aqueduct can be found. There are some interesting Roman and Byzantine mosaics in the Basilica. The site is now fenced off in places and cultivated. Local farmers grow wheat in patches between the old walls and olive trees shade old masonry. Beware of snakes around the ruins which are said to be plentiful, though I have only ever seen one. Nikopolis is not somewhere that you have to go and see, but it is a pleasant place to wander aimlessly around and to dream on sultry summer days. The museum and the site are open 0900–1530 weekdays and 1000–1630 on Sunday.

Ormos Vathi

The inlet immediately N of Preveza. At one time this was a prohibited anchorage, but recently yachts have used it and no-one seems to mind. Anchor in 10m on mud, good holding. Good protection from the prevailing westerlies. There is a boatyard on the N side of the narrow inlet. It is a short and pleasant walk into Preveza.

Amvrakikos Kolpos

(Gulf of Amvrakia)

The landlocked gulf entered from Preveza. The channel into the gulf is well marked by buoys and beacons. The gulf itself has a number of harbours and anchorages and is a pleasant spot to get away from it all – few yachts make the excursion into it. The N side of the gulf is largely low-lying marshy land with shoal water bordering it for some distance off. This is a breeding ground for water-birds of all types and also for estuary type fish such as sole and eels – some of the restaurants have good fresh flat-fish seldom seen elsewhere in the Ionian.

It is a strange experience to anchor off the N shore surrounded by water with little land nearby. At the beginning of this century H M Denham recorded that underwater volcanic activity at the E end of the gulf killed all the fish which floated to the surface and were collected by the locals. The gulf also attracts numbers of dolphins which feed on the rich fish stocks and mercifully, despite the decline in numbers of dolphins in the Mediterranean generally, there are still good numbers in the gulf according to the reports of friends sailing here recently.

Nisis Kefalos

The islet directly off Ak Panayia. In settled weather a yacht can anchor off here in the shallow water fringing the islet, though it is really only suitable as a lunch stop and not an overnight anchorage.

Vonitsa

Pilotage

Approach Once into Ormos Vonitsa the town and the castle on the slopes immediately W will be seen.

Mooring A yacht can anchor in Ormos Ay Markou on the W side of the bay where there is good protection from the prevailing wind. Unfortunately much of the bay is obstructed by a mussel farm so care is needed. It may be better to anchor off in 5m on the S side of the entrance as it quite deep inside (8–15m) and there is reasonable shelter tucked in at the entrance.

Alternatively anchor off or go stern- or bows-to the town quay taking care of the ballasting which projects underwater in places. The new isolated breakwater off the quay does little to provide protection from the prevailing winds.

An alternative anchorage is off the E side of Nisis Koukouvitsa, the wooded islet on the E side of Ormos Vonitsa, tucked as close as

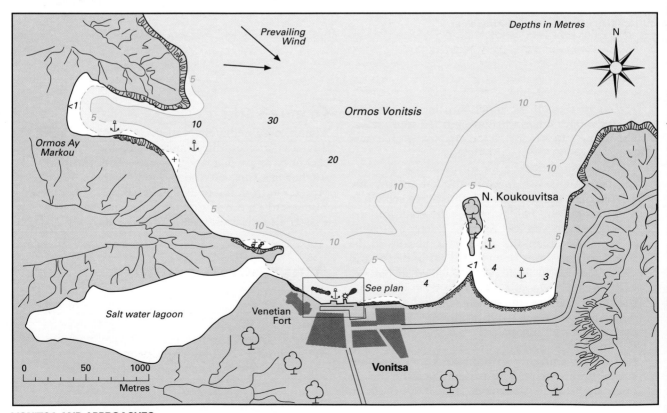

VONITSA AND APPROACHES

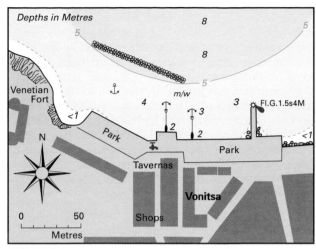

VONITSA

possible into the lee of the island. It is a wonderful place, covered in pine, with a small church on the S end.

Facilities

Fuel and water in the town. Most provisions can be found and there are good local tavernas. PO. OTE. Bank.

General

Vonitsa is a pleasant sleepy sort of place that gets a few tourists in the summer, enough unfortunately for a disco, but not enough to overrun the place. The castle prominent W of the town is largely Venetian, constructed in the 17th century but incorporating part of an earlier Byzantine fortress. It is an interesting place to ramble around with good views out over the gulf from the ramparts.

Vonitsa is said to be the place where the Norman adventurer Robert of Guiscard died of fever, probably malaria, along with 10,000 of his troops. As often seems to happen in accounts of these things, he is also supposed to have died in Fiskardho on Cephalonia where the remains of a Norman church commemorates his death and the name of the place, Fiskardo, is a corruption of his name.

Loutraki

An inlet at the bottom of the large bay immediately W of Ormos Karvasaras. The anchorage in the inlet here and in Ormos

Palaeomylos on the W side are now mostly obstructed by fish farms, but there is usually somewhere that a yacht can find shelter.

Amfilokhia

A village with a small harbour at the head of Ormos Karvasaras. A yacht will normally go alongside the N end of the quay with an anchor laid out to the NE to hold off. It is very deep in the bay, 12–15m, so ensure you have plenty of scope. With the prevailing wind blowing straight down into the bay a considerable swell is kicked up making it uncomfortable and at times possibly dangerous.

Fuel and water in the town. Most provisions can be found and there are tavernas. PO. OTE. Bank.

On a hill behind the town are the remains of ancient Limnaia, a city of some importance mentioned by Thucydides. Little remains today to be seen. The town of Amfilokhia, formerly Karvasaras like the bay, was founded by Ali Pasha as a military garrison. The name Karvasaras is said to be a corruption of *caravanserai*. Today the village is a likeable enough place, but not somewhere you will want to stay for long because of the uncomfortable harbour.

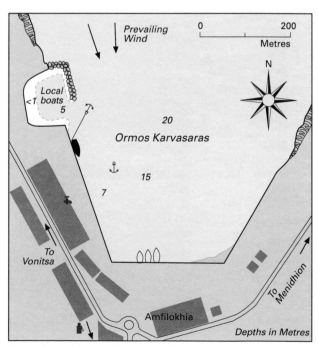

AMFILOKHIA (Ormos Karvasaras)

Menidhion

A small village and harbour in Ormos Kopraina in the NE corner of the gulf. A yacht can go bows-to on the end of the mole or anchor off. The bottom is mud, good holding. Reasonable shelter from the prevailing wind.

Fuel from the petrol station up on the main road. Water from one of the tavernas. Most provisions can be found and there are numerous tavernas ashore. The small village attracts a few, mostly local, tourists and is a popular place for an evening out at one of the many tavernas. You will often find fresh flat-fish caught in the river estuaries flowing into the gulf near here.

Menidhion is the best place to organise a trip to Arta about 20km away – buses pass by on the main road above or you can order a taxi at one of the tavernas. Arta is a pleasant town built on a loop of Potamos Arakthos, the large river that flows into the gulf just W of Menidhion. It is said that you can cross the river bar by dinghy and get up to Arta that way, but as hydro-electric barrages hold back the water and then release it to drive the turbines, this makes a trip impossible because there will either be no water or it will be dangerous because of the turbulence from large amounts of water suddenly released.

Menidhion

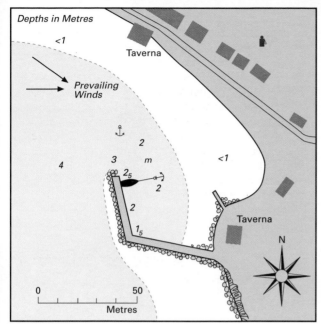

MENIDHION

Nisoi Vouvalo

A group of islands on the N side of the gulf opposite Ak Yelada. The islands are joined by shingle bars with a lagoon in the middle and here a yacht can find excellent shelter from the prevailing wind. Anchor in 2–3m off the beach on the E side of the 'island'. Wonderful deserted surroundings totally away from the hubbub of the resorts.

Koranisia

A new harbour lying approximately 2½M E of Salaora. The entrance to the harbour has silted so only small yachts can use it and even then with some care for the depths. Make the approach from due S and keep very close to the extremity of the W breakwater where there are 1·5m depths – reconnoitre first in the tender if in doubt. Go bows-to the W quay. Good shelter from the prevailing winds. Three tavernas ashore.

Salaora

There is a short rough mole off Salaora where limited shelter can be found. Anchor in 2·5m on the E side of the mole and take a line ashore. A cluster of dilapidated shacks ashore.

A yacht can also anchor off on the W side of Ormos Salaora within what looks like walking distance from Nikopolis.

Arta

Arta is built on the site of ancient Ambracia, the capital of Epirus under King Pyrrhus, though only bits and pieces of the ancient city remain. The population was transported to Nikopolis in 30 BC and it soon declined to become a small provincial town. Its difficult to think of this small provincial town being the most wealthy and powerful ancient city in the region.

It also has interesting remains from the Middle Ages including the quirky church of Panayia Paragoritissa with a dangerous-looking dome supported by antique columns on a primitive cantilever principle.

Still straddling the river is an old Turkish bridge, though it is said to be built on the foundations of a bridge from Alexander the Great's time, which according to legend has the overseer's wife walled up inside it. Poems, songs, a play and even an opera have been written about the bridge and the unfortunate wife. The sacrifice of a human victim to ensure the solidity of the bridge is a common theme in Greece and there are reputed to be other such bridges with victims walled up inside them, notably on the island of Kos and near Thermopylae. According to Lawson quoted in Richard Stoneman's anthology, it was considered propitious in Zakinthos to wall up a Moslem or a Jew in any new bridge right up into the 19th century.

3. The Inland sea. Levkas, Meganisi, Ithaca, Cephalonia and Zakinthos

	Shelter	Mooring	Fuel	Water	Provisions	Tavernas	Plan
Levkas							
Levkas Canal							•
Levkas Town	A	A	A	A	A	A	•
Ligia	C	AC	O	B	C	C	•
Nikiana	B	A	B	B	C	C	•
Nisis Sparti	O	C	O	O	O	O	
Nisis Khelona	C	C	O	O	O	O	
Nisis Madhouri	O	C	O	O	O	O	
Nidri	B	AC	B	A	B	A	•
Tranquil Bay	A	C	O	B	O	O	•
Ormos Vlikho	A	AC	O	B	C	C	•
Ormos Dessimou	C	C	O	B	O	C	•
Stenon Meganisou (Meganisi Channel)	C	C	O	O	O	O	•
Ormos Rouda	B	C	O	B	C	C	•
Ormos Sivota	A	AC	O	A	C	B	•
Ormos Ammousa	O	C	O	O	O	C	
Vassiliki	B	AC	B	A	B	B	•
Skorpios and Skorpidhi							
Skorpios	C	C	O	O	O	O	
Meganisi							
Spartakhori	B	AC	O	B	C	B	•
Vathi	B	AC	O	B	C	C	•
Ormos Kapali and Abelike	A	C	O	O	O	O	•
Port Atheni	B	AC	O	O	C	C	•
Meganisi E coast	O	C	O	O	O	O	
Ithaca							
Frikes	B	B	O	B	C	C	•
Ormos Frikon	C	C	O	O	O	O	•
Kioni	B	AC	O	O	C	C	•

	Shelter	Mooring	Fuel	Water	Provisions	Tavernas	Plan
Kolpos Aetou (Gulf of Molo)	C	C	O	O	O	O	•
(Ithaca Channel)							•
Vathi	A	AC	A	A	B	B	•
Ormos Sarakiniko	C	C	O	O	O	O	
Pera Pigadhi	C	C	O	O	O	O	
Ormos Ay Andreou	C	C	O	O	O	O	
Ormos Pis'Aetou	O	C	O	O	O	O	
Ormos Polis	C	C	O	O	O	C	
Cephalonia							
Fiskardho	A	AC	B	A	B	A	•
Dhiavlos Ithakis							
Anchorages between Fiskardho and Ay Eufimia							
Kalo Limeni	C	C	O	O	O	O	
Ay Eufimia	B	AC	B	A	C	B	
Limin Sami	C	AB	B	B	B	C	
Poros	C	A	B	A	C	C	
Ormos Katelios	C	C	O	O	C	C	
Pessades	C	AC	O	O	O	C	
Argostoli	A	AB	A	A	A	A	
Lixouri	B	A	B	B	B	C	
Ay Kiriakis	C	A	O	O	O	C	
Assos	C	AC	O	B	C	B	•
Zakinthos							
Limin Zakinthos	B	A	A	A	A	A	
Ormos Ay Nikolaos	C	C	O	B	C	C	
Porto Roma	O	C	O	O	O	C	
Ay Yerakas	C	C	O	O	O	C	
Ormos Lagana	O	C	O	B	B	B	
Lithakia	C	A	O	B	C	C	
Ormos Keri	C	AC	O	B	C	B	•
Ormos Vroma	C	C	O	O	O	C	

Opposite: Superb views and close to the action on the quay as well at Nidri

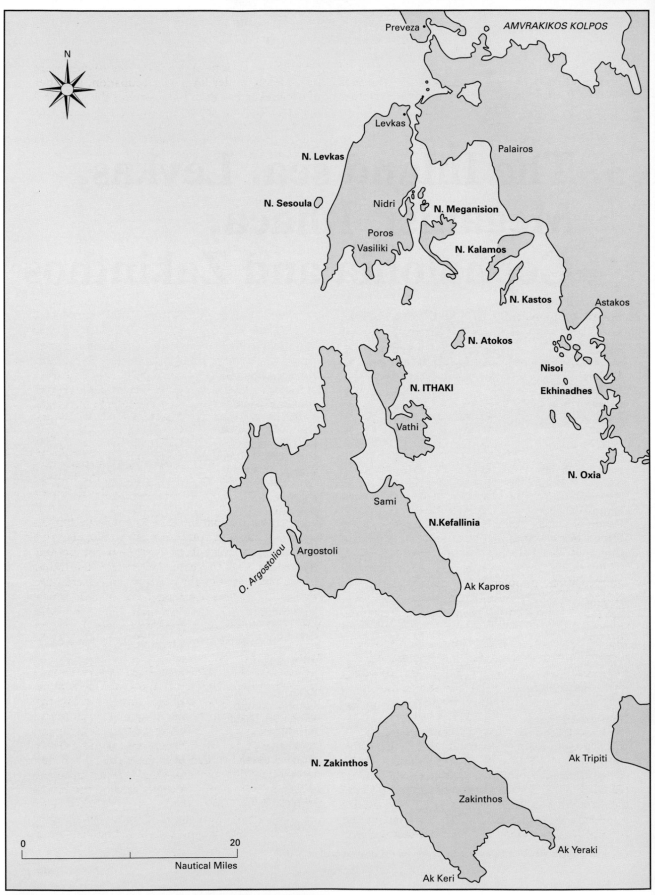

N

AMVRAKIKOS KOLPOS

Preveza

Levkas

N. Levkas

Palairos

N. Sesoula

Nidri

N. Meganision

Poros

N. Kalamos

Vasiliki

N. Kastos

Astakos

N. Atokos

Nisoi

N. ITHAKI

Ekhinadhes

Vathi

Sami

N. Oxia

N.Kefallinia

O. Argostoliou

Argostoli

Ak Kapros

N. Zakinthos

Ak Tripiti

Zakinthos

Ak Yeraki

0   20

Nautical Miles

Ak Keri

NISÓS ZAKINTHOS, NISOS LEVKAS AND NISOS KEFALLINIA

The Inland sea is the area of water enclosed by the islands of Levkas, Cephalonia and Zakinthos on the W and the mainland on the E. Other islands are dotted around the Inland sea and to some extent it resembles a huge lake with land on three sides, or so it seems. It is a wonderful cruising area, one of the best in Greece, and it should be no surprise that it is a popular cruising area for yachts. The area is tailor-made for charter and flotilla sailing and dinghy sailing schools are well established, indeed I spent two seasons as a flotilla skipper in this area many moons ago. Despite the numbers of charter boats here there are so many harbours and anchorages all around the Inland sea that it is possible to get away from it all should you feel claustrophobic during the high season.

Until quite recently there was little tourism apart from yachts and a few determined land travellers. Transport between the islands was not well developed and except for Zakinthos the area was pretty much off the beaten track. Now that new ferry routes have been opened up and regular flights to Aktion, Cephalonia and Zakinthos introduced, the area is better known than it used to be, though no-one could say it was 'touristy' apart from a few patches here and there.

The history of the area is a mixture of influences that broadly follows the history of the rest of the Ionian. Within the group of islands lies the thin hour-glass outline of Ithaca, an island forever haunted by the words of Homer. The ramifications, extrapolations, and metaphorical geography that have been wrung out of Homer's words runs to volumes of commentaries and interpretation, popular and academic, some of which I look at in the introduction to this book. The Greeks and Romans barely bothered with the islands, with the exception of Cephalonia, and though they were all duly colonised and incorporated into the Greek and Roman empires, they were much neglected and subject to piracy and privateering. Under Byzantine rule they fared little better and the coming of the Normans was not unwelcome.

The lasting effect on the islands of the Inland sea was undoubtedly Venetian. From the castles and forts the Venetians built, the churches, the old gnarled olives they encouraged the locals to plant, the architectural influences incorporated into the local houses, to more subtle cultural imports, the Venetians put their stamp on the islands. It is important to remember that with the

singular exception of Levkas, the islands were never really under Turkish occupation, a matter of decades rather than the centuries the mainland opposite had to endure. British influence was confined largely to constructing roads and buildings on Cephalonia and Zakinthos and then the islands were left pretty much to themselves, to some extent forgotten on the western periphery of Greece, at least until tourism touched them here and there in the last few years.

Nisos Levkas

(Nisos Lefkas, Levkadha, Leucas)

Levkas is only an island by virtue of the canal running through the salt marsh between it and the mainland. The present canal is of recent origin, built by the Greeks with British help in 1905, but a canal has existed here since the 7th century BC if we are to believe Thucydides. He also tells us it had silted by 427 BC when the Peloponnesians had to drag their ships over the Levkas isthmus. The Romans repaired the canal, probably under Augustus around the time Nikopolis was built, and after that it is likely it was used under Byzantine and Norman rule though I can find no concrete references. Under the Venetians the canal, or at least the deeper parts of the lagoon, were used to allow ships to pass on the E side of the island. It is likely the Turks used it as well during their occupation. The Russians are known to have dredged a route through the lagoon and built the two small forts, Fort Constantine and Fort Alexander, to guard the 'canal'. The canal we see today is thought not to be anywhere near the original Corinthian canal nor to bear much resemblance to the channel used by the Venetians. Ships then drew much less than they do today and the canal is unlikely to have been more than 1½–2½m deep.

Recently the canal has been widened and dredged though for what purpose no-one is quite sure. There is talk of cruise ships entering the canal and tying up to the quay at Levkas town, but this is more than likely wishful thinking by local entrepreneurs. Tourists are far more likely to arrive overland than over-the-water and to this effect a new floating bridge was recently installed at the N end of the canal to replace the chain ferries. Not that the town council can countenance the new contraption as a bridge: it is the ferry boat *Ag Maura*, the name boldly painted

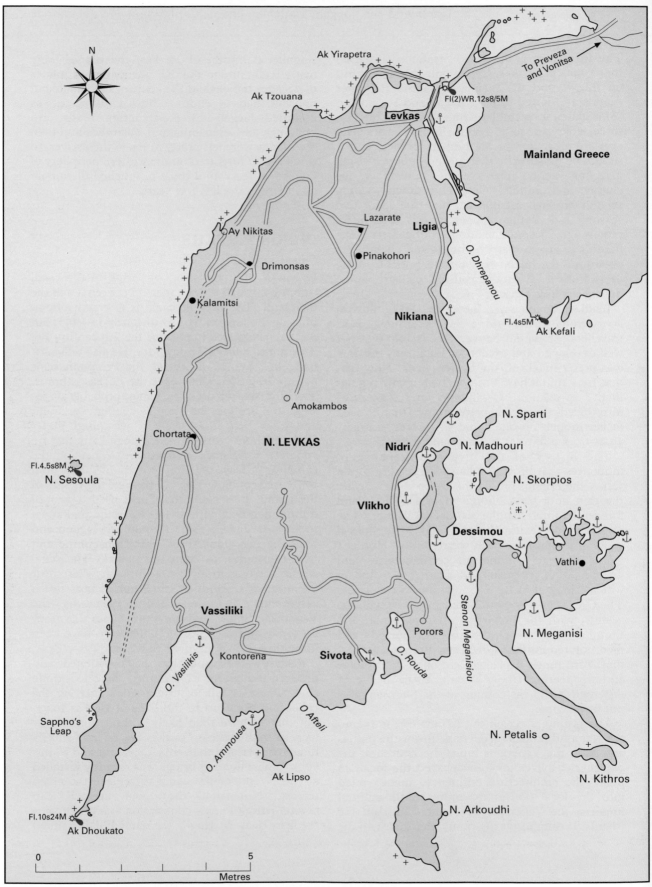

N ↑

Ak Yirapetra

Ak Tzouana

Levkas

Fl(2)WR.12s8/5M

Mainland Greece

To Preveza
and Vonitsa

Lazarate

Ay Nikitas

Drimonsas

● Pinakohori

Ligia

Kalamitsi

Nikiana

O. Dhrepanou

Fl.4s5M

Ak Kefali

Amokambos

N. Sparti

Chortata

N. LEVKAS

Nidri

N. Madhouri

Fl.4.5s8M

N. Sesoula

N. Skorpios

Vlikho

Dessimou

Vathi ●

Vassiliki

Porors

Stenon Meganisiou

N. Meganisi

Kontorena

Sivota

O. Rouda

O. Vasilikis

O. Ammousa

Afteli

Sappho's
Leap

N. Petalis

Ak Lipso

N. Kithros

Fl.10s24M

Ak Dhoukato

N. Arkoudhi

0   5

Metres

NISOS LEVKAS

on the side of the bridge in case anyone should mistake it for anything else, a little island subterfuge designed to keep the special grants and tax concessions that islands in Greece get from the government in Athens.

Though there may be technical quibbles about whether Levkas is an island or not, some guidebooks on the Greek islands do omit it, the place has the feel and look of an island once you are across the causeway and from anywhere other than Levkas town you don't ever ask the question. Even from the canal you can see it is a high island with the main mountain range running down the middle from N to S. Around much of the coast the mountains drop precipitously down to the sea, an impressive coast made beautiful in places by abundant olive groves pierced by tall cypress.

In the SW the steep limestone cliffs give the island its name. Originally it was called Nirikos after the colony established by the Corinthians,

but was changed to Leucas or Lefkos meaning 'white' referring to the white cliffs or possibly to the white (limestone) mountains of which the island is composed. It may be that this was to honour Sappho's lovelorn leap over the cliffs (sometime in the 6th century? BC) or it may be just a piece of straight description. This name, variously bastardized to Lefkas, Levkas, and often the accusative, Levkadha, continued to be used except under Venetian occupation when the name of the fort guarding the land and sea approaches in the N, Santa Maura, was more commonly used. It reverted to Levkas when it became Greek.

For many years Levkas was considered the poor cousin of the islands in the Inland sea, locked into a poverty that was partially historical and partially the result of its geography. Compared to the other islands Levkas has large areas of flat fertile land suited to agriculture and consequently it has been

self-sufficient for many of its needs. It is still the largest wine producer of all the Ionian islands, Zakinthos and Corfu included. This restricted immigration, the lads were needed to work the fields, unlike the other islands where immigration was and still is a part of island life. But whereas the other islands received money sent back by the immigrants once they had established themselves in America or Australia or South Africa, Levkas did not and remained a truly insular place.

The geography aided this history. The island has no deep water port and until recently had only poor road communications with the mainland. Until the F/B *Ag Maura* made getting across the canal easier, the old chain ferries would have traffic backed up for miles at busy times. It was forgotten until the recent incursion of tourism bounced it into the 20th century, though this has been gentle enough and fortunately dispersed around the island.

Getting around inland

On the whole the bus service around the island is patchy. The main bus terminal in Levkas is on the SE quay opposite the yacht quay. A circular route runs around the island several times a day and there are more regular services to Nidri and some other villages. The best way to get around is on a hire motorbike available from several agencies in Levkas and Nidri. Hire cars or jeeps are comparatively expensive and really only worth it if there are four of you.

Roads are good for the main routes, but deteriorate rapidly for secondary routes. It is well worth visiting the villages inland. The countryside is green and wooded in places and there is some magnificent mountain scenery as well. Do not trust the local maps entirely for minor roads which may exist only as tracks or sometimes not at all.

Levkas

Levkas town sits in a corner of the salt marsh where the land starts to rise up to the hills. After midday the sea breeze starts to blow in from the NW and a yacht reaching Levkas in the late afternoon is faced with the terrifying prospect, at least for the first time, of heading for a lee shore with breakers heaping up in the shallowing water until the entrance to the canal is spotted and negotiated.

Pilotage
Levkas Canal
From the N the location of the entrance to the canal is difficult to identify. A long sandy spit extends to the W and NE of the canal entrance. Often a haze obscures the island and the mountains cannot be seen until you are five or so miles off. The wine factory and warehouse on the W of the canal and Santa Maura fort on the E can be distinguished. The buildings of Levkas town will also be seen inland. Closer in the breakwater sheltering the entrance will be identified. From the W two windmills stand out on Yera spit.

A yacht should get all sail off before entering the canal. Rounding the breakwater keep a prudent distance off the end as a sand bank builds up here – it is periodically dredged. On the S side of the entrance off Santa Maura fort there are underwater rocks and debris which are sometimes marked by two 44-gallon drum 'buoys', but not always!

A yacht must normally wait before the floating bridge (the F/B *Ag Maura*) opens which it does on the hour, every hour. For most yachts a section of the bridge at the island end is raised, for very large yachts the bridge is swivelled to lie parallel to the mainland bank. Normally yachts proceeding N go first and yachts going to Levkas town and S go afterwards. There is often a current in the canal, sometimes as much as 1½–2kt, so manoeuvring can be difficult and a yacht is recommended to go alongside the W quay under the breakwater until the bridge opens. The current also makes it difficult to get through the gap left when the bridge section is raised and care is needed. A sense of timing is critical so that you are not too near the yacht in front to get into trouble and not so tardy that the bridge operator throws a tantrum and flusters you as he jumps up and down urging you through.

From the S the entrance to the canal is comparatively easy to spot. In Ormos Dhrepanou aim for Fort Ay Yeoryios conspicuous on a summit on the E side of the canal entrance. Closer in you will see Nisis Volios with a light structure on it and the two conical buoys marking the entrance to the channel. Do not cut outside the two buoys: there is a reef on the E and the remains of an old breakwater on the W. Once into the channel the way is clearly shown by buoys and beacons marking the channel. The channel through the salt marsh is straightforward and clearly marked by poles with cones and baskets.

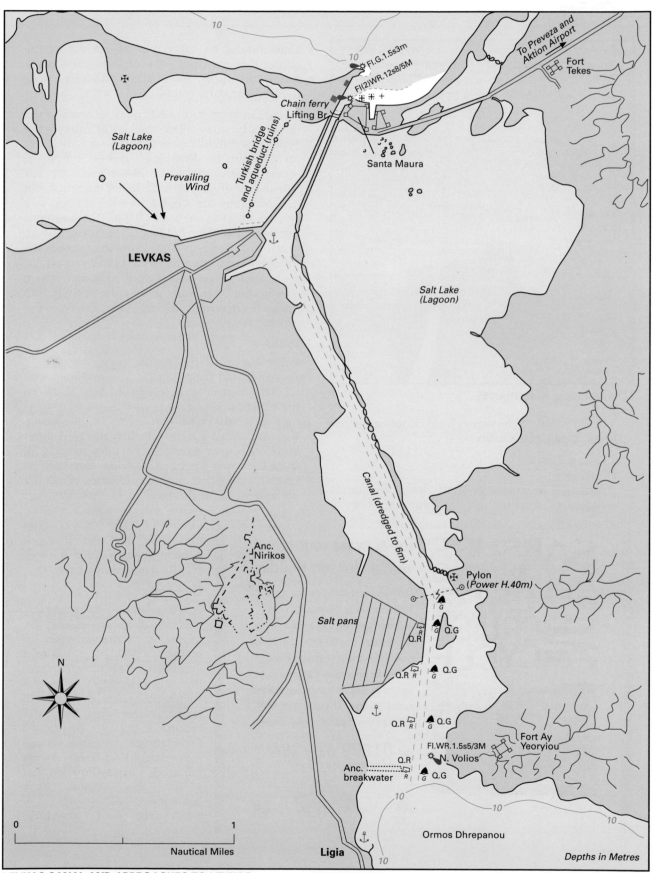

LEVKAS CANAL AND APPROACHES TO LEVKAS

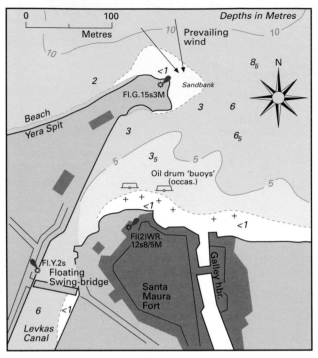

LEVKAS CANAL N. ENTRANCE

The direction of buoyage is from either end of the canal until Levkas town.

Levkas Town
Pilotage
Approach The buildings of the town are readily identified whether coming from the N or S.

Care should be taken not to cut across the corner E of the town – its surprising how many boats end up on the shallow and very sticky mud on the corner here.

Mooring Go stern-to the NE quay or bows-to the E or SE quay. On the latter quays the ballasting extends underwater so it is best not to go stern-to. Protection is best on the E quays where the wind blows you off, but which are often crowded in the summer. On the NE quay the wind is blowing side-on to a yacht so lay the anchor well out – the bottom is mud and excellent holding. A yacht can also go stern- or bows-to the causeway above the bridge where again the wind blows you off.

Shelter is generally good although strong southerlies, especially gales from the SE, can make it uncomfortable and even dangerous at times.

Facilities
Services Water and fuel on the quay.
Provisions Good shopping for all provisions with several supermarkets close to the quay. Ice from the supermarket near the quay.
Eating out Numerous restaurants in the town. Recommended are the 'chicken shack' (I don't know its proper name) in the alley running W from the town square, *Lighthouse Taverna* just off the main street, and the *Adriatica* which is a bit of a walk on the road to Faneromeni, but well worth the walk or a taxi.
Other PO. OTE. Banks. Hire motorbikes and cars. Buses to Athens (usually four a day). Flights from Aktion nearby.

General
It is a strange town, unlike any others in the area, looking like a Greek town that has taken on board Third World architecture from somewhere like downtown Rio di Janero. In recent years it has been tarted up somewhat, but it still retains a distinctive architecture that is remembered if not always admired. The earthquakes that afflict this region have spawned all sorts of earthquake-proof buildings

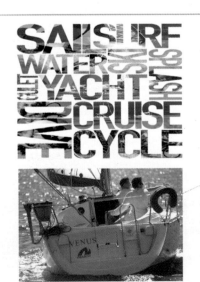

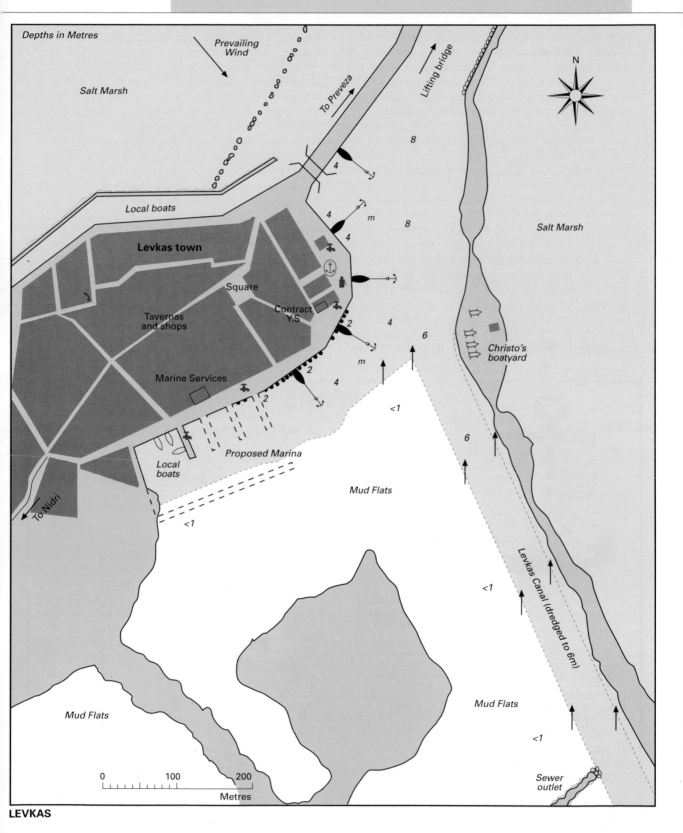

Depths in Metres

Prevailing Wind

Salt Marsh

Lifting bridge

To Preveza

N

Local boats

Levkas town

8

m

8

Salt Marsh

Square

Contract Y.S

Tavernas and shops

Christo's boatyard

4

4

4

4

4

2

2

m

6

Marine Services

2

2

4

<1

6

Local boats

Proposed Marina

<1

Mud Flats

To Nidri

Levkas Canal (dredged to 6m)

<1

Mud Flats

Mud Flats

<1

0   100   200

Metres

Sewer outlet

LEVKAS

and the ones in Levkas are one variation on a theme. The ground floors of the houses look much like the architecture found throughout the Ionian, but the first and in some cases second storeys are usually constructed of corrugated iron or sheet iron over a wooden sub-structure. The roofs too are more often than not corrugated iron. This eccentric architecture is designed to be flexible in the event of an earthquake so it literally sways rather than falling down as stone and bricks do.

The locals are sceptical about reinforced concrete and while there are a few new reinforced concrete apartment blocks on the outskirts of the town, no-one really wants to live there. They may have a point, after all the new reinforced concrete buildings now scattered around the Ionian have yet to be tested by the sort of earthquake that hit the area in 1948 and 1953. Whatever the theory, the town has largely been saved from the soulless architecture that blights some Greek towns and the brightly painted distinctive houses of Levkas

give it a special character that people either love or hate.

For what was a forgotten part of the Ionian, Levkas has a remarkable tradition in the arts and literature. Two of Greece's national poets were born here. Aristoteles Valaoritis (1824–79), a poet who wrote in a rather pompous manner attempting to emulate the epics, is becoming popular again after a period of decline. He was involved with the intricacies of Greek political life until he retired in 1868 to the island of Madhouri off Nidri. Angelos Sikelianos (1884–51) was also born here and is remembered as much for his attempts to rebuild Greek literary and cultural life as for his poetry.

Every year in August the town sponsors a Festival of Arts and Literature which includes the International Folk Dance Festival. For a little over two weeks the town is a riot of events. The Folk Dance Festival attracts groups from all over the world – in different years I have seen groups from most of the Eastern European countries,

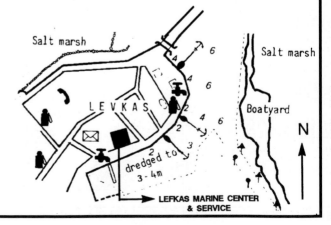

from Russia, Thailand, Malaysia, Indonesia, China, India, Scandinavia, France, Italy, Spain, and Germany, in fact from most of the countries in the world. Every night there is a different group performing and at times you will have to pinch yourself if you are to believe this is a small town in the Ionian. In addition there are many other events going on. In Fort Santa Maura concerts are held – one year I saw Hadzidakis perform a selection of his works, in mine and others opinions his music will be remembered long after the more popular Theodrakis. In other years ballet companies, opera companies, and well known orchestras and conductors have performed here in the spooky shadows of the fort with the last of afternoon wind tugging at the flags around the perimeter and the sound of the sea in the background. Remember to take insect repellent – it is feeding time for the mosquitoes at concert hour.

While Levkas town may not seem the sort of place you would travel a long way to see, in fact those who come here for even a short time often end up staying. I have many good friends here and you can get the sort of insight into Greek life,

warts and all, that is often difficult to find in larger places that hide it and smaller places where local life has been submerged under western influences. Numerous eccentric foreign travellers have succumbed to the discreet charm of the place and settled down in Levkas.

At one time it used to be a base for the cigarette smuggling boats. Fast speedboats like *Channel Breeze*, a forty foot aluminium planing boat with very little superstructure for her size and turbocharged 1300hp diesels, were based here for maintenance between smuggling runs. In Christo's boatyard on the other side of the canal there used to be an assorted selection of speedboats that for one reason or another, too slow or not reliable enough, were left to rot and no-one but no-one would touch them or even tell you who owned them. On the NE quay it was common to see several small tramp steamers that were used to pick up the cigarettes in Albania and ferry them across to just outside Italian territorial waters. When trade died down in the early 80's the port police eventually had them moved to the S end of the canal where they were run up on the mud to rot. Now I wouldn't ask what was being smuggled.

Santa Maura

The fort of Santa Maura at the N end of the canal is well worth exploring. It is not always open at the main gates, but there is always a way in around the walls if you are remotely athletic. The fort has not been restored, but you can easily sort out the different parts of it. One of the most picturesque parts is the old galley port on the E side.

It was originally built in the 13th century by a Latin prince, probably John I. It commands the obvious entry point to Levkas Island along the spit of land from the mainland with the sea on one side and salt marsh on the other. A causeway of some sort connected it to Levkas town at most times. It was enlarged by Charles I Tocco for Spain and the moats and galley port constructed.

The fort takes its name from a chapel erected by an Empress of Byzantium. With variations the story goes something like this. Sometime after the fall of Constantinople to the Turks in 1453, the former empress Helen Palaeologus and mother of the last emperor, Constantine XI, who died defending the city, was caught in a storm off Corfu. She was probably en route to Venice or

The distinctive 'earthquake-proof' town clock in Levkas

Genoa to escape the omnipotent Turk. Her ship was pushed down to Levkas where she was saved on the feast day of Saint Maura. In gratitude she built a monastery inside the fort and, so the story goes, spent the rest of her life here until she died. The saint could not save the fort from the Turks who captured it in 1479. Under Beyazid II a causeway and aqueduct were built. A story, probably apocryphal, relates that Beyazid ordered a causeway that was wide enough for a carriage to pass over it. The costs were enormous: the causeway was over a kilometre long and was reported to have 366 arches. However when finished the causeway was found to be exactly the width of a carriage and therefore impractical for a carriage to pass over. The contractor was duly beheaded.

The fort changed hands again in the early 16th century when it was captured by the Spanish. It was returned to the Turks a year later when a treaty was signed and was to remain Turkish until 1684 when Morosini captured it for the Venetians. Santa Maura and Levkas formally became Venetian in 1698 with the Treaty of Carlowitz and it was to remain thus until Napoleon brought the Venetians to their knees in 1797. During the Venetian occupation the fort was further strengthened and Fort Ay Yeoryios was built at the S end of the canal on the mainland summit overlooking Ormos Dhrepanou. This was to be the last major work carried out on the fort and what we see today is largely Venetian enlarging on the earlier Spanish and Turkish works.

It is a pleasant spot to wander around when the festival is not on. Large cannon lie scattered around the defensive walls and a chapel to Santa Maura still sits in the middle of the fort. There is

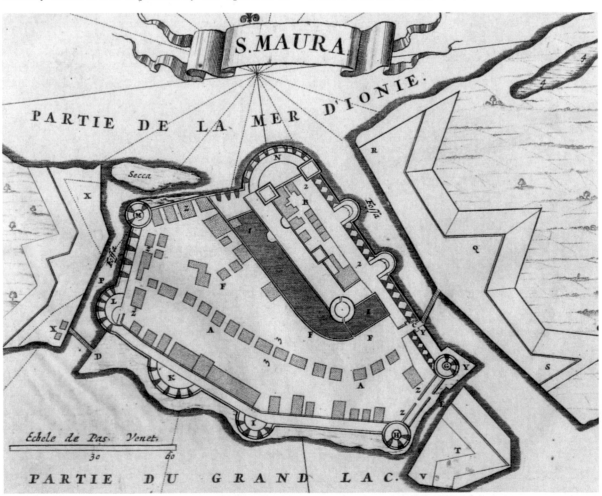

French plan of Santa Maura from the 19th century

The old galley harbour at Santa Maura

nothing of exceptional historical interest to see, just a quiet place with picturesque views out over the sea and salt marsh, a place to sit and dream in the sun.

Canal: south end

At the S end of the canal it is possible to anchor off the W shore. With care a small yacht should head W from between the last and second-to-last set of buoys. The depths here are variable, between 2–4m, with less closer to the shore. Anchor where convenient on mud. The prevailing wind blows from the N to NW off the land.

Note Care must be taken of the old submerged mole running across from the coast to the last set of buoys. A yacht should not attempt to pass between the last buoys and the coast. This submerged mole most likely enclosed a harbour for the ancient city of Nirikos on the slopes above,

although it may have been reconstructed and enlarged in a later age.

Ancient Nirikos

On the slopes above Kariotes are the remains of ancient Nirikos. There is little to see, a section of wall and other large blocks of *ashlar* masonry distributed about the olive groves. No doubt much of the ancient city was incorporated into the various forts built nearby to guard the canal. From the remaining foundations and masonry it can be seen that this was a large city surrounded by substantial walls and fortified towers.

Little is known about the city except that it was established by the Corinthians in the 7th century BC. At this time it may be that the island was joined to the mainland across Paliokhalia. At an early date the name of the city and the island was changed to Leucas. The Leucadians had three

101

ships at the Battle of Salamis. In the Spartan Wars the island sided with Sparta and suffered for it. In 436 BC it was sacked by the Corcyreans and in 446 BC by Athens. It recovered and came under Roman occupation.

At sometime a bridge was probably built from Nirikos to the mainland and it has been suggested that parts of the old bridge can still be seen – though I have never seen anything resembling bridge supports here. The city declined at the end of the Roman era and never recovered with the new settlement built where present-day Levkas town is sited.

Ligia

A small fishing harbour on the W side of Ormos Dhrepanou. From the end of the canal the village and breakwater are easily identified. Most of the deep water berths along the breakwater are occupied by a fleet of *gri-gri* fishing boats and there is not usually room for yachts here. Depths off the village quay are mostly shallow though there may be a space where a small yacht can go bows-to.

Most yachts will have to anchor off the shore in 3–7m on mud and thick weed. Shelter here is not the best in the brisk afternoon breeze which tends to blow straight in from the N to NW.

Ashore some provisions can be found and there are several tavernas including a good local taverna on the waterfront which has excellent fresh fish straight off the boats.

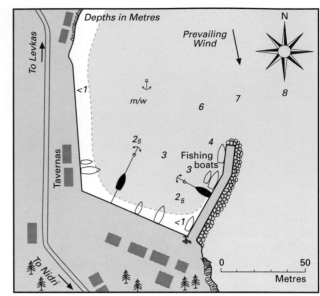

LIGIA

Nikiana

A small harbour recently constructed in Ormos Episkopi, the bay lying just under 2M S of the end of the Levkas canal. There are 2–4m depths along the outer end of the mole where a yacht can berth stern- or bows-to. The bottom is mud and weed, good holding. The harbour is often crowded with charter boats, but there are usually a few berths free. Good shelter behind the mole. A yacht can also anchor off in the bay in 4–10m where there is reasonable shelter from the prevailing wind.

Ashore in the village of Nikiana most provisions can be found and there are several tavernas. The original village has grown considerably to cope with its tourist trade and there are numerous new villas and small hotels along the beach, but it remains a pleasant enough place with a wonderful long beach around the bay and a wooded hinterland.

About 1½M S of Nikiana a number of hotels are conspicuous on Ak Mayemenos. On the S side of the cape there is a small cove that a yacht can use in calm weather, though care is needed of above- and below-water rocks off the coast. A hotel ashore.

Nisis Sparti

A steep-to island lying about ¾M off the coast of Levkas. It is covered in *maquis* and has the

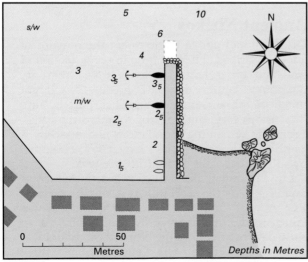

NIKIANA

framework of a reinforced concrete building on it. The passage between Sparti and Levkas is deep and free of dangers except for a rocky shoal patch (see below) off the S end of Sparti. In calm weather a yacht can anchor in the bight on the NW side of the island although it is quite deep here. The anchorage is exposed to the prevailing wind and is untenable in a brisk NW breeze.

Deep draught yachts need to be careful of the shoal (least depth 2·1m) lying about ¼M W of the S end of Sparti.

Nisis Khelona

(Nisis Socava)

A small islet lying close off the coast of Levkas. A yacht can pass between the islet and the coast though care is needed of shoal water off the coast of Levkas and at the S end of Nisis Khelona. In light to moderate NW winds a yacht can anchor off the coast of Levkas to the N and S of Khelona.

Opposite the island there is a quay and pier at Periyiali where a small yacht can go bows-to with care. Much of the quay space is taken up by fishing boats and local *caiques*. Shelter from the prevailing wind in this little bight is surprisingly good.

Nisis Madhouri

(Nisis Modra)

The small island lying S of Sparti and immediately E of Nidri. Madhouri is a wooded island easily identified from the S by the Baroque villa on the SW. This is the family home of the Valaoritis family. The villa was originally built by Greece's national poet and composer of the national hymn, Aristoteles Valaoritis. There is reasonable shelter from the prevailing winds in the anchorage off the SW coast of the island.

Nidri

At the entrance to Ormos Vlikho is the village of Nidri. It is easily recognised by the cluster of buildings and cluster of boats berthed off the town quay.

Pilotage

Approach The approach is straightforward though care needs to be taken of tripper boats, ferries, sailing dinghies, water-bikes, sailboards, and yachts in the immediate approaches. Nidri is something of a Clapham Junction for anything that floats and the water around is constantly churned up by the wake of passing boats in the summer.

Mooring Berth stern- or bows-to where possible on the town quay, leaving the area for the ferries and tripper boats free. The depths drop off quickly from the quay so you will be dropping your anchor in 8–10m depths. The bottom is mud and weed, reasonable holding. Reasonable shelter from the prevailing wind which does not blow home, but does send in a chop. The wake from the tripper boats and ferries also affects the quay.

The quay is crowded in the summer, but you can anchor off to the S in 3–7m. The pier running out from the shore S of the quay at Nidri is the home base of *Sun World* (now *Neilson*) flotilla boats, but you may be able to find a space for a while if no boats are expected back. Do enquire in advance.

The Valaoritis villa on Nisis Madhouri

MINOTAUR CHARTERS INDEPENDENT YACHT CHARTER

BASED AT NIDRI ON LEVKAS

E-mail: Minotaur@hellasnet.gr
Web Site: http://charters.nu/minotaur
Tel/Fax UK 01279 830478
Tel Greece: 0645 92027
Fax Greece 0645 92854

Facilities

Services Water on the quay. Two petrol stations on the road to Vlikho.

Provisions Good shopping for all provisions in the main street.

Eating out Numerous restaurants and bars. When I first came to Nidri in 1977 there were only two tavernas here, *Nick the Greeks* and *Panorama*, both of which still exist. There are now said to be well over twenty at the last count. Take your pick of where to go, local allegiances change along with the quality of the food from year to year, but you cannot complain about lack of choice.

Other PO. OTE. Bank. Hire motorbikes and cars. Travel arrangements can be made by Damianos Gazis at Nidri Travel on the main road.

General

Nidri was once a little fishing and agricultural village. I hesitate to call it a village today, which it was some ten or so years ago, as like many resorts it has grown out of the sleepiness of village life and acquired the fittings and fixtures of a resort, to wit a main street lined with bars, souvenir shops, fast-food counters, ice-cream shops, travel agents and surrounded on the perimeter by hotels and 'village rooms'. In the season the main street is packed with weary tourists looking for yet another recommended taverna or bar and given the choice the process can go on for most of a holiday.

Yet despite its rapid transition from olive oil to sun-tan oil, Nidri retains, just, some of its former character and friendliness. The old widows dressed all in black look on bemused at scantily clad nymphs, shake their heads, and go back to their crochet and embroidery. Nick the Greek, known to the Onassis' before they deserted Skorpios, still runs his taverna and casts a lecherous eye over the girls while Voula toils in the kitchen. On the waterfront there must be one of the most picturesque nautical views around across to the islands and to the wooded slopes of Tranquil Bay – and there is always plenty of activity in the harbour.

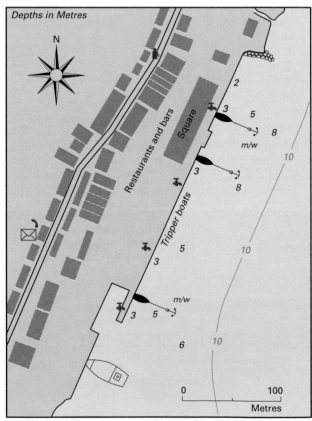

NIDRI

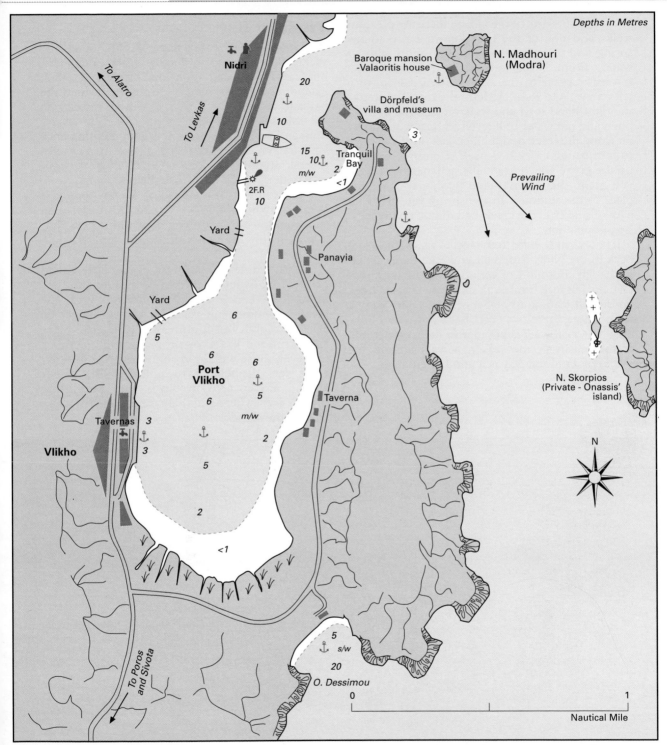

Depths in Metres

Nidri

To Alatro

To Levkas

Baroque mansion -Valaoritis house

N. Madhouri (Modra)

Dörpfeld's villa and museum

20

10

15

10

m/w

2

Tranquil Bay

3

<1

2F.R

10

Prevailing Wind

Yard

Panayia

Yard

6

5

6

Port Vlikho

6

5

6

m/w

5

2

N. Skorpios (Private - Onassis' island)

Taverna

Tavernas

3

Vlikho

3

5

2

N

<1

To Poros and Sivota

5

s/w

20

O. Dessimou

0   1

Nautical Mile

PORT VLIKHO AND APPROACHES

On the outskirts of the village there are pleasant walks and one of the best known is up to the spring and waterfall that supplies Nidri with its water. From Nidri walk along the main road towards Levkas to the sign to Rahi village, turn left and walk to Rahi. At Rahi the road forks, take the right-hand road and walk on past the football pitch and old water mill to Nidri Reservoir. Carry on along the track beside the creek until you have to take to the creek-bed itself. Continue walking up the gorge which gradually gets narrower until you get to the waterfall and pool, a cool shaded place in the summer. In the spring you may find a lot of snakes in the creek-bed dining on the local frog population.

If you want to hike to the top of the waterfall go back to the Nidri Reservoir and take the track off to the left. For a bit of variation on the way back take the left fork from Rahi until you get to a track on the left leading to Neochori and Paliokatouna from where there is a road back down to Nidri. This waterfall walk is popular in the summer and at the height of the season a walk around the slopes of Tranquil Bay is a good alternative.

Tranquil Bay

Opposite Nidri there is a bay much frequented by yachts. The entrance is deep and free of dangers, but care is needed of a shallow muddy shelf extending for some distance from the head of the bay and around the S side. It can be difficult to see unless it is flat calm. Anchor in 8–12m on soft mud and weed. The bottom is good holding once your anchor is properly dug in, but it may take several attempts before it is holding to your satisfaction. Good all-round shelter.

There is a well at the head of the bay though it is not drinking water – take care not to let soap suds run down into it if you do washing here. It is a longish row over to Nidri if you don't have an outboard.

In earlier times when it was a quiet little visited place, H M Denham christened it 'Tranquil Bay' in his *The Ionian Islands to Rhodes*. With the increased number of yachts it can no longer be called tranquil, but it remains a wonderful place and at times it has a certain peace and quiet to it that even those with loud sound systems on their boats feel disinclined to pollute. The slopes around are covered in olives with pencil-thin cypress everywhere and there are wonderful walks around the slopes.

Tranquil Bay opposite Nidri

Wilhelm Dörpfeld

On the far slopes of the headland above Tranquil Bay sits Dörpfeld's villa, now a museum housing some of his collection of artefacts. Wilhelm Dörpfeld assisted the great Heinrich Schliemann to excavate Troy and along with Schliemann believed that Homer should be interpreted literally rather than metaphorically as the academics of Britain and Germany insisted. Schliemann found Troy this way and Dörpfeld set off to look for Odysseus' city state using Homer as his guide.

He was disappointed not to find anything of consequence on Ithaca and for some reason turned his attention to Levkas. His later rationalisation was that Homer's description of Ithaca as an island with estates on the mainland and sheep ferried from the island to the mainland, identified the island as Levkas. Dörpfeld pointed out that Homer's description of Ithaca as 'the farthest out to sea' and 'slanting to the west' did not apply to Ithaca as Cephalonia was the westernmost of the Ionian islands. He hypothesised that the ancients idea of geography positioned the Ionian islands in a line stretching westwards from the entrance of the Gulf of Patras and therefore Levkas was the furthest and in the ancient Greeks mental geography the westernmost island.

He identified a site near Nidri as the capital of this Ithaca, Sivota as the bay where Odysseus was put ashore and met Eumaeus the swineherd, and a cave near Evgiros as the sacred cave of the Nymphs. He unearthed various artefacts dating back to the Mycenean period though there is some doubt about whether they correspond to the time of the Trojan Wars.

So why is Levkas called Levkas and Ithaca called Ithaca? Dörpfeld's answer was that Levkas was originally called Ithaca. The migration of the Dorians from the north in 1200–1100 BC pushed mainland tribes into Levkas forcing the Leucadians westwards where they settled on the island they now called Ithaca. Few historians put much credence in Dörpfeld's theory today, but then there are few viable alternatives. Nidri took Dörpfeld to its heart and he was by all accounts a much loved man in the village. He is buried by the monument, the Mnimion Dörpfeld, on the slopes by the museum. It is a pleasant walk around to the monument with wonderful views over the sea and islands, perhaps to contemplate the geography and compare notes with Homer's brief description of the Ithaca of the *Odyssey*.

Ormos Vlikho

(Port Vliho, Vlihou)

From Nidri the bay of Vlikho extends down through the bottleneck entrance and opens up into a landlocked oval bay with the village of Vlikho on the W side.

Pilotage

A yacht can anchor anywhere where there are sufficient depths. A shallow shelf extends a short distance out around parts of the W and E sides and a considerable distance out at the S end. Depths in Ormos Vlikho are mostly 5–10m in the middle and shelving to less at the edges. There are several favoured anchorages:

1. Off the boatyard in the NW corner.
2. Off the E side either in the NE corner or further down off the taverna.
3. Off Vlikho village.
4. Stern- or bows-to the quay at Vlikho.

The prevailing wind blows in from the NW to N, but usually does not blow home with any great strength though it will blow at 20kt on occasion. Care is only really needed when you are on the quay at Vlikho where a bit of chop is pushed onto it by the wind. The bottom is mud and weed, good holding once through the weed.

Facilities

Water on the quay at Vlikho. Most provisions and several good tavernas in the village. Also a taverna on the E side. Other facilities in Nidri.

General

Vlikho has been little touched by tourism though now it is being tarted up in readiness to latch onto the success of Nidri. The quay has been cleaned up, trees planted, and a water sports base set up. For the time being it remains a quiet relaxed place compared to the bustle and noise of Nidri. There are pleasant walks around the head of the bay – take the main road going S then turn off to the left and follow the road which soon deteriorates into a rough stone and gravel road. Alternatively take a wander up to the boatyard.

Ormos Dessimou

A large bay about a mile S of Nisis Madhouri. It offers good shelter from the prevailing wind, but is quite deep. Anchor in the N corner in 5–10m. The bottom drops off very quickly to 20–30m. Ashore there is a camping ground with a small shop and taverna.

Stenon Meganisiou

Between Levkas and Nisos Meganisi, Stenon Meganisiou or the Meganisi channel gives one of the most beautiful vistas to be seen from the deck of a boat in the Ionian. The channel, ½M wide at the narrowest point, passes between the high slopes and cliffs of Levkas with a number of ravines cutting down to the sea; and on the other side, the lower slopes of Meganisi with a long sandy beach fringing much of it. Cypress and *maquis* grows where it can get a hold on the Levkas side and covers much of the slopes of Meganisi. Towards the N end of the channel Nisis Thilia, a small wooded islet, lies just off the coast of Meganisi.

The wind in this channel is fickle. What usually happens is that it blows from the N to NW at the N end of the channel and from the S to SW at the S end. In the middle there is often a flat spot with no wind or light winds from either direction. It can be disconcerting to be running down the channel with the wind aft of the beam and to see a yacht coming in the opposite direction also with the wind aft of the beam.

There are several pleasant anchorages on the Meganisi side of the channel – the Levkas side is mostly too deep. A yacht can anchor in a small cove on Meganisi above Nisis Thilia. It is also possible to anchor in a bight behind Nisis Thilia, though care is needed of shoal water and rocks close to the island. This anchorage is suitable for an overnight stay in settled weather. Before the afternoon wind gets up it is possible to anchor off the beach on Meganisi S of Nisis Thilia though it is mostly very deep here apart from a few sandy patches off the beach.

At the S end of the channel there are several caves on the Levkas side including the one that features in Hammond Innes' thriller *Levkas Man*. It is worth getting hold of a copy of this book to read while you cruise around as all of the locations can be identified from the descriptions in the book and it is a good holiday read.

Ormos Rouda

A large bay on the SE corner of Levkas, just around the corner from Stenon Meganisiou. There are usually gusts out of the large bay with the prevailing wind. Anchor at the end of the bay in 5–20m, the bottom drops off to considerable depths quite quickly. Shelter here is good although you need to make sure the anchor is well in with the gusts off the high land. On the E side of the bay there is a small harbour used by local *caiques*.

Ashore there are two camping grounds and small holiday bungalows. Most provisions can be obtained from a shop at the camping ground and there are several tavernas. In the village of Poros on the slopes above there is better shopping and more tavernas.

Ormos Sivota

A landlocked bay immediately W of Ormos Rouda.

Pilotage

Approach The entrance is difficult to see from any direction although in the summer yachts will be seen disappearing or appearing as if from the very cliffs along the coast. A cluster of small bungalows on the W side of the entrance and a villa on the summit between Rouda and Sivota will be seen. Closer in a few red roofs will be glimpsed across the isthmus on the E side of the entrance. Once into the entrance the hamlet will still not be seen until you round the dogleg and enter the anchorage proper.

Mooring Sivota is very popular and gets crowded in the summer so you will have to anchor wherever possible. In the inner part of the bay there are 2–10m depths, in the outer part there are 20–30m depths making anchoring difficult.

ORMOS ROUDA AND SIVOTA

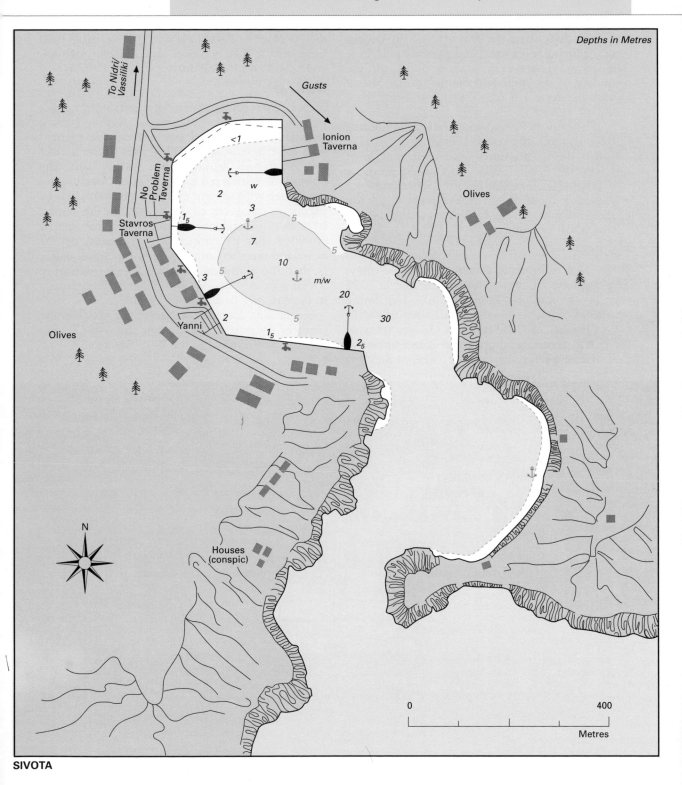

Depths in Metres

To Nidri/
Vassiliki

Gusts

Ionion
Taverna

Olives

No Problem Taverna

Stavros
Taverna

Olives

Yanni

N

Houses
(conspic)

0   400

Metres

SIVOTA

The quay along the W side has 2–3m depths at the S end and a yacht can go bows-to if there is room. There is a shallow patch off the middle of the quay and depths on the N half vary between 1–1·6m, investigate before you charge in here.

The bottom is mud and weed, good holding once through the weed, though this can take some doing at times and will test your anchoring skills. The shelter in here is excellent, fleets of flotilla and charter boats are wintered afloat, but with the prevailing wind there are gusts off the high land around the bay which can be bothersome.

Facilities

Water at a number of points around the quay. The taps have a coin operated meter and in 1999 you got around 40 litres for 100 Dr. Some provisions available from a small shop at the N end of the bay. Several tavernas. *Stavros* towards the N end serves good grilled food and often has fresh fish in a relaxed ambience. Next to Stav's is the *No Problem Taverna* which also has good food right on the water. *Yanni* at the S end also has good food and is a favourite with the flotillas.

General

Sivota relies pretty much for its income on the passing trade from waterborne traffic. It is a wonderful spot, the slopes around are planted with olive trees and the old houses of the hamlet are clustered around the water. But the ubiquitous reinforced concrete is encroaching on the village with several new buildings around the perimeter rising out of earth scars on the slopes. It is so popular in the summer and can get so crowded that its ambience is shattered by the noise and numbers of people. A sad consequence is that the numbers generate lots of sewerage which goes into the bay and it can get very smelly in the summer heat.

Sivota was Dörpfeld's choice for the landing place of Odysseus, the cave of the nymphs was identified as Evgiros to the W of Sivota.

Sivota

Photo *Peter Sewell*

Ormos Afteli

A large bay W of Sivota. In calm weather a yacht can anchor at the head although it is very deep. With the prevailing wind a swell is pushed into here.

Ormos Ammousa

A bay immediately W of Ak Lipso. A yacht can anchor in wonderful surroundings at the N end of the bay in a small cove under a large villa. It is quite deep. When the prevailing wind sets in it blows into here so you will probably have to get out. You get a good slant across to Fiskardho from here or you can run back to Sivota or plug around to Vassiliki.

Ormos Vassiliki

The large bay formed by Ak Dhoukaton on the W side. The prevailing wind tends to gust out of here with some force so care is needed in the approaches.

Pilotage

Approach The white lighthouse on Ak Dhoukaton is easily identified and once into the entrance the buildings at Pondi in the NW corner will be seen. From the E the village of Vassiliki cannot be seen until you are right into the bay. In the summer there are sailboards everywhere operating off the beach at the head of the bay.

Mooring It is possible to anchor at the head of the bay in 2–5m on sand and weed, suitable with moderate winds blowing off the land, but uncomfortable with strong gusts. You are better off going into the harbour at Vassiliki village and going stern- or bows-to the W or S quay. Care is needed in the inner harbour which is silting and there is already a patch with less than 2m approximately where shown. Alternatively if the inner harbour is full you can go on the east quay in the outer harbour. If you do go here make sure your anchor is well in and lay a second anchor just to be sure as the prevailing wind blows straight into here. There are gusts into the harbour, but shelter is good tucked inside and the gusts usually die down at night. In unsettled weather the harbour is uncomfortable and some berths untenable.

Facilities

Services Water on the quay. Fuel on the outskirts of the village.

Provisions Most provisions can be found. Good baker in the village.

Eating out Numerous tavernas around the waterfront.

Other PO. Metered telephone. Exchange facilities. Ferry to Fiskardho.

General

Vassiliki is a pleasant relaxed little place with a wonderful waterfront shaded by trees and festooned with drying nets. In recent years it has played host to packaged watersports holidays, almost exclusively windsurfers who come here for the brisk afternoon wind off the hills. According to the pro's Vassiliki ranks in the top ten places for board-sailing in the Mediterranean. Most of the accommodation for the holidays is at the W end of the beach at Pondi or in hotels behind the beach.

The village is a well-watered place with abundant springs and it is odd to hear water running away into the sea when a short distance away, on the island of Ithaca and parts of

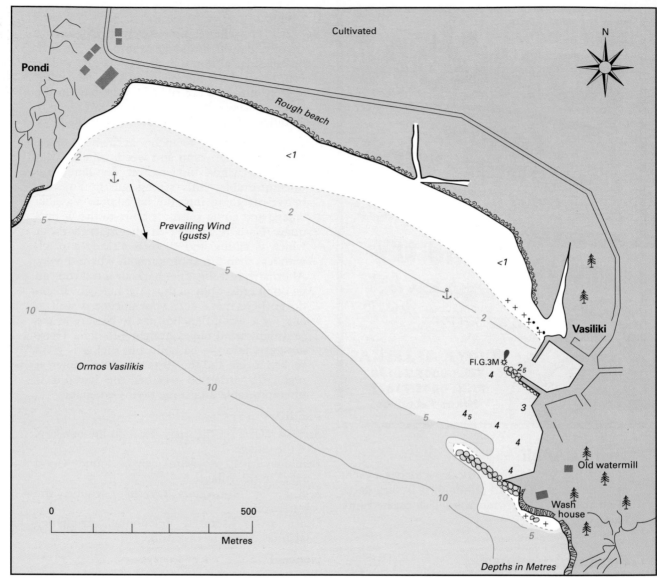

ORMOS VASSILIKI

Cephalonia, it is a precious commodity. If you walk around the coast to the S of the harbour there is an old water mill (converted to a bar) and further around an old public wash-house where ice-cold spring water flows through large tubs and out again into the sea. If you do your washing here tidy up afterwards. On the valley plain behind the beach the river is used to irrigate the rich soil for crops.

Sappho's Leap
Off Ak Dhoukaton, the steep white limestone cliffs that give Levkas its name, the poet Sappho

is supposed to have leapt to her death after being spurned by her lover. For centuries the spot has been known by the name Sappho's Leap and it has appeared thus in poems and prose down through the ages and is even marked on the old Admiralty chart 203. When Byron's Childe Harold sailed past the cape and the cliffs he saw '. . . Leucadia's far projecting rock of woe: And hail'd the last resort of fruitless love'. Despite all the labels there is no conclusive proof that Sappho jumped to her death here or that she even visited Levkas. Nonetheless underneath the myth there is a fascinating trail of animism and human

Vassiliki

sacrifice attached to the cape and the Temple of Apollo that stood here in ancient times.

In antiquity a leap was performed from the cliff-top to the sea below (known as *katapontismos*), though whether this was punishment for crime, sacrifice to Apollo, a trial (much like bungee-jumping or high diving I suppose), or some other pursuit, is unknown. We do know that in the Roman era the jumpers had either feathers or the

branches of trees tied to them depending on the commentator.

In *Pausanias, Volume I, Book X*, there is a short account of a similar cult in Magnesia. 'The Magnesians on the river Lethaios have a place called the Tunnels, where Apollo has a grotto, not very marvellous for size, but the statue of Apollo is extremely ancient and gives you physical powers of every kind; men consecrated to this statue leap from precipitous cliffs and high rocks, they pull up giant trees by the roots, and travel with loads on the narrowest footpaths.' In a footnote Peter Levi who translated this edition of *Pausanias* adds: 'Leaping into the sea from a cliff was a feature of Apollo's festival on the island of Leukas; a shaggy man carrying an uprooted tree of about his own size appears on the imperial coinage of Magnesia. Nilsson believed that leaping into the sea at Leukas was some kind of bird cult . . .'

Little is written or generally known about this shamanistic cult though there is endless speculation. Criminals were believed to be pardoned if they made the leap and survived. Those jumping at the Festival of Apollo were believed to be picked up by boats in the sea below if they survived. Perhaps forsaken lovers did jump here though all the references point to an exclusively male pursuit. If for no other reason Sappho should have the last word.

. . . I know I must die. . .
yet I love the tenderness of life
and this and desire keep me here in
the brightness and beauty of the sun
—and not with Hades.

VASSILIKI

Nisis Skorpios and Skorpidhi

Lying close E of Ormos Vlikho and S of Nisis Sparti are the twin islands of Skorpios and Skorpidhi, the island retreat of the Onassis family or those few who are left. Aristotle the patriarch, his son Alexander and daughter Christina are all buried here, in a simple church under the shade of an old plane tree, a last resting place surprising for its simplicity given the former opulence of the Onassis lifestyle.

Aristotle Onassis bought Skorpios sometime in the 1960's for what the Nidri locals say was a 'song'. Gradually he landscaped the island, built a road right around it, installed security systems that no-one really knows anything about except that they work, installed a small farm on the SW corner to keep horses for riding and cows to supply fresh milk, and built the harbour facilities in the bay on the N for his beloved yacht (read 'ship') *Christina*. Aristotle never slept on the island but stayed on *Christina* at night although there are living quarters ashore for guests. In the late 1970s and early 1980s it was usual to see the *Christina* moored off in the N bay, but after Aristotle's death the yacht went to the Greek government; apparently his will stated that if his daughter did not want it then the state got it – and Christina didn't want her father's toy. (Alexander, the only son, died in 1973 in a plane accident which Aristotle was convinced had been a CIA plot.)

The late Jackie O's chic beach hut on the south side of Skorpios

After her father's death Christina flew into Skorpios on odd occasions though she didn't use it as often as Aristotle had. Since Christina's recent death, like Alexander's shrouded in some mystery, the island has been little used though it is still tended by the island staff. It is very much a park land, carefully planted and pruned, with dazzling green lawns and shaded tennis courts. Staff buildings are on the NE corner with guest buildings further W. The small chapel and the graves of the three Onassis' are on the NW corner. On the edge of a tiny beach, in an idyllic setting, is a small Cyclades-style house Jackie had built so she could get away from it all and swim in the beautifully clear water of the cove. The future of the island is uncertain, but for the meantime the lawns are kept green through the summer and the punters are kept off the beaches.

There are few permanent staff on Skorpios, probably around ten or fifteen, but every day a ferry runs additional staff over from Nidri. Aristotle had a soft spot for Nidri and in Nick the Greeks there are faded newspaper accounts of the Onassis' goings-on in and around Nidri, including photos of Nick himself – looking somewhat younger but no less licentious.

You can sail around Skorpios and Skorpidhi though you cannot land. Greek law states that though you can buy an island, you cannot own anything below the high water mark. This means you can anchor off and swim off the beaches, that you can set foot on the beach below the high water mark, but you cannot wander around it. In the summer there are regular patrols by land and sea keeping an eye on yachtsmen anchored off and on the tripper boats running out of Nidri. I don't know what detection systems are used on the island but they work. A friend coming back from Meganisi one night put a piston through the top of his outboard and the nearest land was Skorpios. He paddled over to the beach on the S side and within fifteen minutes was explaining his predicament to staff who had detected him. They were friendly enough and towed him over to Nidri, but have been known to rough up paparazzi who attempted to sneak ashore at night when Jackie was on the island.

There are several anchorages around the island, but only one really good one. The cove on the SW where Jackie had her 'beach-hut' built is sheltered from the prevailing wind, but is quite deep to anchor in. Further W it is possible to anchor off the W side of a sandy isthmus, though again it is quite deep. The best place is on the E side of the

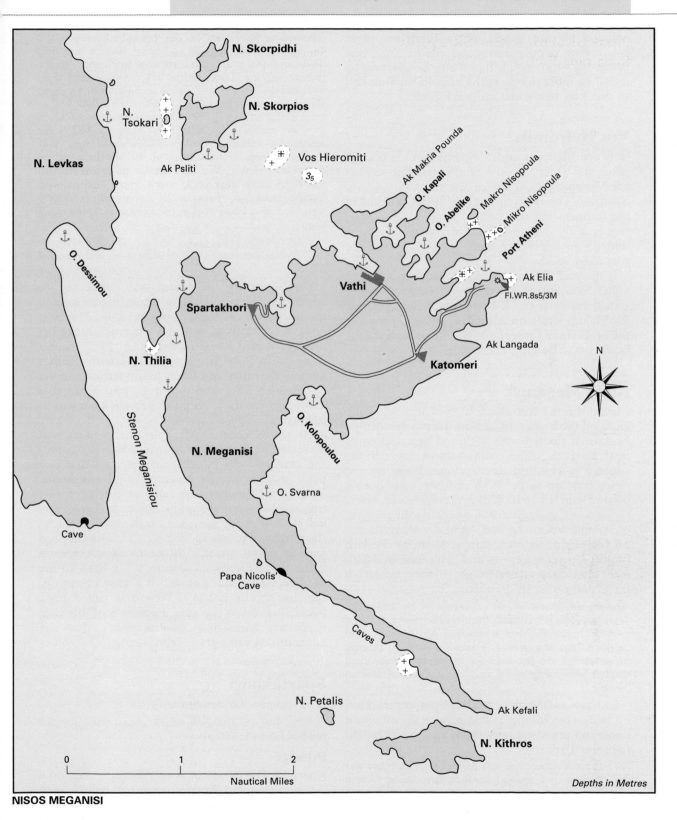

N. Skorpidhi

N. Tsokari

N. Skorpios

N. Levkas

Ak Psliti

Vos Hieromiti

3_5

Ak Makria Pounda

O. Kapali

O. Abelike

Makro Nisopoula

Mikro Nisopoula

Port Atheni

O. Dessimou

Ak Elia

Fl.WR.8s5/3M

Vathi

Spartakhori

Ak Langada

N. Thilia

Katomeri

N

O. Kolopoulou

N. Meganisi

Stenon Meganisiou

O. Svarna

Cave

Papa Nicolis' Cave

Caves

N. Petalis

Ak Kefali

N. Kithros

0   1   2

Nautical Miles

Depths in Metres

NISOS MEGANISI

isthmus off the beach where there are more convenient depths and good shelter from the prevailing wind. You will probably be observed by a staff member in one of the island's mini-mokes, so don't try to wander around ashore.

Vos Heiromiti

Between Skorpios and Meganisi there is a shoal patch and a reef just under the water. The reef lies approximately ½M SE of the midway point of Skorpios. The Heiromiti reef is usually marked in the summer, but this cannot be relied upon. The reef is easily spotted in calm weather, but can be difficult to see when there is a chop with the prevailing wind.

If the reef cannot be seen a yacht should hug either Skorpios or Meganisi. If you keep S of a transit between the SW corner of Skorpios and Ak Makripounda on Meganisi, you will pass S of the reef. Have someone keep a lookout from the bows just to be on the safe side.

Nisos Meganisi

Meganisi is the Rorschach blob of an island lying close off the E coast of Levkas. Its much indented N coast is riddled with sheltered bays and coves next to each other, all of them wonderfully situated in beautiful surroundings. From ancient times right up to the 20th century it has been a pirate haunt. In 1610 William Lithgow of Lanark, (known as Cut-lugged Willie because the relatives of a young woman he had, let us say offended, cut off his ears), was on a ship attacked by Turkish pirates between Levkas and Meganisi in 1610. His account gives a real insight into the dangers of travel and piracy in times past.

'During the course of our passage, the captain of the vessel espied a sail coming from sea; he presently being moved therewith, sent a mariner to the top, who certified him she was a Turkish galley of Biserta, prosecuting a straight course to invade our back: which sudden affrighting news overwhelmed us almost in despair.'

Lithgow rallied the crew and passengers who, he said, were willing at first to give up without a fight, and urged captain, crew, and passengers to fight the Turk.

'In a furious spleen, the first hola of their courtesy was the progress of a martial conflict, thundering forth a terrible noise of galley-roaring pieces; and we, in sad reply, sent out a back-sounding echo of fiery flying shots, which made an equivox to the clouds,

rebounding backward in out perturbed breasts the ambiguous sounds of fear and hope. After a long and doubtful fight, both with great and small shot, (night parting us) the Turks retired till morning, and then were mindful to give us the new rencounter of a second alarm. But as it pleased him, who never faileth his, to send down an irresistible tempest, about the break of day we escaped their furious designs; and were enforced to seeke into the bay of Largostolo (Argostoli) in Cephalonia; both because of the violent weather, and also for that a great hole was sprung in our ship. In this fight there were of us killed, three Italians, two Greeks, and two Jews, with eleven others deadly wounded, and I also hurt in the right arm with a small shot.'

William Lithgow
Totall Discourse of the Rare Adventures and Painefull Peregrinations 1632

Until recently the island was connected to smuggling, mostly cigarette smuggling to Italy in the later years. A number of men from Meganisi have been involved with the cigarette smuggling operations and I well remember in 1977 when I woke up in Port Atheni to find a tramp steamer anchored nearby and boxes being ferried ashore. It left soon after and didn't go into Vathi, the main port for the island. I didn't ask what was in the boxes.

On the W coast of Meganisi, just S of an islet about where the 'tail' of Meganisi begins, there is the cave of Papa Nicolis, a large cave that is a popular stop on the itinerary of tripper boats. Visit it in the morning calm as the afternoon breeze blows straight onto the coast here. You will have to leave someone on the boat and take the dinghy in to have a look around. The cave has various stories attached to it, the most common being that a Greek submarine hid in here during the Second World War, but it is easy enough to see that this is unlikely. Why it is called Papa Nicolis' cave I'm not sure. Further S of this cave there are numerous smaller caves that the adventurous can visit in calm weather.

Spartakhori

(Port Spiglia, Ormos Spiliou)

A large bay on the NW of Meganisi with a small harbour on the W.

Pilotage

Approach The village of Spartakhori perched on a summit on the W side of the bay will be seen and closer in the entrance to the bay.

Mooring Go stern- or bows-to the quay where shown. The harbour is popular in the summer and often full. Take care not to obstruct the ferry berth. The depths drop off very quickly from the quay and you will be dropping your anchor in 12–20m, so make sure you have plenty of scope ready.

Alternatively anchor at the head of the bay where once again there are considerable depths. Shelter in the harbour is good, but at the head of the bay an evening katabatic breeze may blow off the mainland coast making it uncomfortable.

Facilities

Services Metered water tap on the quay. There are only limited garbage disposal facilities so preferably take it elsewhere.

Provisions Most provisions available in the village.

Eating out Two tavernas by the harbour and one at the head of the bay. The *Porto Spiglia* and *The Stars* are favourites with flotillas and their food is good. Tavernas in the village also – *Lakki's* is worth a visit.

General

The bay is an enchanting spot: deep cobalt blue water, steep slopes planted with olives or covered in *maquis*, and the winding road shaded by cypress and pine leading to the village. Even on the hottest day you should climb up to the village, or better still go up in the evening for a drink or

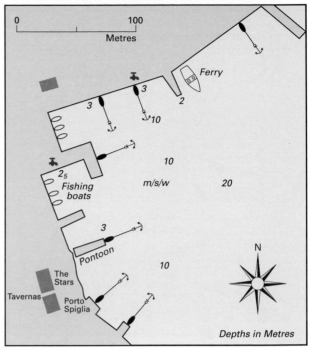

SPARTAKHORI

dinner. The view is wonderful out over Nidri, Madhouri, Skorpios, and right across to the mountains of the mainland on the E. The village is a fascinating warren of alleys and lanes, most too small to get a car through as the village was never designed for motorised transport, but for four-legged transport.

Vathi

(Port Vathy)

The main port of the island immediately E of Spartakhori.

Pilotage

Approach The entrance to the bay is difficult to make out and the houses of the village will not be seen until you are into the entrance, but following the N coast of Meganisi the approach is straightforward.

Mooring Go stern- or bows-to in the harbour where convenient. Alternatively anchor to the W of the mole or in one of the coves on the W or E side. Depths are mostly considerable, usually 10m or more. Shelter from the day breeze is good, but in the evening a katabatic breeze may blow in from the NE making the W side of the bay uncomfortable and sometimes untenable.

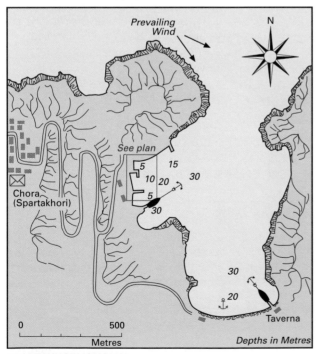

SPARTAKHORI (SPIGLIA)

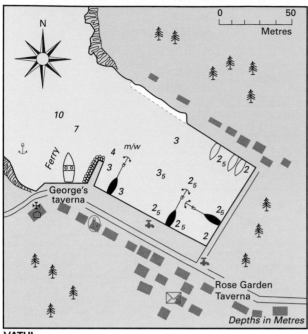

VATHI

Facilities

Services Water on the quay although it is often turned off in the summer.

Provisions Some provisions can be found.

Eating out Several tavernas in the village. Y*eorgiou's* (George's) behind the mole often has fresh fish and the *Rose Garden* further into the village has good food in pleasant surroundings.

Other PO. Metered telephone. Ferry to Nidri.

General

The small village is the main port and capital of the island, though it would be hard to envisage a more sleepy capital in the Ionian. It is a pleasant relaxed place with some fine walks through the olive groves to the bays to the E.

Ormos Kapali and Abelike

Between Vathi and Port Atheni there are two large bays with small coves dotted around the edges. A glance at the plan shows the much indented bays and the different places a yacht can anchor. The heads of these bays are now buoyed off as swimming areas so you will need to anchor clear of the buoys in rather deeper water than in the past.

Vathi on Meganisi

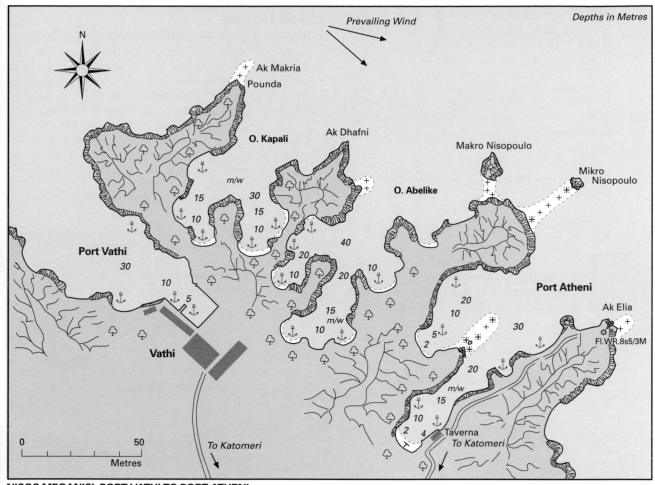

Prevailing Wind

Depths in Metres

NISOS MEGANISI: PORT VATHI TO PORT ATHENI

There are considerable depths in the bays, mostly 8–12m rising abruptly to the shore. The best policy is to anchor and take a long line ashore to a tree or rock. The bottom is mud and weed, good holding once through the weed. Shelter from the prevailing day breeze is good, but in the evening a katabatic wind from the NE can be uncomfortable in some of the coves, though it normally dies down after a couple of hours.

There are no facilities here and nor should there be. The coves are peaceful places surrounded by olive groves and clear water. They are popular places for barbecues and anyone using the bays for this purpose must ensure the fire is built well away from the trees and that a bucket of water is handy. The fire should be damped down before you leave and take any rubbish away with you – there is no point in burying it on the island as olive trees don't exactly thrive on tinfoil and plastic.

Port Atheni
(Ormos Atherinou)

The large bay on the NE of Meganisi.

Pilotage

Approach The two islets of Megalo Nisopoulo and Mikro Nisopoulo can be identified from the W and the light structure on Ak Elia will be seen from the E. A yacht should keep outside Makro and Mikro Nisopoulo as they are connected by a reef to Meganisi. Care is also needed of the reef extending off Ak Elia.

Once into the bay care is needed of the reef running out into the middle of the bay. It appears to be difficult to see if the numbers of yachts running aground on it are anything to go by.

Mooring Anchor in the cove on the W where there are considerable depths, 10–20m, though if you can get near the head of the cove there are 3–8m depths. If you can't get into the head take a long line ashore to the W side.

Alternatively anchor in one of the coves on the E side or near the head of the E cove. Here it is also deep, coming up quickly from 10–15m to 2m and less near the head. If there is room a yacht can go stern- or bows-to the small quay on the E side of this cove where there are mostly 2–4m.

The bottom is sand and rock in the W cove and mud and weed in the E cove. Shelter from the prevailing wind is generally good although there can be strong gusts from the W. In the evening a katabatic wind may blow in from the NE.

Facilities

A metred water tap on the quay.

Jimmy and Spiro's Taverna is situated in the southwest corner and you can park your yacht right outside.

It is about a 30 minute walk to the village of Katomeri inland from Port Atheni. Here some provisions can be found and there are several tavernas. Remember to take a torch for the walk back.

General

The bay is a pleasant spot, like the others surrounded by olive groves and *maquis*. The W cove is the more pleasant as here the water is translucent over the sand and rock bottom, whereas the E cove is murky when the fine silt is stirred up though it is no less clean than the W cove.

Meganisi: East Coast

On the E of Meganisi there are several bays suitable in settled weather. The afternoon wind tends to curl around the bottom of Meganisi and blow from the SW to S making them uncomfortable and sometimes untenable once the morning calm has gone.

In the morning or with light afternoon winds a yacht can anchor in Ormos Langada just above Ak Langada, Ormos Kolopoulou and Ormos Svarna just above the 'tail' of Meganisi. Depths in these bays are considerable and it may pay to take a line ashore.

Nisos Ithaca

Within the Inland sea no other name carries such a burden of myth and historical association with it as Ithaca. I have already talked about the connections with the *Odyssey* and there is really nothing more to say. The places in the *Odyssey* have all been located and signposted on Ithaca, but there can be no certainty that these are the places that Homer described and in the end they are little better than guesses. Ithaca's fame rests on the fact that it survived into the 20th century with the name 'Ithaca'.

There is little actual evidence of a Mycenean kingdom on Ithaca. At Polis in a cave below Stavros finds have included twelve geometric tripods similar to the type described in the *Odyssey*. More importantly terracotta masks, including one from around 100 BC dedicated to Odysseus, indicate a later cult of hero-worship of

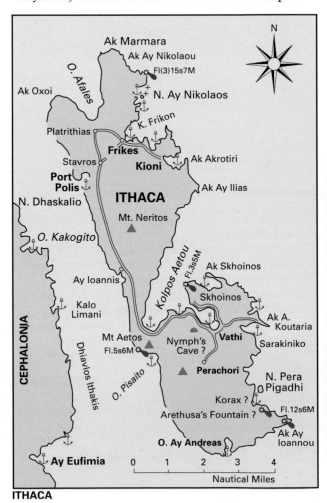

ITHACA

the man. The latter find is the strongest link between the present day island and the Ithaca described in the *Odyssey*. A Mycenean house and pottery shards were also found nearby. Near the village of Stavros on a hill called Pelikata a Bronze Age and Mycenean settlement has been found, but it is too small to be a principal city. On Mt Aetos, on the narrow isthmus joining the two halves of the island, a considerable quantity of pottery from Corinthian and earlier times has been found and it is surmised there may have been a temple or shrine here.

That is basically it in terms of ancient artefacts and sites and in the end does it really matter. The island occupies a mythopoeic geography that has lasted for a good deal longer than the Mycenean kingdoms it describes and the gaps in the finds and the identification enable us to play detective and make our own guesses about the location of the places described. When Byron visited Ithaca from Cephalonia it was suggested by the local dignitaries he visit some of the local sites associated with the *Odyssey*. Trelawny who accompanied him recorded that Byron turned to him and muttered as an aside: 'Do I look like one of those emasculated fogies? Let's have a swim. I detest antiquarian twaddle. Do people think I have no lucid intervals, that I came to Greece to scribble more nonsense?' The bard had good advice to give sometimes.

The island is a delightful place to sail around, if a bit windy in the summer. It is mostly a barren place with just a sprinkling of *maquis* on the slopes and the only wooded places are a few valleys where underground springs enable the vegetation to survive through the hot summer months. The local authorities have declared many of the villages and houses to be of special historical interest and it is prohibited to build large hotels that do not fit into the scheme of things. It's a pity the authorities did not apply the same criteria to the ugly reverse osmosis plant at Sarakiniko, but overall they have succeeded in retaining an architectural cohesion in harmony with the island's history.

Frikes

A small harbour and hamlet tucked into the westernmost corner of Ormos Frikes, the large bay on the NE of Ithaca.

Pilotage

Approach Except for the islets and reefs under Ak Ay Nikolaou, the approaches are free of dangers. However with the prevailing westerlies there can be severe gusts off the land and care is needed. The buildings of the hamlet including two windmills on the rocky bluff immediately E will be seen when close-to.

Frikes

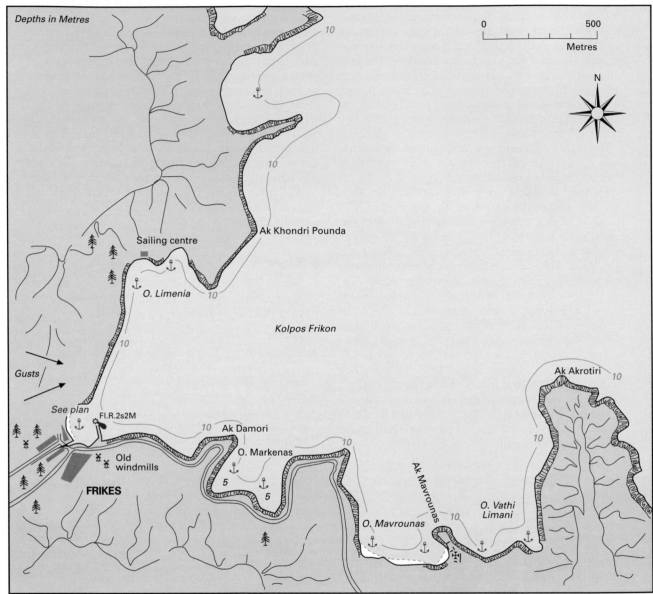

Depths in Metres

0   500
Metres

N

Ak Khondri Pounda

Sailing centre

O. Limenia

Kolpos Frikon

Ak Akrotiri

Gusts

See plan

Fl.R.2s2M

Ak Damori

O. Markenas

Old windmills

5

5

FRIKES

Ak Mavrounas

O. Vathi Limani

O. Mavrounas

KOLPOS FRIKON

Mooring Berth alongside the short mole. There is not a lot of room and it gets crowded in the summer. Alternatively large yachts can go stern-to the outside of the mole with a long line to it keeping well clear of the ferry berth. In light westerlies or calm weather the anchorages around Frikes can be used.

Facilities

Most provisions can be obtained and several tavernas open in the summer. Ferry to Vassiliki.

General

Frikes is a delightful place set at the bottom of a steep and wooded valley, the old houses clustered around the small harbour, and several old windmills standing sentinel on a rocky bluff above, proof of the winds that howl down the valley and off the slopes. The once isolated hamlet has recently seen a little tourism, though not so much as to spoil it. The village is of comparatively recent origin as villages were not commonly built by the sea prior to the 18th and

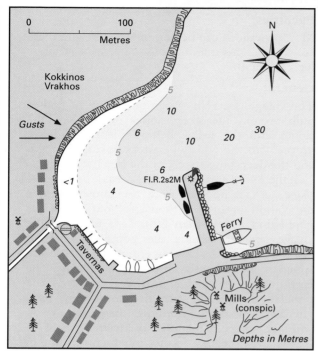

FRIKES

plan as the prevailing winds send a chop in. In calm weather or light westerlies anchor in the SW corner on sand, shingle and weed.

Ormos Mavrounas The next bay along from Ormos Damori. Like Damori shelter is not as good as it looks. In calm weather anchor in the SW corner on sand, shingle and weed.

Ormos Vathi Limani The bay next to Mavrounas on the E side of the rocky headland. In calm weather anchor where convenient. Ashore there are the ruins of the monastery of Ay Nikolaos which was destroyed in the 1953 earthquake, though the church still stands.

Kioni

A village and harbour in Ormos Kioni just S of Ormos Frikes.

Pilotage

Approach From the N and E the three windmill towers on the end of Ak Psigadhi, the S entrance point of the bay, show up well. From the S they will not be seen until close-to if you are hugging the coast. The entrance into the bay is straightforward and free of dangers although there are severe gusts out of the bay with the prevailing westerlies.

Mooring Go stern- or bows-to the quay or anchor off. There are considerable depths off the quay and you will probably be dropping your anchor in 10m or so. If you are anchoring towards the outer part of the bay it is very deep, 20m in line with the breakwater, so put out plenty of scope.

19th centuries because of the risk of pirate attacks. In fact the name of the village may be derived from the pirate Frikon who used it as a base according to some local sources.

Anchorages in Ormos Frikon

There are numerous anchorages in the bay that can be used according to the wind direction and sea state. In most of them the depths are considerable unless you can get in close and if necessary take a long line ashore. From the N these are as follows.

Port Ay Nikolaos A bay directly under Ak Ay Nikolaos. Care is needed of the reef around Nisis Ay Nikolaos. Good protection from the prevailing winds although there are gusts.

Ormos Khondri Pounda A bay just above Ak Khondri Pounda. Good shelter from the prevailing wind, though some swell works its way in during the evening.

Ormos Limenia A two-headed bay under Ak Khondri Pounda. In the W cove there is a watersports centre. Anchor in either cove on shingle, sand and weed. Reasonable shelter from the prevailing winds although there are gusts.

Ormos Damori The bay immediately E of Frikes. Shelter is not as good as it looks on the

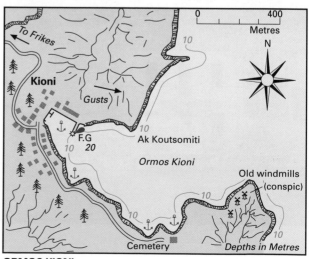

ORMOS KIONI

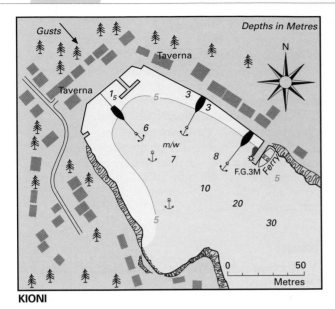

KIONI

The bottom is mud and weed, not everywhere the best holding. Shelter is good although the gusts can be bothersome. In calm weather or light westerlies a yacht can also anchor in the cove on the S off the cemetery although again depths are considerable. The wash from ferries can also be bothersome here.

Facilities

Most provisions can be obtained ashore and there are several tavernas on the waterfront. Caique ferry to Vathi.

General

The village is a gem: an amphitheatre of houses built around the steep slopes of the bay, the slopes and the valley behind planted in olive groves with the odd tall cypress poking through, and the deep blue waters of the bay itself.

In the 19th century the village was a prosperous place, as can be seen from the houses, with a population of over a thousand, but today the population is less than 200. Like many of the villages in the islands the population started drifting away to the cities or emigrated overseas to America and Australia in the 20th century. The earthquake of 1953 further reduced the population when many decided not to move back after being evacuated from the village. Today you will often come across an American drawl or an Aussie twang from a former inhabitant or one of their sons or daughters feeling totally out of place in this little Greek village miles from a metropolis.

Kioni

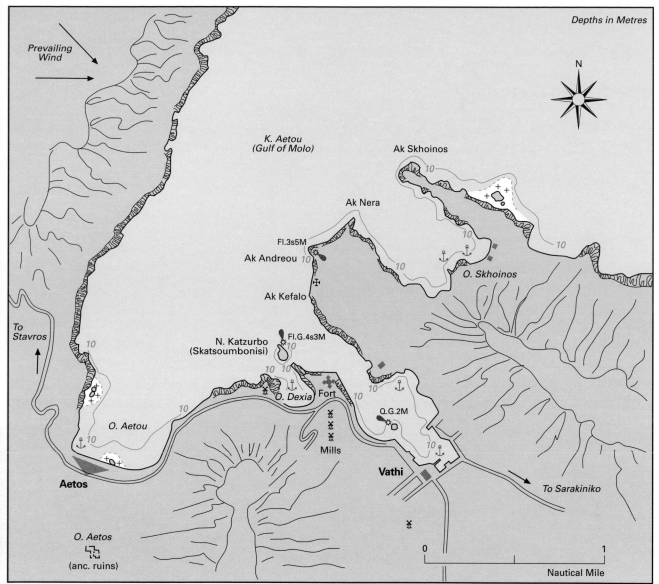

Depths in Metres

Prevailing Wind

N

K. Aetou (Gulf of Molo)

Ak Skhoinos

Ak Nera

Fl.3s5M

Ak Andreou 10

Ak Kefalo

O. Skhoinos

10

10

10

10

To Stavros

N. Katzurbo (Skatsoumbonisi)

Fl.G.4s3M

10

10   10

10

O. Dexia   Fort   10

Q.G.2M

10

10

10

O. Aetou

10

Mills

Vathi

To Sarakiniko

Aetos

O. Aetou

(anc. ruins)

0   1

Nautical Mile

KOLPOS AETOU (GULF OF MOLO)

Kolpos Aetou

(Aito, Gulf of Molo)

The large gulf on the E side of the isthmus joining the two halves of Ithaca. The capital and main harbour, Vathi, lies in a large bottleneck bay on the SE side of the gulf.

Pilotage

In the summer the gulf is a very windy place, one of the windiest in the Ionian. The prevailing wind creeps up over the waist of Ithaca and then tumbles down into Kolpos Aetou. It tends to follow the land and blows from the SW on the W side of the gulf and from the NW down into Port Vathi. Off Kolpos Aetou it tends to blow from the W to NW, but curves around Ak Skhoinos and Ak Sarakiniko to blow from the N to NW.

There are few good anchorages around the gulf suitable with the winds gusting off the hills, but in calm weather or light westerlies a number of anchorages can be used.

Depths in Metres

Taverna

Taverna

3

10

m/w

10

15

<1

NISOS
ITHAKI

Gusts

Limin Vathi

10

AVIN

Ruined
houses

Q.G.2M

10

20

N. Loimokathartirion
(Lazaretto)

10

10

12

10

<1

To Aetos
and Stavros

Ferries

m/w

2

To
O. Sarakiniko

5

2₅

m

7

4

3

2

5

3

3

2₅

Tavernas
and shops

Vathi

0

500

Metres

VATHI (ITHACA)

Vathi looking north from near Palaiochora

Photo *Nigel Patten*

Ormos Aetou The bay in the SW corner of the gulf. Anchor in 5–10m on the W. Care is needed of the reef around the rock off the shore about half way along. The bottom is sand and weed.

Ormos Dexia The bay lying under Nisis Katzurbo. Anchor in 5–12m on mud and weed, not the best holding. The protection from the prevailing wind is not as good as it looks on the plan as it blows straight in here, so the anchorage can become untenable at times.

Ormos Skhoinos The large bay lying immediately under Ak Skhoinos, the E entrance to Kolpos Aetou. Anchor in 8–15m in the SW corner or in 5–12m in the SE corner. The bottom is sand or mud and weed, not the best holding. In light to moderate westerlies some yachts stay in the SW corner, though it is not the most comfortable and if the wind increases you may have to get out.

Vathi

(Port Vathi)
The main harbour of the island on the E side of Kolpos Aetou. Vathi means 'deep' and the approaches and most of the harbour are just this – deep.

Pilotage

Approach The town of Vathi cannot be seen until you are right into the bay. A chapel and light tower on Ak Andreou are easily identified and likewise the light structure and the island of Nisis Katzurbo. Once into Port Vathi the houses of the town will be seen at the head of the bay.

Care is needed in the approaches and in Port Vathi itself as the prevailing wind gusts in from the NW making berthing and anchoring difficult at times. Care also needs to be taken of the large ferries using Vathi, normally they will let you know if you are in the way with a blast from the ship's horn and the basic rule of the road is keep out of the way.

Mooring Yachts can go stern- or bows-to the short mole, along the quay E of the ferry berth, or on the projecting quay at the head of the bay. The quay E of the ferry berth is usually the best place to be although it is quite deep off here – you will be dropping your anchor in 10–15m. The small basin has been largely filled in and what is left is crammed full of local boats. The prevailing wind blows into the bay on all of these berths and you should ensure you put out plenty of scope and that the anchor is holding. The bottom is mud and thick weed, poor holding.

You can also anchor off in the northeast corner or in the area north and east of the short mole. Again the bottom is mud and thick weed, poor holding.

Facilities

Services Water and fuel at the AVIN station on the east side of the bay.
Provisions Good shopping for provisions close by in the town. Ice available.
Eating out Numerous tavernas in the town. A good taverna (*Gregorys'*) with lots of interesting Greek dishes on the E side of the NE corner, and another a little further around to the W.
Other PO. OTE. Bank. Hire motorbikes and cars. Ferries N to Paxos, Corfu, and Brindisi. Ferries E to Patras. Also ferry to Astakos, and to Sami and Ay Eufimia on Cephalonia.

General

The island capital is a relaxed low-key place that only seems to bustle when the ferries arrive. Many of the buildings were destroyed in the 1953 earthquake and some of them to the E and S of the centre have been left as ruins. Many others have been repaired and despite the new buildings, mostly in the centre, Vathi retains a pleasing aspect to it. The proper name of the town is actually Ithaca, but most people refer to the town and harbour as one under the name Vathi.

The island capital used to be Palaeochora on the slopes above Vathi and out of the way of surprise attacks by pirates. When the Venetians brought some law and order to the area, the villagers moved down to Vathi and to Perachori. Under the Venetians the area around Vathi was called Val di Compare and the island itself has also been known by various names including Nerikii (7th century BC), Piccola Cephalonia (Middle Ages), Thrakoniso and Thiakou (Byzantine), Fiaki (Turkish) and Thiaki.

The islet in the harbour is now called Loimokathatirion, though most people still call it by its old name, Lazaretto, after the quarantine station that was built on it. During English rule it was turned into a prison which explains the legend on the old Admiralty chart 1620. It was destroyed in the 1953 earthquake and not rebuilt, although the church of 'Sotiros', originally built in 1668, remains.

Vathi is the best place to leave a yacht and take a motorbike to explore the island and, if you are interested, visit the sites associated with the *Odyssey* that are difficult to visit by sea. Basically the main road goes N from Vathi along the spine of the mountain range to Frikes and you come back the same way. It is an interesting excursion testing your riding skills on the winding road, though much of it is now tarmac so it is quite easy as long as the bike holds up. In Vathi the archaeological museum has been recently reopened and some of the finds from the excavations are displayed here. An inscription outside displays a quotation from Byron: 'If this island belonged to me I would bury all my books here and never go away'. I thought he said the same thing about Naxos in the Cyclades.

Ormos Sarakiniko

A large bay under Ak Koutaria where good shelter can be found with the prevailing wind. A large building is conspicuous on the coast just S of the bay. There is also a pleasant bay just N of Ak Koutaria that can be used.

Pera Pigadhi

Between Ak Sarakiniko and Ak Ioannou at the SE tip of Ithaca, the islet of Nisis Pera Pigadhi lies close to the coast. From the distance it is difficult to distinguish from the coast itself and not until you are close to it will you be able to pick it out.

On the W side of the islet and in Ormos Pera Pigadhi, the bay on Ithaca immediately S of the islet, there is reasonable shelter from light to moderate westerly winds. The prevailing northwesterly does not reach here until late in the afternoon and although it gusts down onto the islet and the bay, there is something of a lee here. However in the summer proper there can be exceptionally strong gusts and it can become untenable. In the morning and early afternoon it makes a wonderful lunch stop with crystal clear

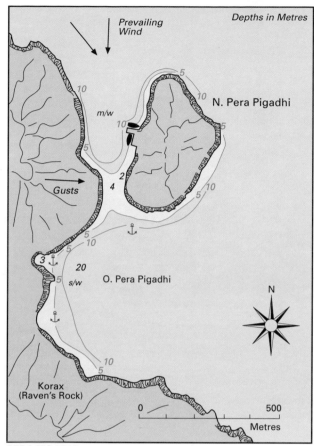

PERA PIGADHI

of Arethusa flowed, and indeed there is a spring here. This is where Eumaeus the swineherd lived and kept his pigs, at least it has been identified as such by those dabbling in mythic geography. In fact there are several other places that could be so identified, Ay Andreou around the corner is one, but the fact that the name Koraka has stuck to the present day in this lonely place is pertinent – the power of old place-names should not be underestimated.

Ormos Ay Andreou

A steep-sided inlet on the S of Ithaca. The exact location can be difficult to identify until close-to. Anchor at the head of the inlet in 8–15m or in the cove on the W side with a long line ashore. There is room for only three or four yachts in here, late-comers will have to anchor in considerable depths further out. The bottom is sand, shingle and

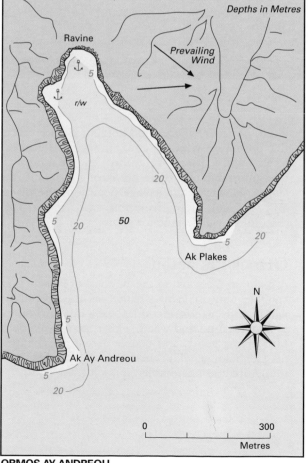

ORMOS AY ANDREOU

water over a sand and rock bottom ideal for swimming and snorkelling.

Either go stern- or bows-to the quay or alongside on Nisis Pera Pigadhi or anchor where convenient just S of the channel or in Ormos Pera Pigadhi. There are 4m least depths through the middle of the channel though the clarity of the water makes it look much less. Out of the channel the depths drop off very quickly and you will usually be dropping the anchor in 10–20m. The bottom is sand, rock and weed, mostly good holding. Anyone staying the night on the quay on the islet should know there have been reports of very big and bold rats living here, so take adequate precautions to prevent them getting on board.

The situation here is wonderful with turquoise water and the steep cliffs of Ithaca rising sheer from the sea. The high rock slope is called Koraka, corresponding to the Korax of the *Odyssey*, the 'Ravens Rock', where the Fountain

Ormos Ay Andreou

weed, not everywhere good holding. Shelter from the prevailing wind is good though a reflected swell will often rebound in making it uncomfortable and there are strong gusts off the slopes. However the savage beauty of the place and its complete isolation will make the discomfort worthwhile for some.

Ormos Pis'aetou

A bight on the waist of the W coast of Ithaca. It is suitable only in calm weather as the prevailing wind sends a considerable swell in. Anchor in 5–20m on mud and weed. This is an age-old port for ferrying goods and people across the channel to Cephalonia. The harbour in the bight is miniature and unsuitable for yachts.

Ormos Polis

A bay on the W coast just down from the N end of Dhiavolos Ithakis. It can be difficult to identify the exact location from the N, but close-to it will become obvious.

Anchor in 5–20m on sand and weed, not everywhere good holding. The bottom drops off very quickly making choosing a spot to anchor critical. Shelter from the prevailing winds which tend to blow down and across the channel is adequate although a reflected swell may be pushed in making it uncomfortable. The small mole in the bay is mostly shallow and usually full of local *caiques*.

The Cave of Louizos where the Bronze Age tripods and masks were found, including the one dedicated to Odysseus, is on the N side of the bay. It is said that in the bay there are the remains of a Byzantine town called Ierousalem, destroyed in an earthquake around AD 967, though I can find few details on it and I have never seen any evidence of it underwater.

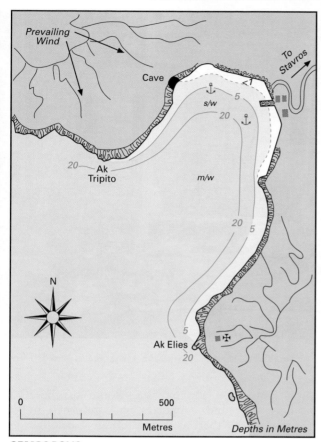

ORMOS POLIS

Nisos Cephalonia

(Kefallinia, Kefallonia)

Cephalonia is the largest island in the Ionian, around twice the size of nearby Zakinthos and about 30% bigger than Corfu. Yet it never seems that big, partially because those on the water seldom cruise right around it and even land travellers are put off by the mountainous interior and tend to stick to a few areas. It is not as green as some of the other Ionian islands because the winter rain is not trapped beneath the rock and tends to run straight off down ravines and gullies to the sea. Consequentially there are no major rivers. Some of the slopes are covered in pine and cypress, including a species of pine named after the island, *Abies Cephalonica*, that grows above 750m to 1700m, though it is not unique to the island as is sometimes stated and in fact is found all over Greece.

The main mountain ridge runs in an L-shape down the middle of the island, approximately from N to S, with another high mountain ridge in

the far W and the SE. These mountains drop straight down into the sea everywhere except for a few small valleys, so you will usually be sailing right at the foot of impressive mountain scenery. This can create a few problems with strong gusts off the high land especially on the S and E sides of the island, though nothing that cannot be coped with if you take care.

Cephalonia has a number of ancient associations, though there are few substantial remains to be seen. Homer mentions Same and Dulichium as neighbours of Ithaca: 'For neighbours we have many peopled isles with no great space between them, Dulichium and Same and wooded Zacynthus'. It is likely that Same is the ancient city of Sami near the present day ferry port of Sami tucked into the bay on the E side of Cephalonia. It has been suggested that Dulichium was one of the other ancient city states on Cephalonia at Pale (Lixuri), Kranoi (Argostoli) or Pronoi (Poros). Then again some authorities believe Dulichium was present-day Levkas.

The four city states were separated by mountainous terrain and largely operated as separate kingdoms with their own coinage and trade agreements. The cities slowly declined in later periods. Cephalonia duly passed to the Romans and in fact the whole island was the private estate of a certain C Antonius at one time according to Strabo. The Normans under Robert Guiscard, the Pisans, various Latin princes including Orsini and the Tocchi, the Turks, the Venetians, the French, and the English, in that order, ruled the island until union with Greece in 1864.

It is an odd mix of an island. It has a definite Italianate feel to parts of it and therein lies an interesting tale. In the Second World War it was occupied in 1943 by 9,000 crack Alpine Acqui soldiers. When the Germans arrived the Italian troops refused to co-operate and then refused to hand the island over to the Germans. For seven days the Italians fought the Germans until eventually the remaining soldiers of the Acqui division, around 3,000 men, surrendered and were executed, it is said on Hitler's personal order. Few survived, but one of those who did, and who was smuggled off the island by the Greek resistance, later became the captain of one of the large ferries operating between Italy and Patras – every time he passed Cephalonia he would salute the island with three long blasts on the ship's horn.

In the disastrous 1953 earthquake over 90% of the buildings on Cephalonia were destroyed. Fiskardho was spared, it is said, because it sits on a bed of clay that absorbed the shockwaves

Cephalonia was recently put on the literary map with a novel by Louis de Bernieres. *Captain Corelli's Mandolin* was one of those wonderful escapees from the publishers list which by word of mouth became a best-seller. It deals with the Italian quasi-occupation of Cephalonia mentioned above and the love affair between Captain Corelli and a young Greek girl Pelagia. Intertwined through it all is the history of the Italian occupation, the arrival of the Germans, the Communist resistance and things just generally Greek. If you haven't read it go out and buy it now, if you have read it take it along to read again.

The island produces some of the best wines in the Ionian, though the impetus for this comes not from nearby Italy, but mostly from local initiative with some help from the French and later an Englishman who developed wine-making here. The Cephalonians themselves, thwarted by their island and its lack of water and flat fertile ground for cultivation, have always been ready to emigrate. Many of the men have worked in the merchant navy and many others have emigrated to America, Australia and South Africa over the years. The big earthquake of 1953 prompted massive emigration and today the island is only thinly populated for its size. Some of these prodigal sons and daughters have returned in recent years so there is a smattering of colonial accented English spoken in the villages dotted around the island.

Getting around inland

During the English administration a number of paved roads were built and these formed the basis for the present road system. For the size of the island the road network is poorly developed – smaller islands like Corfu and Zakinthos are much better served than Cephalonia. To get around the island you really need to hire a motorbike or car, for the rougher roads you will need a four-wheel drive jeep, as the bus service is not comprehensive or frequent.

Motorbikes and cars and jeeps can be hired at Argostoli, Lixuri, Poros, and Fiskardho. In Ay Eufimia there is a car and motorbike agent although he seldom seems to have very much to actually hire! An excursion inland is well worthwhile. The mountain scenery so spectacular from seawards is every bit as spectacular in amongst it, wonderful wooded valleys, steep terraced slopes, bare rocky peaks above the tree-line, and small villages tucked away in the interior.

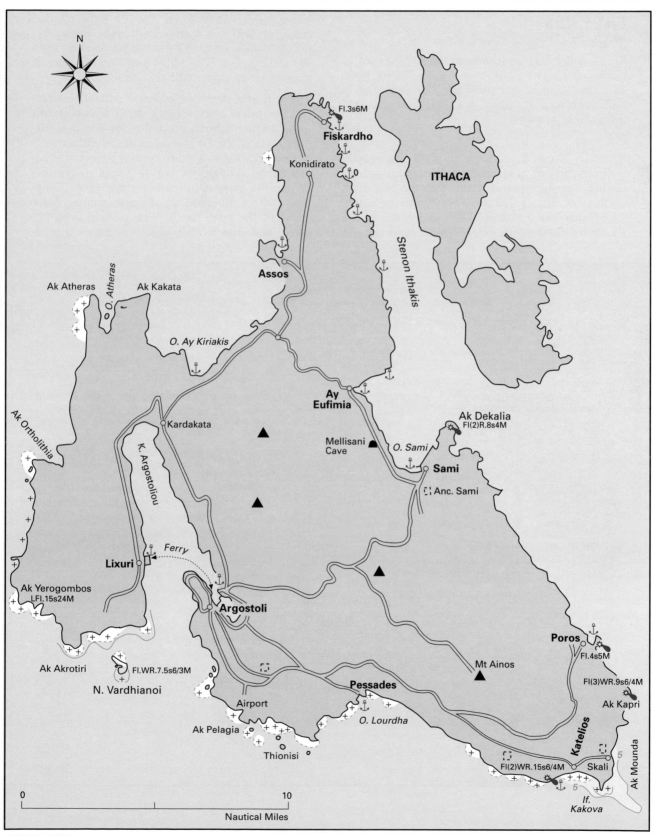

N

Fl.3s6M

Fiskardho

Konidirato

ITHACA

Ak Atheras

O. Atheras

Ak Kakata

Stenon Ithakis

Assos

O. Ay Kiriakis

Ak Ortholithia

Kardakata

Ay Eufimia

Ak Dekalia
Fl(2)R.8s4M

Mellisani
Cave

O. Sami

Sami

K. Argostoliou

Anc. Sami

Ferry

Lixuri

Ak Yerogombos
LFl.15s24M

Argostoli

Ak Akrotiri

Fl.WR.7.5s6/3M

N. Vardhianoi

Poros

Fl.4s5M

Mt Ainos

Fl(3)WR.9s6/4M

Pessades

Ak Kapri

Airport

O. Lourdha

Ak Pelagia

Katelios

Ak Mounda

Thionisi

Fl(2)WR.15s6/4M

Skali

5

5

*If.
Kakova*

0   10

Nautical Miles

CEPHALONIA

Fiskardho
(Phiscardo)

An enclosed bay and harbour on the NE tip of Cephalonia. The harbour is a gem, offers good all-round shelter, and consequently is popular in the summer, though you can always find somewhere to moor.

Pilotage

Approach It can be difficult to work out exactly where the bay is although it is easy enough to work out the general location at the N end of Dhiavlos Ithakis. A cluster of villas in the bay N of Fiskardho are conspicuous and closer in the new lighthouse, the ruined tower, and the old

Venetian lighthouse on the N side of the entrance will be seen – although it can be difficult when coming from the NE looking into the setting sun. The villas and hotel on the S side of the entrance will also be seen.

Mooring Berth stern- or bows-to where possible on the town quay leaving the SW corner for local *caiques*. Care is needed at the E end of the quay where the ballasting extends underwater a short distance. A pontoon has been installed on the W side and is run by *Tassia's Taverna*. When the quay is full, anchor and take a long line to the shore on the N side keeping well clear of the ferry berth. The bottom is sand, mud and weed with a few rocks scattered

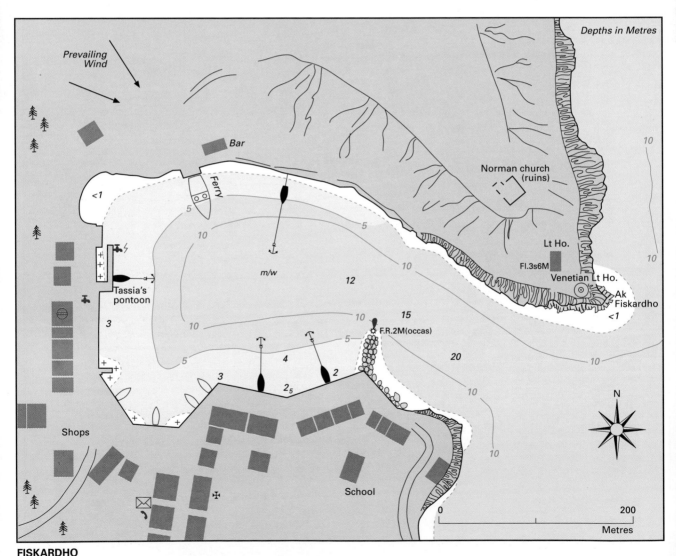

FISKARDHO

The old Venetian lighthouse under the new (-ish) lighthouse on the northern entrance of Fiskardho

around for good measure, mostly good holding once through the weed. Good all-round shelter in the bay.

Facilities

Services Water on the W quay. Water and electricity on the yacht pontoon. Fuel can be delivered.

Provisions Good shopping for provisions nearby.

Eating out Numerous restaurants some of which are excellent. A number of bars offer snacks and drinks with a ringside seat to watch the goings-on in the harbour. *Herodotus* on the road out of the village has a good selection of interesting dishes and repays a visit as does the *Garden Taverna*.

Other PO. OTE. Exchange facilities in the PO. Hire cars and motorbikes. Ferry to Frikes on Ithaca and Vassiliki on Levkas.

General

Fiskardho is a picture-postcard spot, one of the most photogenic places on Cephalonia and a favourite haunt of yachties who generally end up staying longer than intended. It is said that Aristotle Onassis once wanted to buy the N side of Fiskardho, but was thwarted by the multiplicity of owners including an obdurate church, so turned to Skorpios instead. One of the attractions of Fiskardho is that it was one of the few places on Cephalonia to escape wholesale destruction in the 1953 earthquake, (over 90% of the buildings on the island were destroyed), so the buildings around the harbour are all typical of a vanished architecture, mostly 19th-century Italianate-looking houses. Add to this the safe harbour, nearby coves with crystal clear water (there are not what you could call good beaches in the area), pleasant walks around the pine-clad coast, the friendly intimate atmosphere of the place and it is no wonder that Fiskardho is a popular spot and gets more than a little crowded at the height of summer.

It takes its name from Robert Guiscard, the Norman adventurer who challenged Byzantium for its territory in Italy and western Greece and by and large succeeded in taking it. Byzantine rule was harsh in many areas with excessive taxes levied and little given in return. With a few of his companion knights Guiscard stormed through Italy and western Greece. In Fiskardho he succumbed along with many of his men to fever, possibly typhoid or malaria, and died here. The ruins of the Norman church on the N side of the bay are said to have been built to commemorate the man. There is a slight problem here in that he is also said to have died at Vonitsa in the Gulf of Amvrakia. Guiscard or Guiscardo became corrupted over time to Fiskardho, so perhaps the place takes precedence over Vonitsa's claim to the man. On the N entrance point there is an excellent example of a Venetian lighthouse: a round tower with a sheltered top with gaps in it so the oil fire could be seen.

Dhiavlos Ithakis

The channel between Cephalonia and Ithaca is hemmed in by high mountains on either side which funnel the prevailing wind down the channel. There are also gusts, sometimes severe, off the high land and down the valleys on the W side of the channel. Although the wind strength is increased over that on the open sea and the gusts off Cephalonia can be unnerving, there are no real problems that a little prudence cannot cope with; for which read reef well down first and then shake the reefs out if you have been overly cautious.

Anchorages between Fiskardho and Ay Eufimia

Along the coast of Cephalonia on the W side of Dhiavlos Ithakis there are numerous attractive anchorages in bays and coves which can be used according to the wind and sea. The slopes around many of the bays are covered in pine and cypress and offer wonderful solitude and crystal clear water. Many of them cannot be reached by land although a new road has made some of them more accessible for landlubbers.

Boats visiting this stretch of coastline should do everything in their power not to disturb things too much. The Mediterranean monk seal, *Monachus monachus*, inhabits the waters around here, some of the last remaining members of a species that is very nearly extinct. It is a shy animal, easily disturbed, and if you see one do not chase it to get a better look at it, but discretely and quietly leave it alone.

Most of the bays along the coast are very deep, usually you will have to anchor in 10m plus of water. The bottom is mostly sand, shingle and weed, poor holding if you strike thick weed or a lot of shingle, so select the spot you anchor in with care. The water is normally very clear so you can pick out a good spot on the bottom to drop the anchor onto. With the prevailing NW wind there are gusts off the land in most of these anchorages so if possible take a long line ashore. While there are gusts off the land, the wind blowing from the N down the channel sends a swell into some of the bays. From the N the anchorages are as follows:

Ormos Fiskardho In the S of the bay there is an inlet with an old gravel-loading plant on the N side. It is very deep in here so take a long line ashore to counter any gusts off the land. Good shelter.

Palaeokaravo Just under a mile S of the inlet above there is an attractive bay suitable in calm weather or light westerlies.

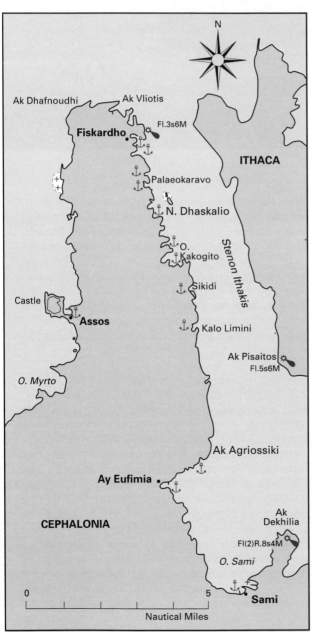

STENON ITHAKIS

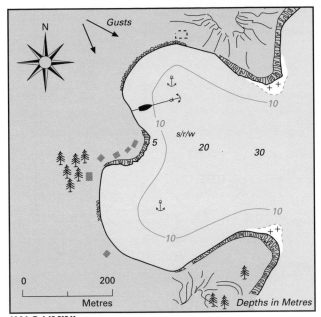

KALO LIMINI

Nisis Dhaskalio A small islet lying close off the coast. A chapel is conspicuous on it. Above- and below-water rocks fringe the islet. On the coast opposite are several attractive coves suitable in calm weather or light westerlies.

Ormos Kaminus A bay about a mile S of Nisis Dhaskalio. Suitable in calm weather.

Ormos Kakogito A large bay about ½M S of Kaminus. The shelter in here is not as good as it looks on the chart as the prevailing wind sends a swell in.

Ormos Sikidi A small bay about ½M S of Kakogito. Reasonable shelter. There are several other similar coves down the coast to Kalo Limini.

Kalo Limini A twin-headed bay just over a mile S of Sikidi. It is easily recognised by the few houses on the shore. Anchor in 10–15m with a long line ashore. The N cove offers the best shelter. Although there are gusts off the land and some swell enters, it is a suitable overnight anchorage in settled weather.

Ormos Sarakiniko An inlet about 1½M S of Kalo Limini. Suitable in calm weather.

Ak Agriossiki Immediately SW of the cape there is a narrow inlet offering some shelter from the prevailing wind. There is usually something of a lee around the cape until you encounter the wind gusting out of Ay Eufimia. Room for a few yachts to anchor in pleasant surroundings.

Ay Eufimia

(Ayias Euphemias, Ag Evfimia, Pilaros Cove)
The large bay and harbour lying on the same parallel as the S end of Ithaca.

Pilotage

Approach Coming down Dhiavlos Ithakis from the N you will not see the village and harbour until you round Ak Agriossiki. From the E and SE the village is easily identified. Closer in the breakwater will be seen. With the prevailing wind there are strong gusts out of the bay, though the sea is usually flat.

Mooring Berth stern- or bows-to the quay on the N or on the old ferry quay under the mole. The prevailing wind gusts down onto the harbour so make sure your anchor is well in and if in doubt lay a second anchor. Much of the quay has been extended so that underwater rubble is not the problem it once was. Alternatively anchor off clear of the anchors of yachts berthed on the quay. The bottom is mud and weed with some rocks, mostly good holding, but with the gusts make sure the anchor is well in. With the prevailing wind there are gusts down the valley and into the harbour, mostly bothersome and rarely dangerous.

Facilities

Services Metered water taps at a number of points around the quay on the N side. Fuel can be delivered.

Provisions Most provisions can be found.

Ay Eufimia

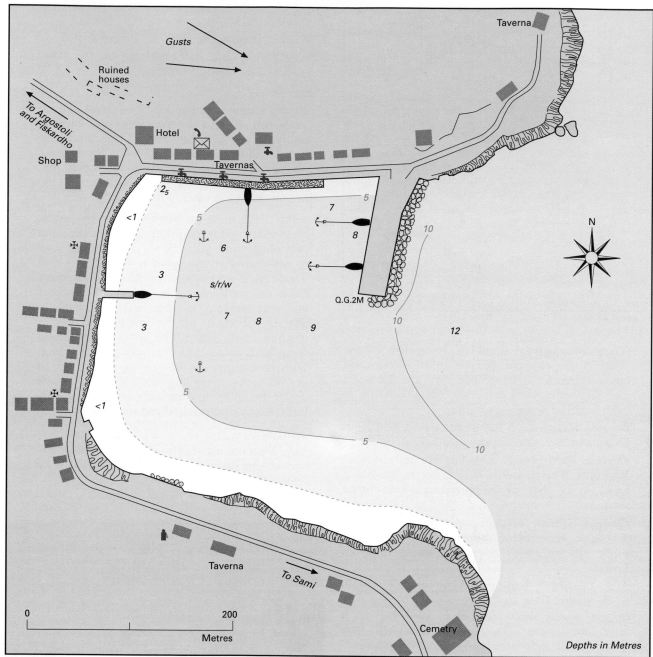

AY EUFIMIA

Eating out Several tavernas including an excellent one situated at the end of the track running along the coast from the harbour breakwater – here you sit with a view over to Ithaca and the food is good (Kefallonian pie served).

Other PO. Telephone. Hire cars although there may not be one available!

General

Ay Eufimia used to be the main ferry port for Cephalonia until the 1953 earthquake destroyed much of it and Sami was developed instead. In Maki's *Asteria Cafeneion* there is an old photograph of Ay Eufimia prior to 1953 showing a substantial village and a busy harbour. For years the village stagnated and few yachts visited here – in 1977 when I first tied up in Ay Eufimia there was one taverna and Maki's *Cafeneion*.

Near the village of Karavomilos on the road between Ay Eufimia and Sami is the Cave of Mellisani. From the entrance you go down through a tunnel to the cave and underground lake of deep inky water with turquoise patches where the sun manages to strike it. A boatman takes you around the cave, about a twenty minute trip, which I suppose gives one an idea of what entering Hades and encountering Charon must be like, though there are generally too many people to set the tone. The boatman will tell you that the roof of the cave did not fall in courtesy of the 1953 earthquake as is often stated, but several thousand years ago. The water of the cave is slightly brackish and is in fact seawater that enters at the water mill on Ak Ay Theodoroi at Argostoli and travels through underground passages to the Mellisani lake, bubbling up into the sea nearby. Apparently the exact source of the water flowing through Mellisani was not determined until the 1950's when a French team used red dye to trace it from Ak Ay Theodoroi. Also nearby is the Cave of Drogarati.

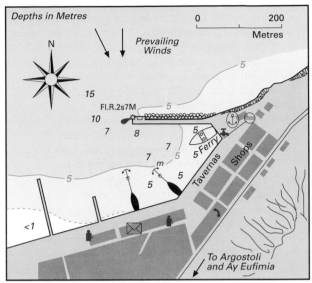

SAMI

Sami

Limin Sami

(Samis)

The main ferry port for Cephalonia in the large bay at the S end of Dhiavlos Ithakis.

Pilotage

Approach Once into Ormos Sami the buildings of the town are easily identified. The approach is straightforward and free of dangers.

Mooring Berth stern- or bows-to the SW end of the town quay or alongside the breakwater keeping well clear of the ferry berth. The prevailing wind blows straight down Dhiavlos Ithakis into the harbour making it uncomfortable at times. Although the wind does not blow home, it tends to lift over the high hills behind, it does send in some swell. The bottom is mud, good holding.

Facilities

Services Water can be delivered by mini-tanker. Fuel nearby or large amounts can be delivered.

Provisions Good shopping for provisions nearby in the town.

Eating out Several tavernas and snack bars nearby.

Other PO. OTE. Bank. Hire cars and motorbikes. Bus to Argostoli that connects with the ferries. Ferries to Patras, Vathi on Ithaca and to Brindisi via Paxos and Corfu.

General

The setting of Sami in the wide bay under the

shadow of the high wooded ridge running NE to Ak Dekalia is magnificent, so Sami itself comes as a bit of a disappointment. It is an entirely modern town built with the help of the British after the 1953 earthquake. Yet after a while the place grows on you. Sit for a while on the waterfront with a cold beer and like the locals watch for the ferry arriving – nothing much disturbs this sleepy little hollow until the ferry comes when there is hectic activity getting people and vehicles on and off and then everything settles back to a more sedate pace.

There are some wonderful walks along the coast to the NE of the town where there are rocky coves suitable for swimming which are usually uncrowded as the locals and most visitors use the beach to the W. The ruins of ancient Sami are just outside the town, but there is little to see except a few sections of wall.

Ormos Andisamis

A large bay immediately S of Ak Dekalia. Although it looks as if it should offer good shelter, the prevailing wind gusts straight in and sends a swell into it. Suitable in the morning before the wind gets up. On the slopes above is the monastery of Moni Agrilion.

Poros

(Pronos)

A small harbour tucked into Ormos Poros 9M SE of Ak Dekalia.

Pilotage

Approach From the N the buildings of the village are easily identified. From the S the village and harbour will not be seen until you are around

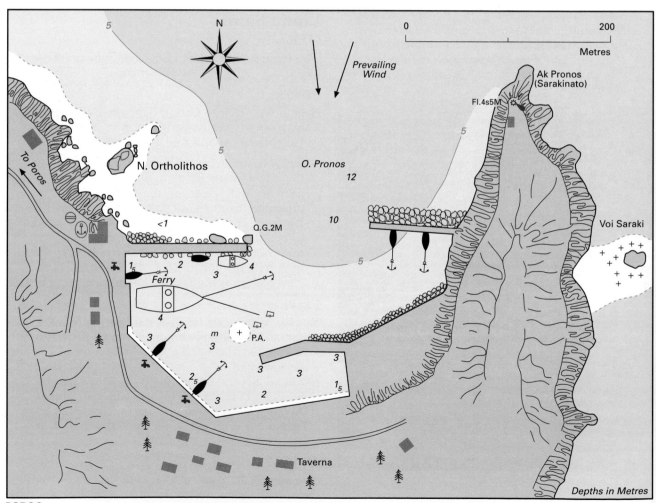

POROS

Ak Poros. Once into the harbour care is needed of an underwater rock reported to lie in approximately the position shown. Keep to the north of it when heading for the south quay.

Mooring Berth stern- or bows-to the quay on the S or under the short breakwater on the east side. The bottom is mud and weed, good holding. The prevailing wind tends to push a chop into the harbour, uncomfortable but usually tenable although it has to be said shelter is not brilliant in here. At night when the wind dies down things are calmer.

Facilities

Services Water on the quay.
Provisions Most provisions can be found in the village.
Eating out Good local taverna by the harbour and others in the village.
Other PO. OTE. Bus to Argostoli that connects with the ferry. Ferry to Killini and to Zakinthos in the summer.

General

Poros is often stated to be one of Cephalonia's major tourist resorts, but it seems to me that most people arriving on the ferry are on the road to Argostoli before they even blink twice at Poros. While Poros does attract numbers of tourists, many local, it is more in the mould of a ferry port like Sami. The setting is spectacular, it sits at the foot of a valley cutting down through the high mountains, on the edge of the sea, but the village itself wins few kudos from most people though I quite like it.

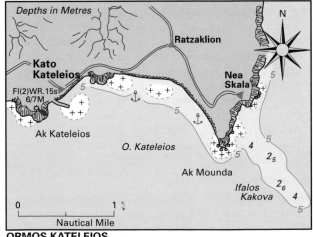

ORMOS KATELEIOS

Ak Mounda and Kakova Shoal

Off Ak Mounda, the SE tip of Cephalonia, Kakova shoal runs out in a SE direction for around 1¾M. There are several 2m patches although there are mostly 4m depths in the inner and outer part. In calm weather a yacht can, with care, pass around ¼M and less than ½M off the coast where there are mostly 4m plus depths. However keep a lookout on the bows. With the prevailing wind a swell heaps up over the shoal water and a yacht should keep well off.

On the old Admiralty chart 203 a number of transits are given. Ak Kapri in line with the W side of Nisos Atoko leads clear of the shoals, however with any haze it can be difficult to see Atoko clearly. The other transit is Ay Yeoryios (Georgis) Castle in line with Ak Koroni which leads clear of the shoal water, but it depends on you being able to identify the castle.

Ormos Kateleios

Under Ak Mounda there is a large bay extending around to Ak Kateleios. With light westerlies a yacht can anchor on the N side of the bay. The prevailing wind tends to blow down the E side of Cephalonia from the N to NW and along the S coast from the W. The W side of the bay should be avoided as a reef obstructs most of it including the approaches to the small harbour. A yacht should not attempt to approach the harbour as the entrance and part of the harbour are rockbound. Ashore there is the village of Kato Kateleios where some provisions can be found and there are several tavernas.

On the slopes behind the village of Markopoulo a remarkable phenomenon occurs in August. Between August 6th and 15th or at least before the Feast of the Assumption on the 15th, small snakes migrate or emerge around and in the church. The snakes are said to have miraculous properties, conferred to whoever catches one, and the ceremony attracts the ill and infirm or whoever is looking for a miracle. It is difficult to know where the association comes from. In Kirkpinar in Anatolian Turkey water snakes appear in early summer and are said to have healing properties. The locals drape them over the afflicted part to cure it. The Christian religion normally associates snakes with Chaos and disorder, but a snake was the symbol of Askeplios, the Greek god of healing, and there are fragments here and there of snakes being used in ancient Greek medicine. Perhaps the ceremony here is one of those distant folk memories of an ancient practice, absorbed by the church because it could not entirely eliminate it.

Ak Kateleios

Directly under the cape there is a small rock-bound *caique* harbour where a small yacht may find room. Great care is needed in the approach and a lookout should con you in from the bows. The area to the W of the breakwater is littered with above- and below-water rocks. The approach should be made from a SE direction passing between the end of the breakwater and a withy. There are 2m depths in the immediate approach and at the outer end of the breakwater. A *cafeneion* ashore.

Pessades

On the W side of Ormos Lourda there is the small ferry port of Pessades for the ferry running across to Ay Nikolaos on Zakinthos. The *caique* harbour here is miniature, but a small yacht may find a berth on the end of the mole. Nearby there is the concrete apron for the ferry.

Argostoli

(Argostolion)

The capital and principal harbour of the island tucked into a bay in Kolpos Argostoliou, the gulf in the SW of Cephalonia.

Pilotage

Approach From the W the tall white lighthouse on Ak Yero Gombos is conspicuous. From the E Nisis Thionisi and a large white hotel on Ak Pelagia are conspicuous. Care is needed of the reef SE of Ak Pelagia and of the reef W of Ak Ay Nikolaos.

Once into the immediate approaches to Kolpos Argostoliou, Nisis Vardiani although low-lying, can be identified. A yacht can pass between Nisis Vardiani and Cephalonia where there are 5·5m least depths in the fairway. On Ak Ay Theodoroi a Doric style lighthouse is conspicuous. Proceed down into the bay where the buildings of Argostoli will be seen. Leave the beacon marking a rocky patch to starboard.

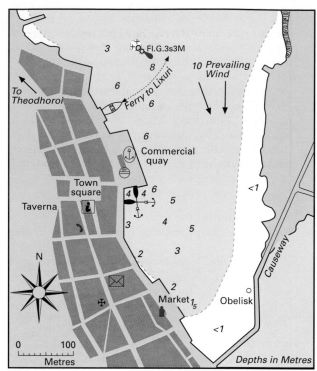
ARGOSTOLI

Mooring Berth stern- or bows-to the S side of the ferry quay or on the N end of the W quay. Yachts clearing into Greece should go onto the S side of the ferry quay within the customs enclosure. Although the prevailing wind blows down into the harbour, there is a good lee under the ferry quay. The bottom is mud and good holding.

Facilities

Services Water and fuel on the quay.

Provisions Good shopping for provisions in the town.

Eating out Numerous tavernas in and near the town square immediately W of the ferry quay. The *Port of Cephalos* near the ferry quay and the *Kanaria* are not bad.

Other PO. OTE. Banks. Hospital. Dentists. Hire cars and motorbikes. Buses to most places on the island. Ferry to Lixuri. Ferry to Killini. Internal and international flights from the airport nearby.

General

Argostoli, like 90% of the rest of Cephalonia, was flattened in the 1953 earthquake and the present city was entirely rebuilt after the event. Argostoli became the capital in 1765 when the Castle of St

George on the heights to the SE, the Venetian capital, was considered beyond repair after a series of earthquakes. The small fishing village developed through the 18th and 19th centuries into what was apparently one of the most beautiful cities in the Ionian, rich in ornate public buildings in the Venetian style and later in a Georgian-Mediterranean style under British rule.

It is difficult to imagine today. The causeway across the lagoon was built under British rule and was one of the few things to survive the earthquake. For the rest Argostoli seems to have been slapped together as quickly as possible after the earthquake and is a nondescript, soulless place, reinforced-concrete-by-sea, that only here and there is relieved by a reconstructed church or an old stone wall. Year by year the town mellows, but not yet enough, and it seems such a waste

The celebrated water wheel at Argostoli. The 1953 earthquake altered the terrain to such an extent that the flow of sea-water is now much reduced

The Doric-style lighthouse conspicuous on Ak Ay Theodoroi in the approaches to Argostoli

when the situation on the edge of the lagoon with high mountains on the other side is so wonderful.

Within the town there are two interesting museums. The Archaeological Museum just S of the main square has an interesting collection of artefacts from Mycenean through Greek and Roman to Byzantine times. The Folklore Museum in the basement of the library is interesting for its exhibits and photographs showing the town before the devastating earthquake.

At the end of the peninsula to the N of the town, close by the Doric style lighthouse, is the Katavotheres water wheel, now clasped in the grasp of a taverna. Prior to the 1953 earthquake seawater poured into a subterranean chasm and a water wheel was built to harness the power for grinding wheat. The earthquake reduced the flow and although the sea still flows underground, it is barely enough to turn the wheel. The seawater seeping into the underground passages finds its way right across the island to the Cave of Mellisani between Ay Eufimia and Sami. To the S of Argostoli at Metaxata, Byron spent the winter of 1823–24 before he went to Mesolongion and his death for the Greek cause. Like so much else the house was destroyed by the 1953 earthquake.

Lixuri

(Lixurion)

A town and small harbour nearly opposite Argostoli on the W side of Kolpos Argostoliou.

Pilotage

Approach The harbour is easily identified and the approach is straightforward. Keep a good lookout for the ferries crossing between Argostoli and Lixuri which have right of way in the harbour.

Mooring Berth stern- or bows-to the N or W quay keeping clear of the ferry berth. The bottom is mud. Good shelter although strong NW winds cause a surge.

Facilities

Services Water on the quay although it is not always turned on in the summer. Fuel in the town.

Provisions Good shopping for provisions.

Eating out Tavernas in the town close to the harbour.

Other PO. OTE. Bank. Hire motorbikes. Ferry to Argostoli.

General

Lixuri is an agricultural town serving the flat farmland around it, terrain that is a rarity on the island. It is a pleasant workaday place that sees a few tourists though most prefer to stay on the other side. The harbour is unfortunately next to the main sewer outlet and gets very smelly in the summer heat. Escape by taking a wander around the back-streets where there are all sorts of interesting workshops.

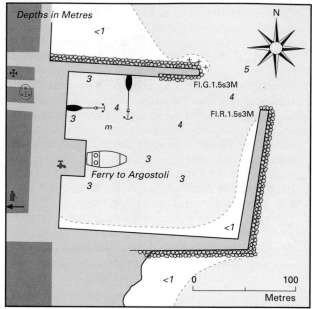

LIXURI

The West Coast

The west coast has little to offer the yachtsman apart from spectacular scenery and delightful coves and beaches that cannot be used because the prevailing NW to W winds send a heavy swell in. Even in the morning before the afternoon breeze has set in there is invariably a considerable ground swell setting onto the coast. In calm weather a small yacht could use Ay Kiriakis and larger yachts can get into Assos. However neither of these two places should be entered with the prevailing NW wind.

Ormos Athera

A large bay about 13M N of Ak Yero Gombas. It is open to the prevailing wind and I mention it only because it looks a wonderful spot to explore.

Ay Kiriakis

A small harbour in Ormos Ay Kiriakis, the large bay W of Athera in the crook of Cephalonia. In the SW corner of the bay there is a miniature fishing harbour where a small yacht could find a berth. It should only be approached in calm weather and not in the prevailing wind which blows straight down onto the entrance.

Ay Kiriakis

Considerable caution is needed in the immediate approach and the entrance which is bordered by underwater rocks. Berth under the outer breakwater with a long line ashore where shown on the plan. Care is needed as the depths inside the harbour are irregular.

Two tavernas ashore which often have excellent fresh fish caught by local boats. The situation under steep mountains and the rocky coast bordered by clear, clear waters is superb, but the harbour should only be used by a small yacht in calm weather.

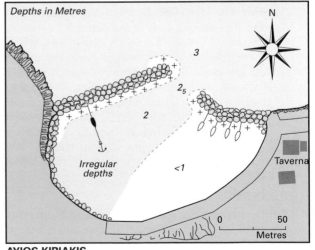

AYIOS KIRIAKIS

145

Assos harbour

Assos

A small harbour on the N side of a short headland lying 6M S of Ak Dafnoudhi on the N tip of Cephalonia. It should only be used in calm weather or light westerlies.

Pilotage

Approach The massive fort on the steep headland partially sheltering Assos is not as easy to pick out as it might appear, but can usually be identified from the distance. Closer in yachts coming from the N will see the houses on the isthmus and the short mole.

Mooring Go stern- or bows-to the mole with a long line ashore as it is bordered by rocks for most of its length. There are one or two spaces where smaller yachts can go close enough so you can get ashore. Alternatively anchor off. It is mostly quite deep in the bay, 7–10m, so ensure you let out enough scope. The bottom is mud, shingle and weed, not everywhere good holding. Shelter in here is adequate in light northwesterlies, but a yacht should leave in moderate or strong northwesterlies which push a swell in.

Facilities

Some provisions can be found. Numerous tavernas in the village. Infrequent bus to Fiskardho and Argostoli.

General

The little hamlet snuggling into the hillside is nearly always mentioned as a popular tourist resort or resort-to-be, but as yet Assos entertains only a few visitors and remains an intimate spot with a small hotel and a few village rooms. It is difficult to reach by land down the winding road from the mountain ridge and its small harbour is not big enough nor safe enough for many yachts or tripper boats. It is a wonderfully picturesque place crammed into the gap between the fort and peninsula and the high cliffs and mountains around it.

The fort on the peninsula is massive and enclosed a large town, but little is known about it. An ancient Greek fort existed here and parts of it have been incorporated into the Venetian fort. This latter fort was built around 1595 and sprawls across the peninsula enclosing an area that is recorded to have included sixty public and over two hundred private buildings. Large water cisterns ensured it could last out a long siege.

In the 20th century a prison was established on the peninsula and though little is known about the type of prisoners sent here, it would have been an ideal location to exile political offenders to. The abandoned prison in the centre of the peninsula is a melancholy place, its watchtowers intact but deserted now, the roof destroyed, the cells abandoned, with only a few goats for inhabitants. The lonely setting casts a gloom over the decaying buildings and perhaps the ghosts of prisoners unjustly kept here linger on. The old fort is a fascinating place to wander around though care is needed of the crumbling masonry and of the underground cisterns. The rough dirt road leads to the cliffs at the W end of the peninsula and the limit of the old stone walls guarding it. Needless to say there are wonderful views from parts of the fort.

Nisos Zakinthos
(Zakynthos, Zante)

Zakinthos is the southernmost of the Ionian islands although Kithera at the bottom of the Peloponnese used to be included in the Heptanisoi for administrative purposes. Geographically it is quite different from its northern neighbours, Cephalonia and Ithaca, which are really mountain tops in the sea with little flat land suitable for cultivation. Zakinthos has a huge central plain surrounded by a horseshoe range of mountains that catch the winter and spring rains and funnel them down to water it. The fertile soil responds to give Zakinthos a huge swathe of green in marked contrast to the barren slopes of Cephalonia and Ithaca and in this it resembles Corfu – indeed there is an age-old rivalry between the two islands over which is the more beautiful. To this bounteous island add its strategic position in the southern approaches to the Gulf of Patras and it is obvious why it has long been historically important and consequently colonised by anyone who wished to control the sea routes to the south around the Peloponnese and into the Gulfs of Patras and Corinth.

Being close to Ithaca it is naturally enough mentioned by Homer in the *Odyssey* where it is called 'wooded Zakynthos', a description that not only mentions it by the name it bears today, but describes its principal asset. Homer also tells us that the name of the island comes from a son of Dardanos, an ancestor of the Kings of Troy, who was called inevitably, Zakinthos. He arrived with ships and men from Arcadia and built an acropolis he called Psophida, and so gave his name to the island. There are other versions of where the name comes from including a derivation from the Greek word for the hyacinth which grows everywhere.

Little is known of the ancient period until the Peloponnesian War when the Athenian fleet under Tolmidis sacked the island and the Zakinthians had little choice but to support Athens during the war. Later it came under Philip of Macedon and passed in turn to the Romans. After the end of Roman rule the island was subject to neglect and to the depredations of every passing pirate and invader. It was sacked by the Goths, the Vandals under Gizarich who left the island with 500 aristocrats who were systematically butchered and thrown overboard

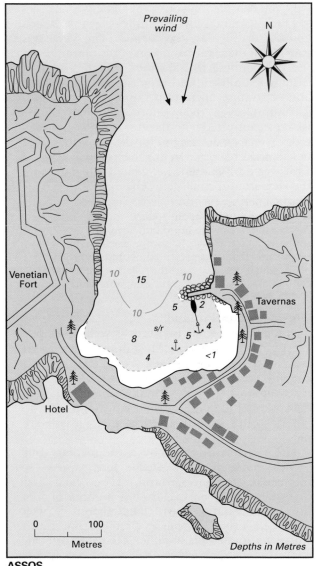

ASSOS

on the way home, the Saracens who regularly plundered Zakinthos, the Normans who razed the island, and then the Turks who in 1479 depopulated the entire island.

This catalogue of disaster and carnage ended in 1489 with the arrival of the Venetians who needed Zakinthos to safeguard their trade route around the Peloponnese and on to the E. The Venetians restored order and immediately settlers flocked to the island such that by 1515 the formerly depopulated island had a population of more than 20,000 people. The Venetians remained until 1797 and the fall of the Republic. When the French took Zakinthos they were the beneficiaries of what has been described as one of the most beautiful cities in the Ionian. Their version of the name of the island, Zante, has stuck right up into the 20th century. The English arrived in 1809 and did what they were best at, building roads and public buildings, until in 1864, along with the other Ionian islands, Zakinthos became part of Greece.

Spinning on Zakinthos

As with many of the other islands, the enduring architectural legacy has been Venetian. The city of Zakinthos was flattened in the 1953 earthquake, but was rebuilt along the lines of the old city and so it is possible to get a glimpse of what old Zakinthos looked like. Some who saw the old city are harsh on the modern one, Lawrence Durrell described it as a '. . . beautiful woman whose face had been splashed with vitriol. Here and there, an arch, a pendant, a shattered remains of arcade, all that is left of her renowned beauty', though I think this goes a bit far. If you search out some of the old buildings, ignore the reinforced concrete, wander through the reconstructed arcades and then make an effort of will, you can see, only just, the old city.

The Venetians left another legacy which endures to this day: the currant. The Venetians supervised the transplantation of the currant from the Peloponnese to Zakinthos with the hope of cashing in on lucrative European trade. It worked and currant cultivation spread throughout Zakinthos, even today more than half of the island is cultivated with the currant vine although today's recipes do not call for the quantities used in Victorian recipes. On this theme when Edward Lear was on Zakinthos he penned a few lines on the view from the village of Galaro.

'The old nursery rhyme –
If all the world were apple-pie,
And all the trees were bread and cheese –
supposes a sort of food-landscape hardly more remarkable than that presented by this vast green plain, which may be, in truth, called one unbroken continuance of future currant-dumplings and plum-puddings.'

Getting around inland

The road system on Zakinthos is well developed except in the very north. Most of the major roads are paved and minor roads are usually in good condition. Like some of the other islands the local maps are not entirely truthful about the road network or the grade of the road. Some just do not exist and some marked as major roads are not.

The interior is served by a rudimentary bus service, but you really need a hire car/jeep or motorbike to get around. Hire cars and motorbikes are available from a number of hire firms in Zakinthos town. The interior is well worth exploring, especially parts of the south where it is impossible or difficult to get to by boat.

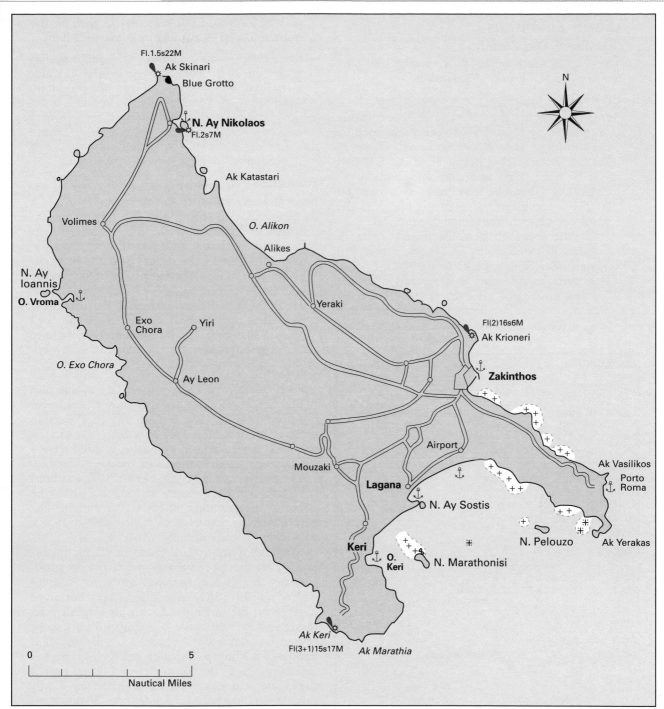

Fl.1.5s22M
Ak Skinari
Blue Grotto

N. Ay Nikolaos
Fl.2s7M

Ak Katastari

Volimes

O. Alikon

Alikes

N. Ay
Ioannis
O. Vroma

Yeraki

Fl(2)16s6M
Ak Krioneri

Exo
Chora

Yiri

Zakinthos

O. Exo Chora

Ay Leon

Airport

Mouzaki

Ak Vasilikos
Porto
Roma

Lagana

N. Ay Sostis

Keri

**O.
Keri**

N. Marathonisi

N. Pelouzo

Ak Yerakas

Ak Keri
Fl(3+1)15s17M

Ak Marathia

N

0   5

Nautical Miles

NISOS ZAKINTHOS

Limin Zakinthos

(Zakynthos, Port Zante)

The capital and major port, really the only harbour, on the E side of Zakinthos.

Pilotage

Approach From the N the SE peninsula dominated by Mount Skopos and separated by the central plain looks like an island. Closer in the hotels on Tsilivi Beach N of Ak Krioneri will be seen. The buildings and harbour of Zakinthos will not be seen until you are around Ak Krioneri. From the S the buildings of the town can be seen from some distance off.

In the approach from the S and E care is needed to avoid Ifalos Dhimitris, a reef and shoal water lying approximately 900m ESE of the harbour entrance; it is marked by a red conical buoy (Fl.R). Closer to the coast there is a group of unlit mooring buoys off the end of an oil pipeline. In the immediate approaches and the harbour itself keep an eye open for the numerous ferries coming or going to Killini.

Mooring Berth stern- or bows-to the yacht station under the N breakwater. The bottom is mud, good holding. Good shelter from the prevailing wind although sometimes a slight surge is set up. Strong southeasterlies (rare in summer) cause a considerable surge and in these conditions it is better to anchor off in the SE of the harbour leaving the ferry quay clear.

Facilities

Services Water and fuel on the quay.

Provisions Good shopping for all provisions nearby in the town.

Eating Out Numerous tavernas of all types in the town and around the square near the harbour. For a town of this size the quality of food in the tavernas is surprisingly poor.

Other PO. OTE. Banks. Hospital. Dentists. Hire cars and motorbikes. Ferry to Killini and occasional service to Katakolon. Internal and international flights.

General

Prior to 1953, that catastrophic date in this part of the Ionian, Zakinthos was one of the most beautiful cities in the Ionian, rich in Venetian architecture from the 17th and 18th centuries. It was also a centre for the arts. It produced a number of well known men of letters.

The poet Hugo Foscolo (1778–1827) was born here although he is better known in Italy as he wrote in the language of his Italian father. The best known is Dionysis Solomos (1798–1857), who like Foscolo initially wrote in Italian, but then forged demotic Greek into a vehicle for his poetry. He composed the *Hymn to Liberty* which became the Greek national anthem. Andreas Kalvos (1792–1863) was born here, but lived most of his life in England with his English wife, though his remains were later shipped back to be buried on Zakinthos. These are only the best known of a whole panoply of writers that marked Zakinthos out as the cultural capital of this part of the world – it can even be seen in the locally produced guide book which instead of snatching likely looking words from a dictionary to enthuse about beaches and hotels, by contrast with others is well written with a solid chunk of text on the arts, past and present.

After the earthquake the city elders decided not to clear away the rubble and build a totally modern city, but to rebuild the old city as best

APPROACHES TO LIMIN ZAKINTHOS

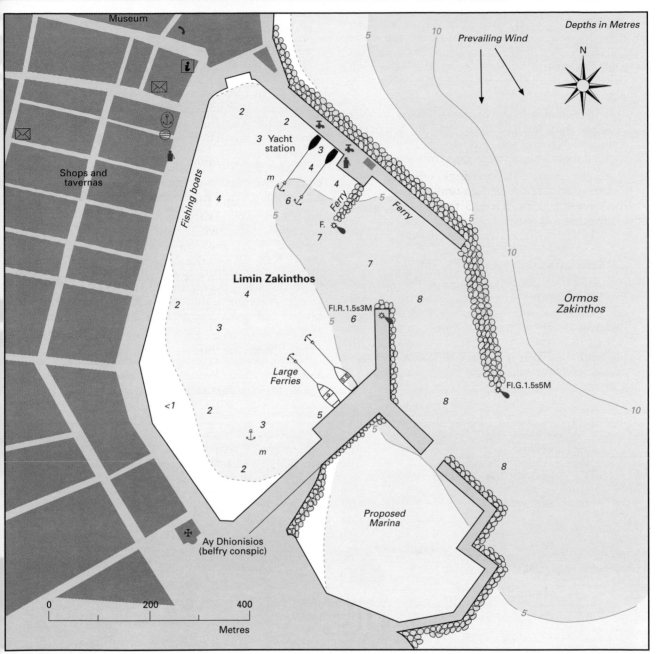

LIMIN ZAKINTHOS

they could. Some would say they failed utterly with the project, but for me the new city at least gives glimpses of the old. The streets parallel to the waterfront are in the arcaded style for which it was previously known. Some of the landmarks such as the church of Ay Dionissiou which survived the earthquake at the W end of the harbour and the buildings around the town square are in the old style, but perhaps because too many obviously modern buildings intrude or perhaps because the reinforced concrete used in the reconstruction does not weather like old Venetian mortar and plaster, the city needs years yet to mellow and acquire a distinct character of its own.

There are several interesting museums in the town should you need to enquire into the past of the town and island.

Zakinthos Museum Situated in Solomos Square right by the harbour, it houses an impressive collection of church art, especially Byzantine and post-Byzantine icons rescued after the earthquake, as well as other items relating to the island.

Solomos Museum In Ay Markou square just N of Solomos Square. Contains exhibits relating to Solomos, Kalvos, and Foscolo, as well as other writers, painters and musicians from the island.

Resistance Museum Situated in the library in Solomos Square, it contains exhibits relating to the resistance in the Second World War as well as exhibits on folklore.

Zakinthos Marina

A marina is under construction on the outside of the S breakwater. For a good number of years now work has not proceeded after the initial building of the basin and it is next to impossible to discover when work will start again. At the moment the basin is not really usable and most yachts go onto the yacht quay in the main harbour.

Ormos Ay Nikolaos
(Korynth)

A bay on the E side of the N tip of Zakinthos. Nisis Ay Nikolaos lies in the entrance to the bay and a yacht can pass on either side of it though care needs to be taken of the N entrance where a reef extends out from the islet and from the N entrance point. There are good depths in the fairway.

Anchor in 5–15m where convenient or go bows-to the outside of the short breakwater with a long line to it. The depths drop off quickly in the bay so ensure you let enough scope out. Keep well clear of the ferry berth and the area where it manoeuvres. The berths inside the short stone breakwater are for the local *caiques*. There is a wooden quay in front of one of the tavernas with room for a few yachts in 2m depths. There are severe gusts into the bay with the afternoon breeze and most yachts stop here just for the morning calm and then proceed on to Limin Zakinthos for the night.

Ashore several tavernas open in the summer. The ferry from Pessades on Cephalonia runs across to here in the summer. Local boats run

Limin Zakinthos looking down from the slopes to the north

Photo *Neville Bulpitt*

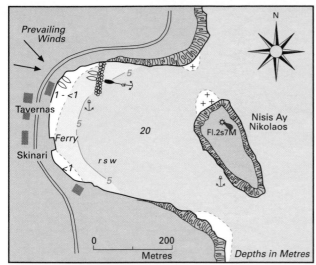

ORMOS AY NIKOLAOS

trips to the local 'Blue Grotto' on Ak Skinari which is said (don't they always) to rival that on Capri. It would be best to make the trip in the morning before the afternoon breeze sets in.

Porto Roma

A beautiful anchorage under Ak Vasilikos suitable in calm weather. Taverna on the beach and others a short walk away.

Boating restrictions in Kolpos Lagana

Reproduced below is the recent advice note from the Greek authorities restricting navigation and mooring in Kolpos Lagana. I have reproduced the advice note and zones rather than my interpretation of it so there can be no doubt regarding the wording and advice given.

Boating restrictions in the Bay of Laganas

The Bay of Laganas on Zakythnos is the most important nesting area for the loggerhead sea turtle (*Caretta caretta*) in the Mediterranean. Apart from specific legislation (Presidential Decree of 5/7/90, Government Gazette 347/D) that has been enacted to protect the nesting beaches and a broader surrounding area, the Coast Guard of Zakythnos has issued two Local Port Regulations (Ref. Num. 19/91 and 20/94 Government Gazettes 585/B/91 & 591/B/94). According to these, the Bay is divided into three

zones, in which the following laws are effective from 1 May through to 31 October each year.

Maritime Zone A: It is forbidden for any boat vessel to enter or moor within this zone. Fishing with any kind of fishing gear is prohibited.

Maritime Zone B: It is forbidden for any boat or vessel to travel at a speed greater than 6 knots, and to moor or anchor within this zone.

Maritime Zone C: It is forbidden for any boat or vessel to travel at a speed greater than 6 knots, within this zone.

The protection of sea turtles is the responsibility of us all!

Help us to ensure the effectiveness of the protective measures!

What this effectively means is that Yerakas, Ormos Lagana and Lithakia cannot be used from 1 of May to 31 October. Yachts should observe the restrictions diligently as there have been a number of fines (around £200) for infringements of the regulations.

Now the sea area is effectively policed it is to be hoped that the beach development will be policed as well so the turtles get a chance to breed safely without interference from the lager louts and their like who tend to inhabit parts of this resort area.

I have left the plan and notes on the anchorages in this restricted area intact in this edition in case any yachts want to go there out of the restricted times between May and the end of October. Even outside of the restricted period yachts should exercise caution and it may be prudent to enquire with the authorities at Limin Zakinthos on the legality of navigating and anchoring in these zones outside the time limits given.

Ak Yerakas

On the W side of the cape there is a large bay suitable in calm weather. The entrance is fringed by reefs on both sides, so every care is needed when threading a way through them. Entry should be made on approximately 040° towards the beach. Anchor off the beach where convenient. Reasonably good protection from the prevailing wind.

Ashore there are several tavernas. The beach is a turtle breeding area and the restrictions above should be stringently heeded.

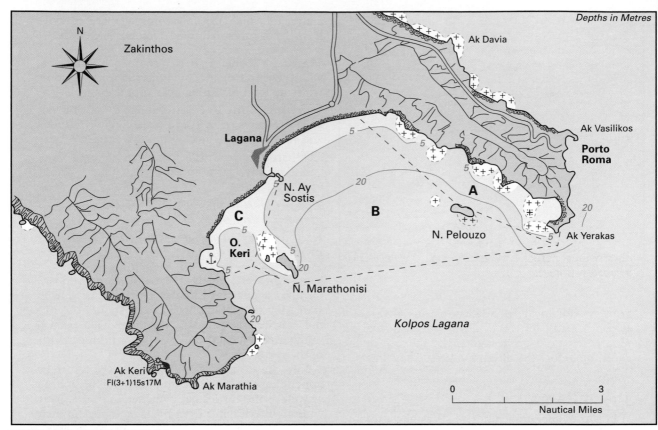

ZAKINTHOS: KOLPOS LAGANA
For restricted areas A,B,C see text.

Ormos Lagana

The wide bay fringed by a long sandy beach on the N side of Kolpos Lagana. In settled weather a yacht can anchor off here. The sandy bottom shelves gently to the shore. Numerous tavernas and most provisions can be obtained in Lagana village. The restrictions above should be stringently heeded.

The area has been much developed for tourism with hotels along the beach and tavernas, bars and discos to service the large numbers that arrive here in the summer. Lagana village/resort has little to recommend it and has little to do with things Greek on Zakinthos. The small village has expanded into an unwieldy resort lined with bars and souvenir shops that resounds to the monotonous beat of disco music and the equally monotonous chatter of those listening to it.

One of the casualties of the development along the beach has been the loggerhead turtle, *Caretta caretta*, which comes ashore in June to lay its eggs.

Unfortunately the same thing that draws turtles here, the fine white sand in which they dig a nest to lay their eggs, is the same stuff that attracts tourists. The turtles are scared off by loud noise from the discos and bright lights in the hotels and tavernas. The egg nests themselves can be damaged by people digging in the sand. And worst of all the young turtles which hatch on a night of the full moon can lose their direction when distracted by bright lights. Instead of heading for the light of the moon over the water they head for the bright lights of hotels and tavernas and consequently never make it to the water.

If you are swimming around and you come across a lot of jellyfish, then reflect on the fact that the loggerhead eats large numbers of jellyfish and the decline in numbers, they are currently half what they were in 1973, may be responsible for the rise in the number of jellyfish in the Mediterranean. Thankfully access to the beach is now prohibited at night, but there is still much to be done. In the summer a Turtle Information Centre operates on the beach and organises volunteers to guard the nests and the turtles. You can contribute by getting in touch with the Sea Turtle Protection Society of Greece, PO Box 511, 54 Kifissia, 14510 Greece.

Lithakia

At the W end of Lagana beach a small headland juts out towards a small islet, Nisis Ay Sostis. A small *caique* harbour has been built on the E side of the headland. There are 1·5–3m depths in the harbour, but even a small yacht will have problems finding a berth amongst the local boats. Care is needed of long mooring lines stretching underwater across the harbour. Tavernas and discos on the beach nearby.

Ormos Keri

(Kieri)

A large bay lying under Nisis Marathonisi, the island lying on the W side of Kolpos Lagana. A yacht should pass outside the island as above-water rocks and a reef partially connect it to Zakinthos. On the W side of Ormos Keri there is a cove, Port Keri, where there is reasonable shelter from the prevailing wind. The restrictions above on speed limits should be stringently heeded.

Anchor in 2–8m on either side of the rough stone mole. The mole has underwater ballasting extending out from it in most places, but it is possible to anchor and take a long line to the outside of it. The bottom is mud and weed, good holding once through the weed. Mini-markets ashore and numerous tavernas.

In ancient times Keri was famous for its pitch wells mentioned by no less an authority than Herodotus:

'There are a number of lakes – or ponds – in Zacynthus, of which the largest measures seventy feet each way and has a depth of two fathoms. The process is to tie a branch of myrtle on to the end of a pole, which is then thrust down to the bottom of this pond; the pitch sticks to the myrtle, and is thus brought to the surface. It smells like bitumen, but in all other respects it is better than the pitch of Piera.'

The Histories Book IV

Today there is a concrete pool by the quay though this is claimed not to be pitch. In a marshy lake nearby you can go and poke a pole into the

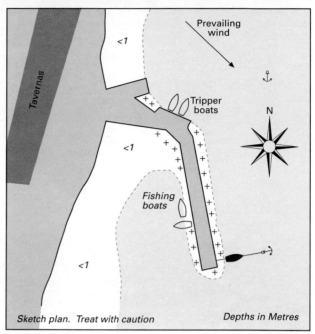

Sketch plan. Treat with caution
Depths in Metres
ORMOS KERI

bottom after the method described by Herodotus. The pitch used to be much in demand for caulking boats, but I suppose modern synthetic alternatives have all but usurped the old-fashioned product. In recent years visitors have claimed there is more oil on the beach from the large numbers of inflatables here in the summer than there is in the lake.

Ormos Vroma

(Port Vromi)

An inlet close to the NW corner of Zakinthos under the islet of Nisis Ay Ioannis. It is difficult to make out the location of the inlet until close to it. It affords reasonable shelter from the prevailing wind but can be untenable in southerlies. Anchor and take a line ashore on the N side on the dogleg of the inlet. There can be a katabatic wind off the mountains at night.

A road has been cut down to it and its remote and savage charm has thus evaporated. A taverna and mobile canteen. Tripper boats visit on their route around the island.

In a bay just N of Vromi is a beautiful white sandy beach with the wreck of a coaster half-covered by sand that is much featured in the publicity photos of the Greek Tourist Organisation.

4. The mainland coast from Levkas to Nisis Oxia and adjacent islands

	Shelter	Mooring	Fuel	Water	Provisions	Tavernas	Plan
Vathi Vali	B	C	O	O	O	O	
Palairos (Zaverda)	A	A	B	A	B	B	•
Vounaki Marina	A	A	A	A	C	C	•
Mitika	C	AC	B	B	B	C	•
Kalamos							
Port Kalamos	B	A	O	B	C	C	•
Port Leone	B	AC	O	O	O	O	•
Episkopi	B	AB	O	O	O	O	•
Ak Aspro Yiali	O	C	O	O	O	O	
Kastos							
Port Kastos	B	AC	O	B	C	C	•
Anchorages around							
Kastos	BC	C	O	O	O	O	
Dhragonera and Echinades							
Ormos Aspro Yiali	C	C	O	O	O	O	
Port Marathia	B	C	O	O	O	O	
Boulder Bay	C	C	O	O	O	O	
Astakos	B	A	B	A	B	B	•
Port Pandelimon	A	C	O	O	O	O	•
Plati Yialos	B	C	O	O	O	O	•
Nisis Petalas	B	C	O	O	O	O	•
Ormos Oxia	O	C	O	O	O	O	
Ormos Skrofa	C	C	O	O	O	O	
Nisis Oxia	O	C	O	O	O	O	

Like the mainland coast to the N this is a remote and lost area, even more so than the area N of it. From Levkas the coast rises abruptly to high mountains, the Akarnanika Oroi some 1590m (5167ft) high, which drop sheer into the sea. The mountains are mostly barren and rocky, little vegetation escapes the browsing of sheep and goats, and are cut by deep gorges and gullies that become torrents with the winter rain. Further S, below the agricultural town of Astakos, the coast flattens out around a huge river delta from the Akheloos, the longest river in Greece, to marshland and lagoons. This combination of inhospitable terrain, the precipitous mountains and swamp land, made it difficult to settle and even more difficult to control, so it is not surprising that it was little colonised by anyone over the ages.

Near Neokhorion in the middle of the marshland are the ruins of ancient Oiniadai, established sometime in the 6th century BC. At the time it was probably built on the coast, but the silting of two and half thousand years has locked it into the middle of this water land. It is the only major ancient site. This area has always been the domain of the dispossessed and of hardy farmers and fishermen. It is little changed to this day and despite a number of new roads winding up and over the mountains or across barrages in the swamp land, retains a feeling of isolation and supports only small communities who can put up with the rigours of life here. Even the two major islands off the coast, Kalamos and Kastos, are rugged places with small populations, though swelled by numbers of noisy campers in noisy inflatables in July and August.

Opposite: The anchorage under Nisis Petalas looking out from the cave Photo *Nigel Patten*

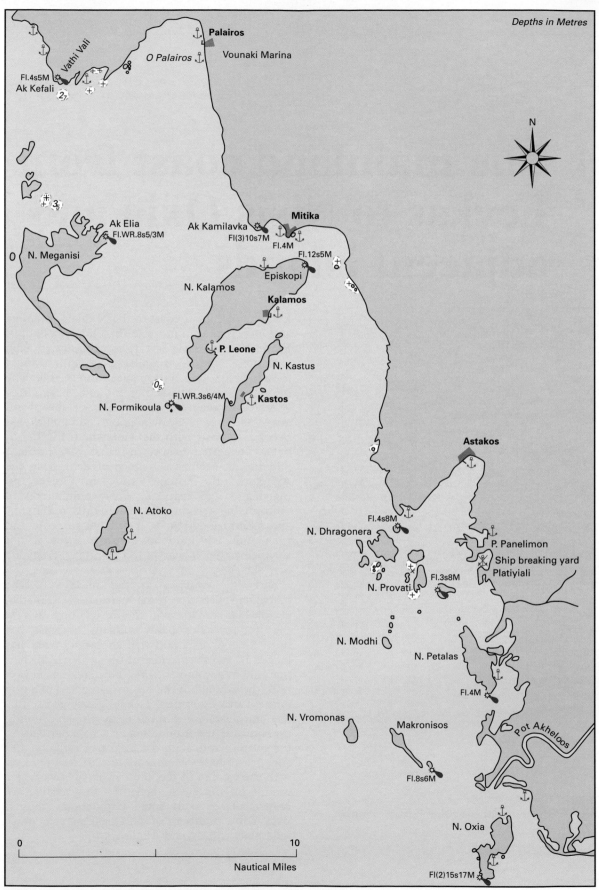

Depths in Metres

Palairos

O Palairos

Vounaki Marina

Vathi Vali

Fl.4s5M
Ak Kefali

2₇

3₅

Ak Elia
Fl.WR.8s5/3M

N. Meganisi

Ak Kamilavka
Fl(3)10s7M

Mitika

Fl.4M

Fl.12s5M

Episkopi

N. Kalamos

Kalamos

P. Leone

N. Kastus

0₅

Fl.WR.3s6/4M
N. Formikoula

Kastos

Astakos

N. Atoko

Fl.4s8M

N. Dhragonera

P. Panelimon

Ship breaking yard
Platiyiali

N. Provati

Fl.3s8M

N. Modhi

N. Petalas

Fl.4M

N. Vromonas

Makronisos

Pot Akheloos

Fl.8s6M

N. Oxia

Fl(2)15s17M

0   10

Nautical Miles

THE MAINLAND COAST AND ADJACENT ISLANDS (Levkas to Nisis Oxia)

Palairos. Mending the nets   Photo *Graham Sewell*

Levkas Canal to Palairos

On the coast from the S end of the Levkas canal to Ak Kefali there are a number of attractive coves that can be used depending on the wind and sea. With light northwesterlies blowing out of Ormos Dhrepanou there are several coves affording adequate shelter, but with strong northwesterlies they become untenable. Care needs to be taken of the isolated reef (2·7m least depth) lying approximately ½M SSE of the light structure on Ak Kefali.

Vathi Vali

This inlet immediately E of Ak Kefali is now mostly obstructed by a fish farm and although you can still anchor in here, the ambience of the place is dented by the ramshackle fish farm.

In the large bay next to Vathi Vali there are several coves in attractive surroundings that are suitable in light northwesterlies. Anchor where convenient. Care needs to be taken of the reef and islet (Ay Nikolaos) off the entrance.

On the W side of Ormos Palairou just around the corner are Nisidhi Pogonia, a group of islets lying close off the coast. In calm weather there is an attractive anchorage tucked in immediately N of them.

Palairos
(Zaverda)

A village and small harbour sitting under the high mountains in the NE of Ormos Palairos.

Pilotage

Approach Once into Ormos Palairos the buildings of the village straggling up the hillside are easily identified although haze may sometimes reduce visibility to 3M or so. The entrance to the

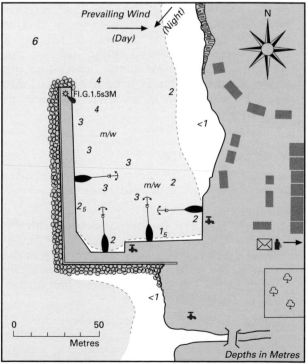

PALAIROS (ZAVERDA)

harbour is straightforward although do not stray too close to the coast where there is a shoal bank.

Mooring Berth stern- or bows-to the mole on the W or bows-to the S mole or the quay on the E. The harbour is used as a base by a charter company and at times can be crowded with yachts on a turn-around. The bottom is mud and good holding. Good shelter from the prevailing breeze although a katabatic wind may blow down off the mountains from the NE at night making it uncomfortable for a few hours.

Facilities

Services Water on the quay. Fuel in the town.

Provisions Good shopping for provisions in the village.

Eating out Several tavernas near the harbour. The *Old Mill* restaurant run by the effervescent Kitty is now located in the village and not at the top of the hill – the food is still good although the location is not quite as pleasing.

Other PO. OTE. Taxis. Infrequent bus to Vonitsa.

General

Like Mitika and Astakos further down the coast, the village here has mostly concerned itself with the farming population in the area, only recently have yachts and its adoption by a charter company turned it to the sea. It remains a predominantly agricultural village and one can see the local inhabitants metaphorically scratching their heads in bewilderment at these foreigners paying lots of money to go sailing on the sea.

Vounaki Marina

A small marina, the home of *Sunsail* charter boats, situated just south of Palairos.

Pilotage

Approach The hotel complex associated with the marina is easily identified south of Palairos. Make the final approach to the marina from the west as the dinghy mooring area immediately north of the entrance is shallow. The marina listens out on VHF Ch 10.

Mooring Berth where directed. There are laid moorings tailed to the quay. Good shelter inside although strong westerlies might cause some bother. The first night here is free.

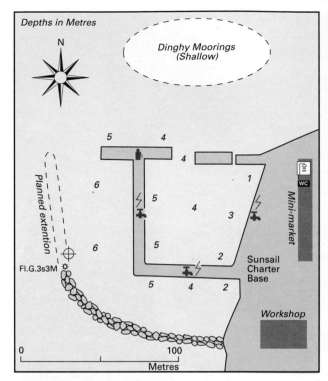

VOUNAKI MARINA

Facilities

Services Water and electricity at every berth. Shower and toilet block. Fuel on the T-pier.

Provisions Mini-market. Palairos is not too far away with better shopping.

Eating out Taverna ashore. Other tavernas in Palairos.

General

Vounaki is a major *Sunsail* charter base and the hotel is used as a Sunsail Club for shore-based holidaymakers. Visitors are free to use the marina facilities, taverna and shops, but cannot use the hotel facilities which are for *Sunsail* clients.

Mitika

(Mytikas)

An agricultural village and now a small ferry port for the islands in the Inland sea.

Pilotage

Approach The buildings of the village are not easily seen until you are into Ormos Mitika. However Nisos Kalamos is easily identified and a yacht should simply head for the NE end.

Mooring In calm weather a yacht can anchor off the village on the W side and this is quite the most pleasant place to be. With the prevailing wind a yacht should go to the new harbour. There are mostly 2–3m depths in the outer half sloping gradually to the beach. Go stern- or bows-to the NE side taking care of the numerous floating moorings. Alternatively anchor and take a long line to the breakwater on the SW side. Good shelter.

Facilities

Services Water on the quay. Fuel is some distance out of town.

Provisions Good shopping for provisions.

Eating out Several tavernas on the waterfront.

Other PO. OTE. Local *caique* ferry to Kalamos and Kastos.

General

Like Palairos this village has traditionally been occupied with agriculture and only recently experienced a little tourism. It sits on a flat coastal plain hemmed in between mountains on either side and until the new road was built it was largely locked into itself. Now it plays host in July and August to a fleet of inflatables which occupy themselves, somewhat noisily, around Nisos Kalamos.

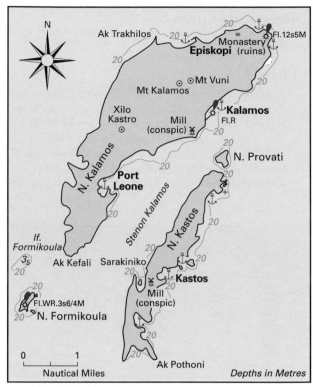

NISOI KALAMOS AND KASTOS

Nisos Kalamos

This high island looking like a colossal stranded whale off the mainland coast is easily identified from afar. It rises up from the tail in the SW to 750m (2438ft) at Oros Vouni near the NE end. The slopes drop mostly sheer into the sea and are covered sparsely in *maquis* at the S end, but surprisingly are thickly covered in pine at the N end. The name is said to be derived from the reeds (*kalami*) which used to grow here, but to anyone who has been to the island this is baffling as it has none of the marshy ground that reeds need. It may be that the name was transferred from the area around Mitika where there is swampy ground. Perhaps the inhabitants of the mainland were forced to flee to the island from pirates or invaders from the N. Now the process has reversed itself and the villages on the island are dying places and in the case of Port Leone (Kefali) in the S, entirely deserted.

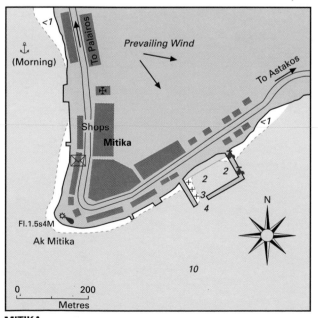

MITIKA

Port Kalamos

The small village that serves as the island capital on the E side.

Pilotage

Approach Proceeding up Stenon Kalamou between Kastos and Kalamos, several mills on a short spit, including one on a rocky bluff by the sea, will be seen. Closer in the village and small harbour are easily identified. From the N the village will only be seen once you are around the N end of the island.

Mooring Berth stern- or bows-to on the breakwater wherever there is room. The bottom is mud, sand and weed, mostly good holding. Although the small harbour is popular at the height of summer you can usually find somewhere to berth. In a pinch anchor off on the W side of the harbour and take a long line ashore to the beach.

Facilities

Two tavernas open in the summer, but don't expect lightning fast service – after all, as the old lady in one of them explained, 'it's difficult to

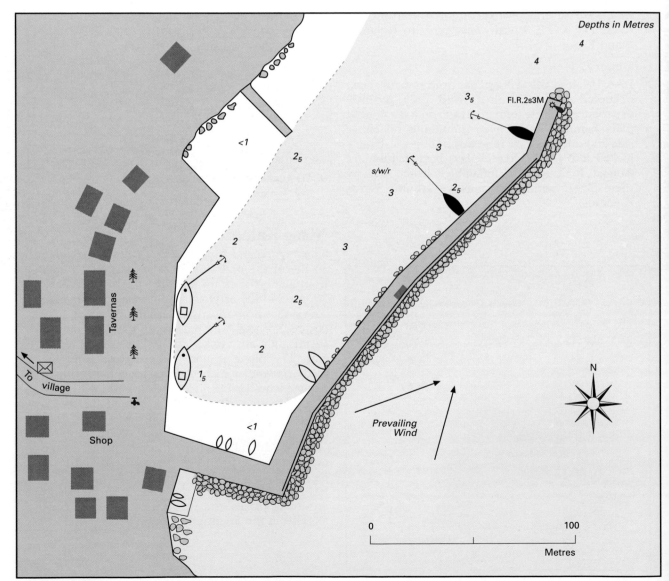

PORT KALAMOS

One of the last trading *caiques* in Kalamos harbour

cook and add up the bill as well'. Small grocery shop and a bakery in the village. PO.

General

The small village is a wonderful place that somehow handles its summer visitors entirely on its own terms. One of the last trading *caiques* in the Ionian still putters across from the mainland to supply the island. But the population is decidedly skewed to the older age group and I fear for the survival of villages like this except as some sort of summer resort. Recently I watched a funeral procession here and of the forty or so mourners, there were only a couple under late middle-age and the bulk of them were sixty or older. The young leave for the fleshpots of Athens and once there, few return to the simple life on the island.

Port Leone

(Kefali)

A large deep bay on the S of the island. The entrance is difficult to see from the S, but if you head for the general vicinity of the bay it is difficult to miss. From the N two old mills will be seen on the E side of the entrance and closer in the houses and the church of the deserted village.

The bay is very deep and you will have to anchor in 10–20m of water. A few yachts can go bows-to the short stone jetties with a long line ashore. The bottom is sand, mud and weed, good holding. Good shelter in here although gusts may occasionally swirl down off the high slopes.

The village was deserted after the 1953 earthquake which destroyed the water supply. The inhabitants decided not to rebuild the village,

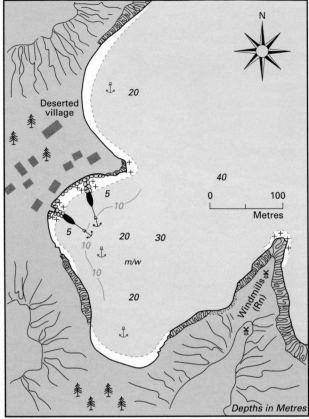

PORT LEONE

Port Leone and the village deserted after the 1953 earthquake

but moved to the mainland or migrated. The village church is still in good repair and every Sunday a few villagers come from Kalamos village to clean it, renew the oil in the lamps and put fresh flowers on the altar. The village, the ruined houses, the abandoned olive press, the cisterns now empty, the church still cared for, all contribute to a poignancy that cuts through the crackle of cicadas and rustling wind.

Episkopi

A small village and harbour on the N side of Nisos Kalamos. The houses of the small village can be seen and also a ruined monastery further E of the village. Closer in the miniature harbour will be seen. It is suitable only for small yachts drawing 1½m or less. The entrance is hairy with the afternoon wind and you will need to have everything ready before you enter.

Go alongside the rough quay taking care of the rocks protruding underwater or go bows-to. The bottom is mud and thick weed, mediocre holding. Good shelter. There is room in here for only a couple of yachts. The ferry berth is used only intermittently, but yachts would probably have to move out to let it in.

The village no longer really functions as such anymore, but is used as a summer residence by most of the families or their relatives. A few families live here all year round. There is a very small general shop that never seems to be open, but that is all. No tavernas, no shops, just cicadas and neglected olive groves. From the village there is a pleasant walk along the little-used road to the ruined fortified monastery with wonderful views over the strait to the mainland.

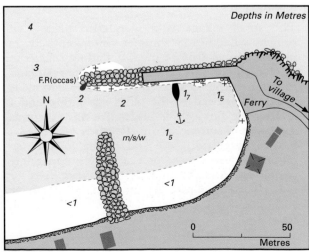

EPISKOPI

Ak Aspro Yiali

Around the cape on the N end of the island there are several anchorages protected from the prevailing winds. It is mostly quite deep here. In July and August campers with inflatables base themselves here creating noise pollution, littering the area with rubbish, and defiling the cemetery though it clearly has a notice up saying No Camping. I can understand why they flock here: the water is a wonderful turquoise and cobalt, the rocks and cliffs are eroded into fantastic shapes, and the whole area is thick with green pine providing cool shade.

Nisis Kastos

The scraggly sister island lying parallel to Kalamos. Although it is nearly as long as its neighbour, it is thinner and lower. The only village on the island is Kastos on the E side, but there are a number of anchorages that can be used in the summer.

Port Kastos

Pilotage

Approach From the S the exact location of the village and harbour is difficult to make out until you are close to it. A mill on the S side of the village and the harbour will be seen before the village and tiny harbour. From the N the islet of Prasonisi is easily identified and closer in the houses of the village, a mill on a ridge above the village and another on the S side will be seen.

Mooring Go bows-to off the short mole if there is room. Alternatively anchor in the bay although this can be a bit rolly from the ground swell that works its way around. With care you can anchor off the beach with a long line ashore or a kedge out the back where you escape the worst of the ground swell. The bottom is mud and weed, good holding once through the weed. Good shelter from the prevailing winds.

Kastos harbour

Facilities

Two tavernas, one by the harbour and another on the opposite side where it is best to row your dinghy across and climb up the steps rather than walk around. The latter has wonderful views from the balcony. Very limited provisions from a wonderful small village shop.

General

The small village is a charmer. It has only recently come back to life after the villagers were evacuated in 1976 because of a suspected typhoid outbreak – so don't drink the water. The inner harbour shelters a few fishing boats and the adjacent square has a few trees for shade so the fishermen can sit around talking about the fishing and the visitors while they mend their nets. Outside the village the land shimmers in the heat and there are only a few olive groves and a lot of prickly pear cacti.

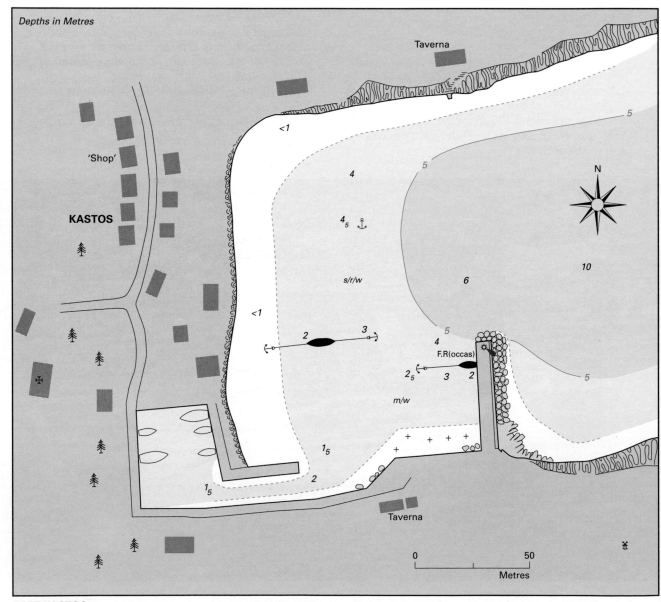

PORT KASTOS

Anchorages around Nisis Kastos

Port Sarakiniko A bay on the W side of the island directly opposite the village. It is suitable only in calm weather as the prevailing wind pushes a swell in and at night a strong katabatic wind may blow down off the mainland coast straight into it. In calm weather it makes a wonderful lunch stop.

South Bay On the S tip of the island there is a bay that also provides an attractive early lunch stop. By afternoon the prevailing breeze pushes a sizeable swell into it.

Southeast Bay On the E coast near the S end of the island there is a deep bay suitable for an overnight stay in settled conditions. It is quite deep so you will be anchoring in 10–20m.

Prasonisi Cove The cove opposite Nisis Prasonisi affords reasonable shelter in settled weather and some yachts spend the night here. Some ground swell works its way in, but it is more uncomfortable than dangerous.

Northeast Coves On the E coast at the N end of the island there are several coves that make attractive lunch stops in settled weather.

Nisis Atoko

This large lump of an island sits almost in the middle of the Inland sea. It is easily identified from some distance off because of its height (303m/985ft) and because it sits by itself away from the other islands. It has two anchorages that can be used in settled weather.

Cliff Bay At the S end there is a wide double-ended bay suitable in calm weather or light westerlies. With strong westerlies a swell penetrates. It is everywhere very deep and you will have to anchor in 10–15m at either end. The steep cliffs and rocky pinnacles provide an imposing backdrop, fine for a lunch stop in calm weather but, I imagine, threatening in bad weather.

One House Bay On the SE side there is a bay providing reasonable shelter with the prevailing westerlies. Anchor in 5–12m on sand, good holding. In settled weather yachts stay overnight here although a katabatic wind off the mainland coast may push some swell in at night.

The anchorage is a wonderful place with high cliffs and huge eroded rocks on the S side and a fine beach at the head of the bay. A single house

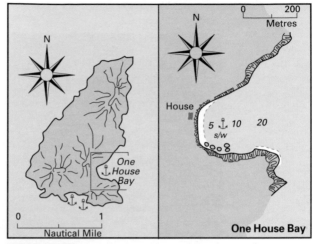

NISOS ATOKO

stands on the shore used occasionally by a fisherman and his family.

Nisoi Dhragonera and Echinades

This group of islands and islets scattered down the coast nearly to the entrance of the Gulf of Patras (Patraikos Kolpos) hide the low mainland coast and call for some attentive eyeball navigation to get you safely through them. They are all uninhabited and there are few safe anchorages in the islands – though luckily there are several down the adjacent mainland coast. The name echinades means sea urchin and in this it is accurate as these are spiky rocky islands sitting in the sea and looking just like their namesake.

Anchorages around the Dhragonera and Echinades

Nisis Dhragonera The comparatively large island lying close off Ak Tourkoviglas. On the N side there are two coves suitable in calm weather, but open to the prevailing westerlies. On the SE tip of the island there is a miniature crack of an inlet that a small yacht can use. Take a long line ashore to the W side.

Nisis Karlonisi Lies close E of Nisis Dhragonera. With care a small yacht can tuck itself into the cove lying in the narrow channel separating the island from Nisis Provati immediately S of it. Care needs to be taken of a reef running out on the W side. Take a long line ashore.

One House Bay on Atoko

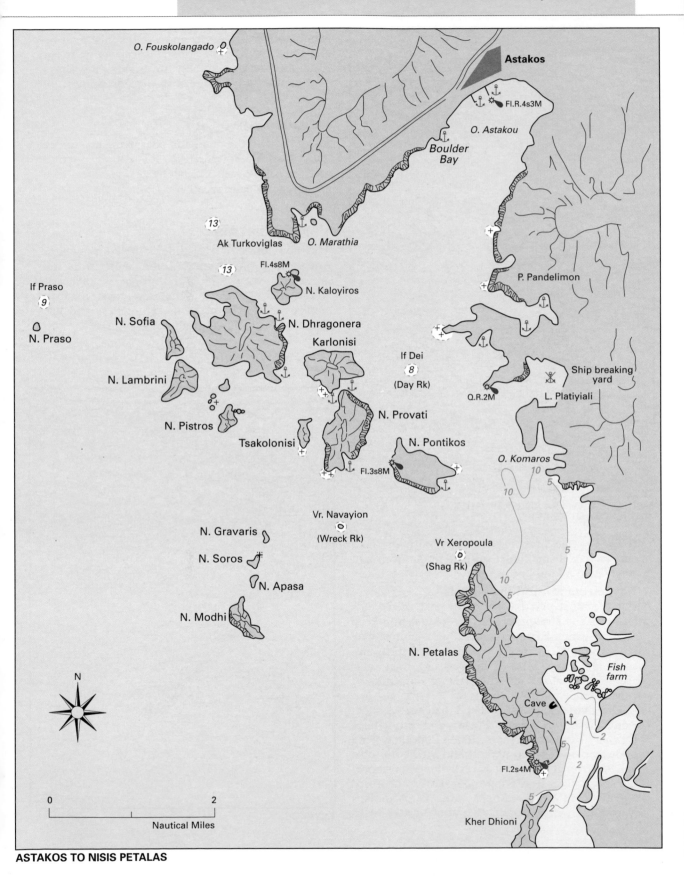

O. Fouskolangado

Astakos

Fl.R.4s3M

O. Astakou

Boulder
Bay

13

Ak Turkoviglas O. Marathia

13

Fl.4s8M

N. Kaloyiros

If Praso

9

N. Sofia

N. Dhragonera

Karlonisi

If Dei

8

(Day Rk)

P. Pandelimon

N. Praso

N. Lambrini

Ship breaking
yard

N. Pistros

Q.R.2M

L. Platiyiali

N. Provati

Tsakolonisi

N. Pontikos

O. Komaros

10

10

Fl.3s8M

5

Vr. Navayion

5

(Wreck Rk)

Vr Xeropoula

N. Gravaris

(Shag Rk)

10

N. Soros

5

N. Apasa

N. Modhi

N. Petalas

*Fish
farm*

Cave

N

Fl.2s4M

5

2

2

0   2

5

2

Nautical Miles

Kher Dhioni

ASTAKOS TO NISIS PETALAS

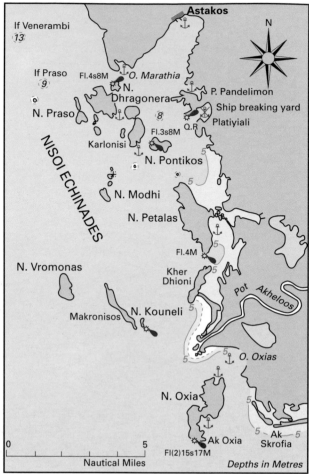

NISOI DHRAGONERA AND ECHINADES AND ADJACENT COAST

Nisis Provati Lies close S of Karlonisi. On the S end there is a small inlet suitable for an overnight stay. Take a long line ashore.

Navigating around the islands

For the most part navigation around the islands and rocks is straightforward so long as you keep tabs on which island is which by diligent eyeball navigation. Most of the islands are steep-to and easily identified. Most of the reefs and shoal water are either close to the islands or not of consequence for most yachts.

The two shallowest isolated patches of shoal water have 9m (Ifalos Praso) and 8m (Ifalos Dei/Day Rock) over them. Ifalos Pondikou lying midway between Pondikonisi and Stenigonia also has 8m over it though it is really an extension of the shoal water bordering the coast. Vrakhonisos Navayion (Wreck Rock) and Vrakhonisos Xeropoula (Shag Rock), two above-water rocks

lying S of Nisis Provati and Pondikonisi, can be identified with care. Shag Rock, as the old Admiralty name implies, invariably has shags sitting on it and is white with their droppings.

Ormos Asproyiali

A large bay on the mainland coast lying just under 2½M N of Ak Tourkoviglas. It is entirely open to the prevailing wind, but makes an attractive anchorage in calm weather.

Port Marathia

The bay immediately under Ak Tourkoviglas. Anchor in 4–6m on mud. Good shelter from the prevailing wind. The anchorage is pleasant although the traffic on the new coast road to Mitika removes some of its remoteness and has also brought campers to the bay.

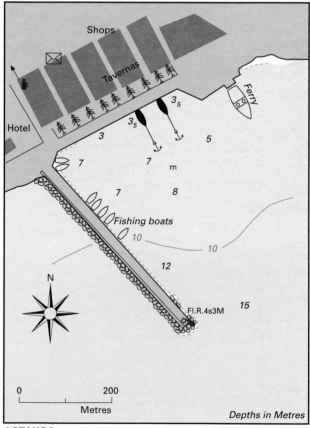

ASTAKOS

Boulder Bay

An attractive bight just under the legend 'boulder' on the old Admiralty chart 3496 (now deleted) and near the church marked Ay Yeoryios on Imray-Tetra chart 121 just under a mile SW of Astakos. With light westerlies, which tend to blow alternately from the SW and gust off the land here, it makes a good lunch stop before going on to Astakos itself. Beach ashore and pine and cypress on the slopes.

Astakos

A small agricultural town sitting on a flat coastal plain at the end of the mountains and the beginning of the low water land to the S.

Pilotage

Approach Once into Ormos Astakou the buildings of the town will be seen and closer in the breakwater is easily identified. A new low breakwater has been built to the SW of the old one, but there is no good quayed area and so it is best to go on the town quay.

Mooring Go stern- or bows-to leaving the ferry quay clear. Alternatively go on the mole as on the N quay you are obliged to move off some afternoons for the hydrofoil. The bottom is mud, good holding. Good shelter from the prevailing breeze.

Facilities

Services Water on the quay. Fuel delivered by mini-tanker.

Provisions Good shopping for provisions. A good baker behind the waterfront.

Eating out Several basic tavernas including one on the waterfront which usually has spit-roast lamb and chicken.

Other Banks. PO. OTE. Ferry to Ithaca and Cephalonia.

General

Astakos has long been locked into this remote part of Greece, cut off by the mountains and the swamp land and away from the sea-routes, it still feels a remote insular sort of place. There are only a few concessions to the Greek holiday-makers who come here in July and August and the few yachts which turn up through the summer.

Astakos

It remains very much an agricultural town dealing in shovels and hoes, fertiliser and weed-killer, baggy denim overalls rather than designer jeans. As well as the farmers it has a sizeable fishing fleet which harvests the rich waters around the Dhragonera and Echinades islands. The name of the town, *Astakos*, means lobster, but I have never seen any on offer in the tavernas or even brought ashore, though the rocky islets appear to be an ideal habitat for the rare crustacean.

The town was known as Dragomestre in the 19th century. In 1828 Richard Church made it the base for his operations during the Greek struggle against their Turkish masters. Church was one of many eccentric British Philhellenes, (Byron was only the most famous), who came to help the Greeks in one way or another. By all accounts Church was an arrogant man with a desire for pomp and power, but not a commander who led his troops from the front. In the battle for the Acropolis at Athens he and Cochrane commanded the land troops from the safety of a ship anchored off and not surprisingly the attack was a fiasco. Despite his blunders Church lived to a ripe old age in Athens in a free Greece.

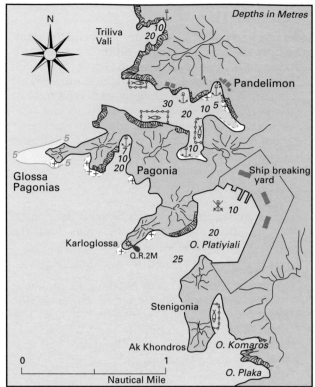

PANDELIMON AND PLATI YIALI

Port Pandelimon

(Panteleimon, Pandelemona)

A twin-headed inlet now partially obstructed by fish farms but still usable with care.

Pilotage

Approach The inlet lies 2½M almost due S of Astakos. The exact location of the entrance is difficult to make out from the distance, but is easy enough to see when closer in. Care needs to be taken of the two fish farms shown on the plan. The perimeter of the farms is marked by small plastic buoys.

Mooring Anchor in the E or S creek, the latter affords the better shelter. Recently the fish farm operator has been flashing a legal looking piece of paper in several languages at yachts coming in here, but there is some doubt over the legality of this – play it by ear. The bottom is mud and weed, good holding once through the weed, though this can take some doing. Good shelter from the prevailing wind although the E creek can be uncomfortable from the chop pushed in by the westerlies, though rarely dangerous.

General

There are no facilities here although you may be able to negotiate for a fish or two from the fish farm. Personally I am suspicious of fish reared in this artificial way. Until the fish farms were recently established there was only the small farm on the N which seems to have been abandoned. The anchorage still has a remote feel to it despite the muffled sounds of heavy machinery at Platiyialos and the debris of the fish farms littering the rocky slopes.

Note

The fish farms are moved around the bay from time to time, mostly I suspect because of the toxins and debris which build up on the sea bottom after a period and aggravate diseases in the fish. Consequently the position of the buoyed-off areas will vary and I have not moved the positions of the farms in the plans because they may well be situated back in the original positions by the time this is printed. Prudence is needed wherever fish farms are located as their exact locations in a bay will change from time to time.

Glossa Pogonias

The tongue of land separating Pandelimon and Platiyialos. Care needs to be taken of the reef and shoal water running out from the tip of it. On the S side of the tongue there is a pleasant bay sheltered from the prevailing wind. Anchor in 7–10m and take a long line to the W side.

Platiyialos

(Plateali)

The large bay lying immediately S of Pandelimon. For some time now a massive project has been underway to make it a ship-breaking yard. Huge concrete aprons slope into the water and there are quays and piers right around the bay. The amount of concrete used to ring this large bay with quays, aprons and hard-standing is difficult to comprehend. Effectively it has demolished any charm the bay had and in any case it will be likely that berthing will be prohibited – should you for some inconceivable reason wish to stop here.

Recently there were rumours that part of the facility would be used for processing chemical waste products, a price demanded by the EU countries for Greece's admission to the club, but to my eyes the facility looks designed for ship-breaking only. Should anyone sailing around the area hear or see anything that hints of chemical waste, I suggest you get in touch with Greenpeace or someone similar. The area is too beautiful in its own remote way to be stained by anything more than rusty hulks.

Ormos Komaros

A small inlet immediately S of Platiyiali that is now so obstructed by a fish farm that it is virtually unusable.

Nisis Petalas

The large, quite high island (250m/815ft) lying close off the coast 2½M S of Platiyialos. It is connected to the swampy coast by several lower islets and shallow water which is walled off by the reed fences of a large fishery.

A yacht can find a solitary anchorage around the S tip (Ak Aspro) tucked under the E side of the island. The bottom slopes very gradually up so you can putter in slowly and anchor in 1·75–2·5m. The bottom is mud and thick weed, good holding once through the weed. Shelter from the prevailing wind is good and the anchorage is useful in strong southerlies when you can anchor at the S end of the bay under Khersonisos Dhioni.

There are no facilities nearby and nor should there be. On the slopes of Petalas there is a large cave. On one visit with an ornithologist friend we spied a huge bird sitting outside the cave at dusk. From a pinion feather retrieved from the cave he later identified it as a tufted vulture with an estimated wing span of around eight feet. They are shy birds, much reduced in numbers since some of the remote places have been opened up, and it is unlikely you will see one except in early spring or late autumn.

Ormos Dhioni

Around the S end of Khersonisos Dhioni a yacht can find some shelter from moderate westerlies tucked under the peninsula. Shelter is better at Petalas.

Potamos Akheloos

The river Akheloos (Acheloos or Aspropotamos) empties into the sea just over 3M S of Ak Aspro on Nisis Petalas. The exact mouth of the river is difficult to identify precisely being surrounded by sandbanks and low islets. The whole area around the delta is low-lying and for over a mile off the mouth the sea is shallow and obstructed by banks just under the water.

The shoal water off the mouth appears to extend for a greater distance than charted with a considerable area of 2–3m depths. Anyone proceeding past the river mouth should keep a prudent distance off or he might, like me on the last occasion I lazily cut the corner full of confidence that I knew these waters well, suddenly find shallow water all around and have to thread a passage out with an adrenaline overload. It is very easy to keep cutting across if taking the inside passage around Nisis Oxia and the only thing to do is make an acute dogleg right around the river mouth taking transits on Nisoi Vromonas, Makronisos, Kounelli, and Oxia. Keeping the N end of Vromonas and the S end of Makronisos in line as shown on the old Admiralty chart 3496 still leads clear of the shoals, though the limit of the shoals is not correct and today they extend further than shown.

The Akheloos is the longest river in Greece, starting in the Pindus and winding its way to the sea here for 135M. It is now dammed for hydroelectric power and its waters diverted for irrigation. Like most river deltas it is rich in fish and there are invariably *caiques* fishing off it.

Ormos Oxia

The wide bay N of Nisis Oxia and under the sandy delta of the Akheloos. It offers indifferent shelter from the prevailing wind but may be useful in an emergency.

In 1823 this remote place was visited, though accidentally, by Byron en route to his appointment with fever and death at Mesolongion. He had left Cephalonia in a small fast ship in company with a larger one for the baggage and equipment, both local boats and therefore sailing under the neutral Ionian flag. In the night the two ships lost contact and in the dawn found they were close to another ship, a Turkish brig. The skipper decided to run into Ormos Skrofa and anchor to escape from the Turk. At some point he decided the anchorage was unsafe and fled N to Astakos. Three days later three ships sent by Mavrocordato found him and escorted the small boat and its occupants to Mesolongion, though not without incident as David Howarth records in his excellent *The Greek Adventure*.

'The passengers in this boat were a landlubberly lot, except perhaps Tita the gondolier, and the crew seem not to have been much better. Fletcher the valet had caught a cold and had to lie down on the only mattress on board, Dr Bruno was prone to wring his hands and weep at any threat of disaster, and Loukas could not swim. Byron himself liked boats, but had never learned much about them. And as they returned through the Oxia channel, the boat missed stays and ran aground in a squall. Two thirds of the crew climbed out on the bowsprit and jumped ashore, Byron told Loukas he would save him, and Dr Bruno stripped to his flannel waistcoat and running about like a rat (it was Byron's description) shouted 'Save him indeed! By God, save me rather – I'll be the first if I can.' Thereupon, after striking twice, the boat blew off again. The crew was removed from the rocks by one of the escort ships, and that evening, without any more alarms, Byron reached the entrance to Missalonghi.'

Ormos Skrofa

Under Ormos Koutsilapis, the high land enclosed by the river delta E of Nisis Oxia, there is a small bay with Nisis Skrofa in the entrance. It is used by local fishing boats, but offers only indifferent shelter from strong westerlies. With gales from the W or S the boats are run up on the beach, so it is best avoided by yachts.

Immediately S of Ormos Skrofa work is in progress reclaiming land and constructing a huge rock barrage. Running out from the reclamation work is Ifalos Skrofa, a huge shoal patch extending up to a mile off the coast. Like the shoal water off the mouth of the Akheloos, it is prudent to keep well off and take a dogleg course around the shoal water.

Nisis Oxia

The high island lying off the N side of the entrance to the Gulf of Patras (Patraikos Kolpos). There are only two indifferent anchorages.

North Bay The bay at the N end of the island. Unfortunately it is now occupied by a fish farm and effectively unusable. A shame as it was a spectacular anchorage in a beautiful remote location.

East Bay On the E side at the narrowest part of the island there is a bay affording reasonable shelter from moderate westerlies. Again it is very deep and you will have to anchor in 15–20m with a long line ashore. Joe Charlton from Levkas recommends a trek up to the ridge and along it to the highest point on the island, an expedition he assures me is not as tough as it looks, though that may be by his fairly tough standards an exercise in survival for others.

The island itself is impossible to mistake once seen. The craggy razor-ridged island is just the sort of sentinel you would expect to find at the entrance to a gulf. I imagine the lighthouse keeper on Ak Oxia at the S end has a lonely job and must be cheered to see the new aquatic travellers mad enough to go to sea for pleasure – I know on several windswept trips around the cape that he has emerged to give me a wave and little things like that do a lot for your spirits.

Appendix

I. GLOSSARY

Common Greek terms and abbreviations used in the text and plans

Akra (Ak)	Cape
Andi (Anti)	Opposite
Ayios (Ay)	Saint
Dhiavlos	Strait or channel
Dhiorix	Channel or canal
Dhromos	Roadstead
Faros	Lighthouse
Ifalos (If or I)	Reef
Isthmos	Isthmus
Kavos	Cape
Khersonisos	Headland
Kolpos	Gulf
Limin (L)	Harbour
Molos	Breakwater or mole
Moni	Monastery
Nisaki	Islet
Nisos/Nisi/Nisia (N)	Island(s)
Notios	Southern
Ormos (O)	Bay
Ormiskos	Cove
Oros	Mountain
Pelagos	Sea
Pirgos	Tower
Porto	Small harbour
Potamos (Pot)	River
Pounda	Cape or point
Stenon	Strait
Thalassa	Sea
Vorios	Northern
Vrakhonisis	Rocky islet
Vrakhos	Rock

A few useful words in Greek
General

yes	ne
no	okhi
please	parakalo
thank you	efharisto
OK	endaksi
hot	zeste
cold	krio
here	etho
there	eki
hello	herete
goodbye	adio
good morning	kalamera
good evening	kalaspera
good night	kalanikta
good	kalo
bad	kako
today	simera
tomorrow	avrio
later	meta
now	tora
I want	ego thelo
where is	pou inai
big	megalo
small	mikro
one	ena
two	thio
three	tria
four	teissera
five	pende
six	hexa
seven	hepta
eight	octo
nine	enai
ten	theca

Shopping

apples	mila
apricots	verikoka
aubergines	melitzana
baker	fourno
beans	fassolia
beef	mouskhari
biscuits	biscottes
bread	psomi
butcher	hassapiko
butter	voutiro
carrots	carotta
cheese	tiri
chicken	kotopoulo

175

chocolate	socolata
coffee	kavé
cucumber	angouri
eggs	avga
fish shop	psaroplion
flour	alevri
garlic	scordo
green pepper	piperi
grocer	bakaliko
ham	zambon
honey	meli
jam	marmelada
lamb	arinaki
lemon	limoni
margarine	margarini
meat	kreas
melon (water-)	karpouzi
milk	gala
mutton	arni
oil	lathi
onions	kremidia
oranges	portokalia
parsley	maidano
peach	rodakina
pepper	piperi
pork	khirino
potatoes	patatas
rice	rizi
salt	alati
sugar	zahari
tea	tsai
tomatoes	dhomates
water	nero
wine	krassi
yoghurt	yaourti

II. USEFUL BOOKS

Admiralty Publications

Mediterranean Pilot Vol III Covers the Ionian Sea.
List of Lights Vol E Covers the Mediterranean, Black and Red Seas.

Yachtsman's Pilots

Greek Waters Pilot Rod Heikell Imray. Covers all Greek waters in a single volume.
The Ionian Islands to Rhodes H M Denham John Murray. Covers the Ionian islands through Crete to Rhodes. Classic guides though no longer revised and kept up to date.
Imray Mediterranean Almanac. Ed. Rod Heikell. Imray. Biennial publication covering all major Mediterranean harbours and marinas although of course not in detail.

Other Guides

Blue Guide to Greece Edited by Stuart Rossiter A & C Black.

Yacht Charter Handbook Rod Heikell. Imray. Covers charter destinations worldwide.
Berlitz Guide to Corfu Berlitz Good compact guide.
Kefallonia and the South Ionian Islands John Fawssett Roger Lascelles.
Corfu & the Ionian Islands Grocs Candid Guides.
The Greek Islands Lawrence Durrell Faber. Good photos and eloquent prose.
The Greek Islands Ernle Bradford. Collins Companion Guide.
The Rough Guide to Greece Ellingham, Jansz and Fisher. RKP. Down to earth guide.
Prospero's Cell Lawrence Durrell. On Corfu.
Fortresses and Castles of Greek Islands and Fortresses and Castles of Greece Vol II Alexander Paradissis Efstathiados Group. Detailed guides available in Greece.
The Venetian Empire Jan Morris Penguin. Readable account of the Venetian maritime empire.

General

A Literary Companion to Travel in Greece Edited by Richard Stoneman Penguin.
The Ulysses Voyage Tim Severin Hutchinson
Eleni Nicholas Gage Fontana/Collins
Hellas Nicholas Gage Collins Harvill
Captain Corelli's Mandolin Louis de Bernieres. Penguin. A 'must' read.

Flora and Fauna

Flowers of Greece and the Aegean Anthony Huxley and William Taylor
Flowers of the Mediterranean Anthony Huxley and Oleg Polunin. Both the above have excellent colour photos and line drawings for identification.
Trees and Bushes of Britain and Europe Oleg Polunin Paladin.
The Hamlyn Guide to Birds of Britain and Europe Bruun, Delin and Svensson Hamlyn.
The Hamlyn Guide to the Flora and Fauna of the Mediterranean A C Campbell Hamlyn Good guide to marine life.

Food

Greek Cooking Robin Howe
Food of Greece Vilma Chantiles
The Best of Greek Cooking Chrissa Paradissis

III. BEAUFORT WIND SCALE

B'fort No.	Wind Descrip	Effect on sea	Effect on land	Wind speed knots mph	Wave ht (metres)
0	Calm	Like a mirror	Smoke rises vertically	less than 1	
1	Light	Ripples, no foam	Direction shown by smoke	1–3 1–3	–
2	Light breeze	Small wavelets, crests do not break	Wind felt on face, leaves rustle	4–6 4–7	0.2–0.3
3	Gentle breeze	Large wavelets, some white horses	Wind extends light flag	7–10 8–12	0.6–1.0
4	Moderate breeze	Small waves, frequent white horses	Small branches move	1–16 13–18	1.0–1.5
5	Fresh breeze	Moderate waves, some spray	Small trees sway	17–21 19–24	1.8–2.5
6	Strong breeze	Large waves form, white crests, some spray	Large branches move	22–27 25–31	3.0–4.0
7	Near gale	Sea heaps up, white foam, waves begin to streak	Difficult to walk in wind	28–33 32–38	4.0–6.0
8	Gale	Moderately high waves	Twigs break off trees, walking impeded	34–40 39–46	5.5–7.5
9	Strong gale	High waves, dense foam, wave crests break, heavy spray	Slates blow off roofs	41–47 47–54	7.0–9.75
10	Storm	Very high waves, sea appears white, visibility affected	Trees uprooted, structural damage	48–56 66–63	9.0–12.5
11	Violent storm	Exceptionally high waves, wave crests blown off, badly impaired	Widespread damage	57–65 64–75	11.3–16
12	Hurricane	Winds of this force seldom encountered for any duration in the Mediterranean.			

IV. USEFUL CONVERSIONS

1 inch = 2.54 centimetres (roughly 4in = 10cm)
1 centimetre = 0.394 inches

1 foot = 0.305 metres (roughly 3ft = 10 metres)
1 metre = 3.281 feet

1 pound = 0.454 kilograms (roughly 10lbs = 4.5 kgms)
1 kilogram = 2.205 pounds

1 mile = 1.609 kilometres (roughly 10 miles = 16 km)
1 kilometre = 0.621 miles

1 nautical mile = 1.1515 miles
1 mile = 0.8684 nautical miles

1 acre = 0.405 hectares (roughly 10 acres = 4 hectares)
1 hectare = 2.471 acres

1 gallon = 4.546 litres (roughly 1 gallon = 4.5 litres)
1 litre = 0.220 gallons

Temperature scale
t°F to t°C is $5/9(t°F - 32) = t°C$

t°C to t°F is $9/5(t°C + 32) = t°F$
So 70°F = 21.1°C   20°C = 68°F
   80°F = 26.7°C   30°C = 86°F
   90°F = 32.2°C   40°C = 104°F

Index